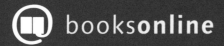
booksonline

Read this book online today:

With SAP PRESS BooksOnline we offer you online access to knowledge from the leading SAP experts. Whether you use it as a beneficial supplement or as an alternative to the printed book, with SAP PRESS BooksOnline you can:

• Access your book anywhere, at any time. All you need is an Internet connection.
• Perform full text searches on your book and on the entire SAP PRESS library.
• Build your own personalized SAP library.

The SAP PRESS customer advantage:

Register this book today at *www.sap-press.com* and obtain exclusive free trial access to its online version. If you like it (and we think you will), you can choose to purchase permanent, unrestricted access to the online edition at a very special price!

Here's how to get started:

1. Visit *www.sap-press.com*.
2. Click on the link for SAP PRESS BooksOnline and login (or create an account).
3. Enter your free trial license key, shown below in the corner of the page.
4. Try out your online book with full, unrestricted access for a limited time!

Your personal free trial **license key**
for this online book is:

ghjw-bfze-apcq-tks3

 PRESS

SAP PRESS is a joint initiative of SAP and Galileo Press. The know-how offered by SAP specialists combined with the expertise of the Galileo Press publishing house offers the reader expert books in the field. SAP PRESS features first-hand information and expert advice, and provides useful skills for professional decision-making.

SAP PRESS offers a variety of books on technical and business related topics for the SAP user. For further information, please visit our website: *www.sap-press.com*.

Ray Li, Evan Delodder
Creating Dashboards with Xcelsius – Practical Guide
2010, 587 pp.
978-1-59229-335-3

Ingo Hilgefort
Inside SAP BusinessObjects Advanced Analysis
2010, 340 pp.
978-1-59229-371-1

Jim Brogden, Mac Holden, Heather Sinkwitz
SAP BusinessObjects Web Intelligence
2010, 550 pp.
978-1-59229-322-3

Mike Garrett
Using Crystal Reports with SAP
2010, 440 pp.
978-1-59229-327-8

Jason Kraft

SAP® NetWeaver BW 7.x Reporting— Practical Guide

Galileo Press

Bonn • Boston

Galileo Press is named after the Italian physicist, mathematician and philosopher Galileo Galilei (1564–1642). He is known as one of the founders of modern science and an advocate of our contemporary, heliocentric worldview. His words *Eppur si muove* (And yet it moves) have become legendary. The Galileo Press logo depicts Jupiter orbited by the four Galilean moons, which were discovered by Galileo in 1610.

Editor Erik Herman
Copyeditor Mike Beady
Cover Design Graham Geary
Photo Credit fotolia/ihor khudo; iStockphoto.com/LPETTET, shironosov
Layout Design Vera Brauner
Production Manager Kelly O'Callaghan
Assistant Production Editor Graham Geary
Typesetting Publishers' Design and Production Services, Inc.
Printed and bound in Canada

ISBN 978-1-59229-357-5

© 2011 by Galileo Press Inc., Boston (MA)

1st Edition 2011

Library of Congress Cataloging-in-Publication Data
Kraft, Jason.
  SAP NetWeaver BW 7.X reporting : practical guide / Jason Kraft. — 1st ed.
      p. cm.
  Includes index.
  ISBN 978-1-59229-357-5
  1. SAP NetWeaver. 2. Web site development. I. Title.
  TK5105.8885.S24K73 2011
  006.7'8—dc22
                                                2010042772

Contents at a Glance

Dear Reader,

As an SAP NetWeaver Business Warehouse (BW) and business intelligence professional, you know the importance of creating a data warehousing and reporting environment that instills a sense of confidence in your users and compels them to be proactive in the way that they process and interact with the data. If you don't offer your end-users smartly designed, intuitive tools that provide the right information, in the right manner, the success rate of your projects will suffer mightily. But "if you you build it [correctly], they will come."

This book provides you with all the information necessary to create powerful, user-friendly, front-end business intelligence tools with the BEx suite and an SAP NetWeaver BW system. It's written in a very readable, accessible manner. The pages are full of practical, real-world tips and guidance that you can start using today!

I'm confident that what you learn in the pages of this book will make you a more agile, efficient, and sought after SAP professional. Once you've finished reading the book, I'd love to hear your feedback, so feel free to drop me a line at the email address below.

Thank you for purchasing a book from SAP PRESS!

Erik Herman
Editor, SAP PRESS

Galileo Press
100 Grossman Drive, Suite 205
Braintree, MA 02184

erik.herman@galileo-press.com
www.sap-press.com

Contents

4   Running Queries on the Web: Business Explorer (BEx) Web Analyzer 69

5   Running Queries in Excel: Business Explorer (BEx) Analyzer ... 95

6 Developing Workbooks with BEx Analyzer Design Mode 119

7   Customizing Web-Based Analytics with Web Application Designer 183

Prepare for a journey through the frontend SAP NetWeaver Business Warehouse (BW) 7 platform. From the sands of Query Designer, through the seas of Excel workbook design, we will land on the shore of BW web applications, leading to the holy grail of highly usable business intelligence for your users.

1   Introduction to BW 7 Reporting

When you hear someone talk about Business Intelligence (BI), they could be discussing one or more of a variety of different topics. According to Thomas H. Davenport, an expert on business process reengineering and knowledge management, business intelligence can be divided into a number of different subdomains, including querying, reporting, online analytical processing (OLAP), alerting, and business analytics. The first four BI subdomains are relatively straightforward — in definition, if not implementation — but what exactly is business analytics?

There are many differing opinions on this question, but one answer is that business analytics involves discovering patterns in an enterprise's data and finding out why those patterns exist in the first place. Once you have that understanding, you can drive your business to the next level by extrapolating those patterns into the future and making decisions that will optimize your business for the predicted future state.

Sounds great, right? But to reach the level of sophistication necessary to have robust business analytics in place, you first need to have a solid foundation, consisting of the first four components of BI. This book deals primarily with the querying and reporting components, as we examine the tools available in the Business Explorer (BEx) suite of the SAP NetWeaver platform.

In the context of this book, reporting refers to the analytical applications you will be building that can run on the Web or in Excel. These applications will be fed data from a query, which in turn is fed from an InfoProvider. Data in the InfoProvider is typically populated from another source system through an extraction process, but this process, along with the backend data warehousing side of the system, is beyond the scope of this book.

The primary focus will be on the end user's experience. SAP implementations often resemble an iceberg in several respects — in this context, the vast majority of system development happens behind the scenes, out of view of most end users. Harmonizing business processes, integrating disparate source systems, and architecting a systems landscape are all critical to the success of your implementation, but these activities are not typically noticed by your end user population.

The two pieces of an implementation that are noticed most by end users are change management, and the new frontend interface of the system. The topic of change management is covered by *Managing Organizational Change during SAP Implementations* from SAP PRESS. In this book, we will help you improve the experience of your end user populations by providing a highly usable frontend interface to your BI applications.

We will begin our endeavor by outlining the various user-facing components of the SAP NetWeaver platform relating to BW 7. From there, we will start by building a query on a previously existing InfoProvider, looking at the Query Designer interface in detail. Throughout the text, we will be calling out specific "User Experience Tips" that will help make life easier for you and your users.

Once we have covered the query design process, we will look closely at both the web-based and Excel-based query runtime environment, examining the features available in each environment and the differences between the two.

Next, we will start building our own BI applications. Our first application will be embedded in Microsoft Excel and built using the BEx Analyzer toolset. Then we will move to the Web application designer (WAD) tool to build web applications that will run on the SAP Portal framework.

Finally, we will explore the different tools available in WAD in detail, including the items that can be added to a web application and commands that can be executed at runtime to provide additional functionality.

Without further ado, let's start with an overview of the SAP NetWeaver platform as it relates to user-facing BI applications.

What you need to know about the current and future SAP Business Intelligence (BI) platform, our focus on the Business Explorer (BEx) toolset, and how BW integrates with other components.

2   User-Facing SAP NetWeaver BI Components

At a high level, SAP NetWeaver 7.0 is a comprehensive platform consisting of several technologies. This platform forms the base for a number of different SAP components, which are divided into a number of areas. Let's start by taking a brief look at all of the components of the SAP NetWeaver platform.

2.1   SAP NetWeaver Components

Team Productivity tools make up frontend user interfaces and collaboration tools, including the SAP Portal, to provide role-based views for applications based on BW 7 or other SAP components, a framework for building mobile applications, and an enterprise search tool.

Information Management tools include Master Data Management (MDM), a tool that allows for the consolidation and centralized management of master data; Business Warehouse (BW), including data warehousing, integrated planning, and analytical applications; BW Accelerator, which helps improve the performance of queries and searches; and Information Lifecycle Management (ILM), which handles data retention, storage, and regulatory issues. The BW component of the SAP NetWeaver 7.0 platform is referred to as BW 7 throughout this book.

There are also tools available for business process management and business rules management. In addition, there are three different types of composition environments to allow the development of business applications: the SAP NetWeaver Composition Environment (CE) is based on Java Enterprise Edition (EE) 5 and supports development with several different SAP NetWeaver components; Developer Studio is based on Java 2 Enterprise Edition (J2EE) and can deliver Java Server

Pages (JSPs), servlets, and Enterprise JavaBeans (EJBs); and the Visual Composer (VC) toolset is focused on modeling business applications without manual coding, and building Flash-based user interfaces for other applications, including BW 7.

The SAP NetWeaver platform includes middleware components that work with a service-oriented architecture environment, specifically the Process Integration (PI) component. Finally, the technical foundation for these applications includes the SAP NetWeaver Application Server (AS) for application deployment, Identity Management to handle user authentication, and Solution Manager for administration.

2.2   SAP's Future BI Roadmap

It's no secret that SAP's acquisition of BusinessObjects (BO) has altered its road map for delivering BI functionality. The BO BI suite is being positioned by SAP as a premium offering, with the existing BEx technology continuing to be supported through 2016. Customers who have purchased the SAP NetWeaver platform already have access to the BEx toolset, and adding BO to the mix would require additional expense. That said, it would be prudent for businesses that currently use the BEx toolset to start planning for a migration to BO by 2016.

SAP's future direction for formatted reporting points to Crystal Reports, which is included in the premium BO BI suite. A basic version of Crystal Reports will be made available to SAP NetWeaver BW, along with the existing BEx report designer tool.

For online analytical processing (OLAP) analysis, the BO BI suite includes an Advanced Analysis tool, which combines the features of the BO Voyager toolset with BEx Analyzer. OLAP analysis will still be handled by BEx analyzer and BEx Web analyzer in the SAP NetWeaver BI suite.

Dashboard design in the BO world is handled by the Xcelsius tool, along with BO Dashboard Builder or the SAP NetWeaver CE (including VC) if the SAP NetWeaver platform has already been deployed.

Finally, the Web Intelligence (WebI) tool is used in the BO BI suite for ad hoc reporting. There is no directly comparable component in BEx, but it is possible to provide limited ad hoc reporting functionality through commands in Web application designer (WAD).

For a comparison of the different tools offered by the two BI suites, *see* Figure 2.1.

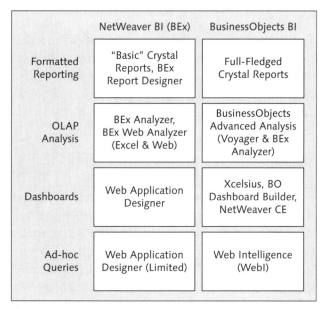

	NetWeaver BI (BEx)	BusinessObjects BI
Formatted Reporting	"Basic" Crystal Reports, BEx Report Designer	Full-Fledged Crystal Reports
OLAP Analysis	BEx Analyzer, BEx Web Analyzer (Excel & Web)	BusinessObjects Advanced Analysis (Voyager & BEx Analyzer)
Dashboards	Web Application Designer	Xcelsius, BO Dashboard Builder, NetWeaver CE
Ad-hoc Queries	Web Application Designer (Limited)	Web Intelligence (WebI)

Figure 2.1   BEx versus BO BI

2.3   The BW 7 BEx Toolset

Because this book will be covering the BEx toolset, let's look at the different components available. A BI application created with this toolset can be deployed on the Web or embedded within an Excel workbook. In the former case, the application would be built with the WAD tool, which would bring in data from one or more queries created with the Query Designer tool. For an Excel-based application, the design mode of the BEx analyzer Excel plug-in would be used for workbook design, with queries again being created with the Query Designer tool.

The runtime environment for a BI web application, BEx Web analyzer, is an XHTML template run on the user's web browser. Excel-based applications utilize the analysis mode of the BEx analyzer tool. The toolset also includes the report designer, which is used to create formatted reports.

Another interesting component of the BEx toolset is Information Broadcasting. This component can be used to distribute web applications, queries, and workbooks a number of different ways: publishing them in the SAP portal as a Knowledge Management (KM) document, pushing them to a BW role, or sending them via email. The options for output formats include HTML files or a link to current data (similar to a bookmark).

The BEx toolset is built on top of a data warehouse layer, which handles extracting data from source systems, aggregating it, and storing it in multidimensional cubes, and managing master data. For more information on the data warehouse layer, see the end of Chapter 9, Business Warehouse 7 Reporting Wrap-Up, for a list of other SAP PRESS books that cover this topic.

2.4   BW 7 and the Portal

The SAP NetWeaver Portal is an integral part of most implementations, because it is necessary to take full advantage of the functionality available in BW 7 web applications. A "federated" portal environment is often recommended when implementing BW 7, as the Java-based BW toolset includes its own portal. The BW portal is set up as a "producer" portal, which supplies content to the main "consumer" portal. Users access the consumer portal directly, while the consumer portal connects to the producer portal via Single Sign-On (SSO).

With this environment, you can maintain all content on the producer portal, so the consumer portal administrator just has to use remote role assignment to assign the content to consumer portal users. Alternatively, you could have some content located on the producer portal, while other content is built directly in the consumer portal.

KM is an important piece of the portal that relates directly to BW 7. KM is essentially a document management solution that has been integrated into the portal. KM has several advanced features, such as taxonomies, subscriptions, and workflow functionality, which are only available on a consumer portal, but for the purposes of KM's integration with BW 7 applications these advanced features are not utilized.

In BW 7 implementations, a KM repository is typically set up on the BW producer portal to allow users to save BI objects such as queries, web applications, and workbooks as documents. The repository on the producer portal is then connected to a consumer portal via WebDAV, as discussed in Online Service System (OSS) Note 969040.

These KM documents are saved in one of three locations within the repository: Favorites, My Portfolio, or BEx Portfolio. See Chapter 4, Section 4.5, Opening and Saving Queries at Runtime, for more information on this topic, including the specific paths within KM for each location. This functionality largely replaces the traditional "bookmark" feature, although it is still possible to create bookmarks in web applications. A KM document can contain historical data from a web application or query, or a link that will run the web application or query with current data. BEx analyzer workbooks can also be stored as a document.

The Information Broadcasting feature of the BEx toolset also utilizes KM, as users can broadcast BI objects such as queries, web applications, and workbooks to any location within the KM repository they have access to.

Another point of integration between BW 7 and the portal is found in Query Designer and WAD — both tools allow you to publish a query or BI web application directly to the portal as an iView, which is a self-contained application typically displayed within a portal page.

2.5 Visual Composer

There has been a lot of discussion about the VC environment...but what exactly is it, and how does it relate to BW 7? In a nutshell, VC is a tool that allows nontechnical users to model applications by dragging and dropping reusable components, similar to how one would design a business process flow in a modeling tool like Visio. The idea is to get business process experts working directly with the system to create applications without the need to communicate business requirements to a technical analyst or programmer.

VC is integrated within the portal, and business applications are deployed as iViews within the portal framework. VC can grab data from several different sources, including SAP R/3 transactional systems, BI analytical systems, and non-SAP systems via Java Database Connectivity (JDBC).

The ability to easily connect to several systems makes VC ideal for designing business applications that have both transactional and analytical components. For example, you could create a VC application that would connect to a BW system to display a list of employees for a cost center, but would also allow users to maintain employee information within the same application by connecting to an R/3 system.

While VC applications can display data from BW systems, the data is shown in a tabular format, and multidimensional analysis (such as adding and removing drill-downs) is not possible. Hierarchies are also not presented in an ideal fashion in VC applications built with the currently available toolset.

Due to these limitations, if you have a business application that only requires analytical reporting using data available in your BW system, you are probably better off using the WAD tool instead of VC. Nonetheless, VC is still a powerful tool for building truly integrated business applications for delivery in the portal environment.

2.6 Conclusion

This concludes our brief look at the SAP NetWeaver platform and its components relevant to BI. We discussed SAP's future BI roadmap, comparing the SAP NetWeaver BI/BEx toolset with the BusinessObjects BI suite, and taking a closer look at the different applications within the BW 7 BEx toolset.

We also introduced the SAP NetWeaver Portal, which shares several integration points with BW 7, and VC, a tool for building comprehensive business applications with both transactional and analytical components.

Now it's time to dive in to BEx and start down the path of building BI applications. The first step we will cover in this book involves using the Query Designer tool to build a query, structuring data to enable efficient multidimensional analysis.

The foundation of a quality Business Intelligence (BI) user experience is effective query design.

3 Building Effective Business Warehouse (BW) Queries: The Basics of Query Designer

Once you have a basic idea of which user populations you will be targeting, you can begin creating the building blocks of your BI user experience: queries. Query design is critical, as a little time invested in creating efficient and relevant queries will save you tons of effort down the road.

This chapter will walk you through the basic process of creating a query from scratch using the Business Explorer (BEx) Query Designer tool (found under the BEx folder of your SAP installation). More advanced functionality related to query design will be covered in Chapter 5, Running Queries in Excel: Business Explorer analyzer.

3.1 Where Is My Data Coming From?

A query without data doesn't provide a whole lot of value to users. Before we begin the process of creating a query, we must first select which InfoProvider the query will be based on. Because this book is focused on the frontend user experience, it is assumed that you already have an InfoProvider such as an InfoCube, MultiProvider, or InfoObject read, but is that InfoProvider the right choice for your query?

3.1.1 Use MultiProviders for Greater Flexibility

When you create a new query, selecting the correct InfoProvider is important, because you'll have to recreate the query if you change your mind. However, if you use a MultiProvider as a layer of abstraction between the query and the Info-

Providers, you can change the components of the MultiProvider without having to completely recreate your query — although a major change like this might still require some changes to the query design. Even if you are only reporting on a single InfoCube, it may prove beneficial to create a MultiProvider consisting of only that InfoCube in case the backend design changes in the future.

3.1.2 Selecting an InfoProvider

Now that you have an InfoProvider (preferably a MultiProvider) ready to go, you can start creating your query. SAP provides a number of ready-made queries in business content, but you can often get a better grasp on query design by starting from scratch.

Open BEx Query Designer and connect to your BW 7 system. Once you are connected and the blank BEx Query Designer window appears, click the 🗐 icon at the beginning of the top toolbar to create a new query. The system will prompt you to select an InfoProvider, as seen in Figure 3.1.

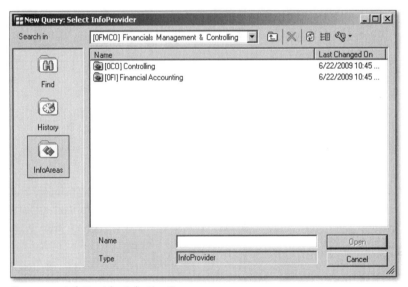

Figure 3.1 InfoProvider Selection Screen

Click the INFOAREAS button, navigate through your system until you find the Info-Provider in question, and double-click the InfoProvider. The BEx QUERY DESIGNER window will now show information about your chosen InfoProvider in the left pane of the window, as seen in Figure 3.2. In this book, we will be using a MultiProvider containing InfoCubes from cost center accounting and project systems (0CCA_C11 and 0PS_C04) as an example. If you have not implemented project systems, using a cost center accounting cube on its own would also work.

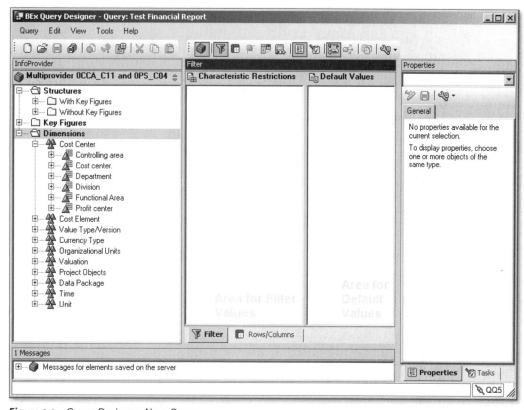

Figure 3.2 Query Designer: New Query

3.1.3 The InfoProvider Pane

The left pane of the BEx QUERY DESIGNER window shows you the STRUCTURES, KEY FIGURES, and DIMENSIONS associated with your InfoProvider. The STRUCTURES displayed in this pane are reusable query components consisting of a number of different selections; we will discuss structures in detail later.

Your InfoProvider's KEY FIGURES are shown in the BEx QUERY DESIGNER window. This section also holds Restricted Key Figures and Calculated Key Figures, two more types of reusable query components that will be examined later. For now, examine the available key figures in the InfoProvider and note which ones you'll want to include in the query.

The DIMENSIONS section of the pane holds the different characteristics of the Info-Provider, organized by dimension as per the InfoProvider's design. We will be using these characteristics to define restrictions on which data is displayed in the query, including both fixed and variable restrictions. We will also use these characteristics to tell the query which rows and columns to display.

As you'll see later in the chapter, structures, key figures, and characteristics are all necessary to create a viable query. Characteristics are often used on their own as rows and/or columns, but the core of the query is the structure, which holds selections combining key figures and characteristic restrictions.

3.2   Restricting Data at the Query Level

InfoProviders typically have a very large amount of data, so it is a good idea to set up some high-level data restrictions for your query. The CHARACTERISTIC RESTRICTIONS and DEFAULT VALUES components of BEx Query Designer will help you set up these high-level restrictions. As seen in Figure 3.2, these two panes to the right of the InfoProvider pane will start out blank, but they won't be empty for long.

We will first discuss the differences between these two components, followed by examples of how to set up different types of restrictions.

3.2.1   Characteristic Restrictions: Set in Stone

The main difference between CHARACTERISTIC RESTRICTIONS and DEFAULT VALUES lies in their flexibility after the report has been run. Items in the CHARACTERISTIC RESTRICTIONS section cannot be changed after query runtime, and are effectively global filters. For example, let's say we set up a restriction on Business Area 0001 and 0002 in Characteristic Restrictions. When we run the query and try to filter on Business Area, only 0001 and 0002 will be available. The option to remove filter values from Business Area will also be grayed out, because according to the query there are no other Business Areas to show.

Characteristic Restrictions are useful when you want to make sure users of a specific query only have access to a specific set of data. For example, imagine a financial report that will never need to show data outside of Business Area 0001 — you can safely set up this restriction in the Characteristic Restrictions section, as it will prevent users from seeing data in other Business Areas. However, if you include a variable for a characteristic in Characteristic Restrictions, users will be able to select which characteristic values using the variable screen of the report.

3.2.2   Default Values: Set Now, Change Later

The second option for setting up global restrictions, the DEFAULT VALUES pane, allows for more flexibility after the query has been run. Restrictions to any characteristic in this pane can be changed by the user after query runtime, as long as the characteristic appears somewhere in the Rows/Columns tab of BEx Query Designer or has a variable associated with it (more on this later).

Expanding on the previous Business Area example, if we set up a restriction on Business Area 0001 in the Default Values pane, and we also include the Business Area characteristic in the Free Characteristics pane of the Rows/Columns tab, users will be able to use the Remove Filter Value or Select Filter Value options on the characteristic after the query is run to see data in other Business Areas.

3.2.3   Setting Up Hard-Coded Restrictions

Now that we know the difference between Characteristic Restrictions and Default Values, we can start setting up restrictions on characteristics to narrow down the data being delivered to the query. Restrictions set up in either of these sections will impact the entire query; we will examine restrictions that only affect individual rows or columns later in the chapter.

Let's say we want to use the Business Area example in Section 3.2.1, Characteristic Restrictions: Set in Stone, and hard-code Business Area 0001 as a Characteristic Restriction so users cannot see data from other Business Areas. The procedure to set up this restriction follows.

Procedure 3.1: Query-Level Hard-Coded Characteristic Restriction

1. Locate the Business Area characteristic in the InfoProvider pane on the left by expanding the relevant dimension.

2. Drag the Business Area characteristic over to the Characteristic Restriction panel.

3. Right-click the new Business Area entry that appeared in the Characteristic Restriction pane and select Restrict. The SELECT VALUES screen will appear (see Figure 3.3).

4. Click the SHOW dropdown menu and select SINGLE VALUES.

5. Click one of the Business Area values on the left side. In this example, we will select Business Area 0001.

6. Once Business Area 0001 is selected, click the right arrow button.

7. Now that Business Area 0001 appears in the CHOSEN SELECTION pane on the right side of the dialog box, click OK to confirm.

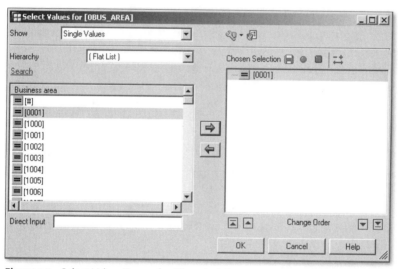

Figure 3.3   Select Values Screen for Characteristic

Business Area will now be in the Characteristic Restriction pane of BEx Query Designer, and if you expand it you can see that Business Area 0001 is now a hard-coded restriction.

By default, BEx Query Designer only shows values contained in the query's Info-Provider. If you'd like to add a restriction on a value that is not yet in the Info-Provider, there is a way to see the entire master data list instead: click the ☐ icon at the very top of the Select Values screen, click the Value Restrictions tab, and change Read Mode Setting to Custom, selecting Values in Master Data Table from the dropdown menu. If you wish to always read directly from the master data table, check the Always Use These Settings box and click OK.

3.2.4   Other Options for Restrictions

The procedure in the previous section is relatively basic and only deals with setting a restriction on a single value. To select multiple single values, at step 5 of the previous procedure you can either `Shift` + click to select multiple contiguous business areas, or `Ctrl` + click for multiple noncontiguous selections). You can also individually select values and move them over one at a time — double-clicking the value on the left is a shortcut to clicking the right arrow button. If necessary, you can click the Wrench icon at the top right to switch between technical names and descriptions.

If you have a hierarchy built for the characteristic, you can select single or multiple hierarchy nodes in addition to individual values. Select the relevant hierarchy from the Hierarchy dropdown menu to display the hierarchy. Nodes are added to the selection the same way, by either double-clicking them or selecting them and clicking the right arrow button.

The default option for both individual values and hierarchy nodes is to include them in the selection, as indicated by a green equal sign or hierarchy symbol. However, you can also specifically exclude an item from a selection by clicking on the value or node on the right side and clicking the Red Square icon. This will change the appearance of the item to indicate that it is now excluded. You can switch the item back to being included by clicking the Green Circle icon.

Value Ranges are another method for setting up restrictions: in step 4, if you select Value Ranges, you can specify restrictions using relational operators such as Between, Greater Than, or Contains Pattern. As with the Single Values section, you can add multiple value ranges with different operators to the same selection.

If you have a complex selection that you'd like to reuse, you can save it by clicking the Disk icon above the right pane of the dialog box. You can see a list of saved selections by clicking the Show dropdown list and selecting Favorites. When you add a saved selection from the Favorites list, the components of the saved selection will be added to any existing selections you may have already included.

The History option under the Show dropdown list is also very useful, as it will show you the recent selections you have made. You can add items from this list in the same way, just be careful if you are adding nodes from multiple hierarchies, as the history list does not include hierarchy names. The hierarchy names are only visible after you add hierarchy nodes from the history list to the right side.

3.3   Variables

One of the most powerful tools available in BEx Query Designer is the variable. Adding variables to characteristics allows the user to modify the restrictions for several characteristics at once through the variable screen (see Figure 3.4). If a characteristic does not have a variable associated with it, the user must rely on filtering functionality to set up restrictions on that characteristic.

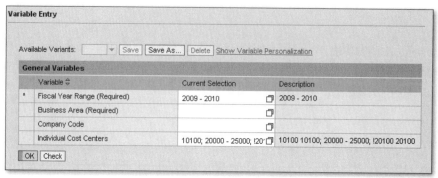

Figure 3.4 Sample Variable Screen

3.3.1   Optional versus Mandatory

There are several different settings available for creating different types of variables, but we'll start by looking at the three different options that control which variables must be populated before the query is run:

▸ A variable with the OPTIONAL setting does not require the user to enter a value before the query is run.

▸ The MANDATORY setting means that the user must enter a value (any value) in the variable before the query can be run.

▸ Mandatory (Initial Value Not Allowed) is the same as Mandatory, except that the user cannot enter # (indicating all data records where the characteristic is not assigned). If the user attempts to enter # into this type of variable, they will see an error message and they will be prompted to enter an actual value. The description of this setting is a little misleading, as it is perfectly fine to assign this type of variable a default value in the query design, but users would not be able to change the default value to # and still successfully run the query.

From a user experience perspective, it is important to map out which variables in your query will have which settings. If any variables in your query are either Mandatory or Mandatory (Initial Value Not Allowed) and do not have a default value assigned, the user will be presented with the SAP variable screen when they try to run the query. The user must then correctly identify the variables that must be filled out and populate them with data before the query will run. This can be a significant hurdle, especially to casual BI users.

User Experience Tip 3.1: Variable Naming Conventions

To address this issue, make sure variable descriptions clearly and consistently identify which variables are optional and which are mandatory. One way is to label all mandatory fields with the suffix (Required) — the term "Mandatory" can seem a bit severe — while leaving optional fields without a suffix. You can add (Optional) as a suffix to optional variables if you wish, but it seems redundant. If you have occasion to use variables with the Mandatory (Initial Value Not Allowed) setting, you can use a slightly different suffix such as (Value Required). It is also helpful to group all required variables at the top of the variable screen, especially if they do not have default values.

User Experience Tip 3.2: Bypassing the Variable Screen

Once you have consistent variable naming conventions, you should closely examine whether it is necessary to have the variable screen appear before the query is run. Some user populations prefer jumping right into the query itself instead of being forced to fill out a preliminary screen. In order for this to be a viable option you must have proper query optimization procedures in place (query performance is covered later in the book), and it is also important to have clearly available interface elements to allow users to set up their own restrictions (also covered later in the book).

It is simple to allow users to bypass the initial variable screen: simply assign a default value to all required variables, or make your required variables into optional ones. The idea behind this Best Practice is to better control the user's first impression of your query: because the SAP variable screen allows for relatively limited customization, many users will be better served by starting off with the rich interface options available through Web application designer (WAD) (covered in a later chapter).

The variable screen will still be available to users even if it is not displayed before the query runs — an easily accessible interface element allowing the user to display the variable screen is more important in this case.

In Figure 3.4, you can see at a glance that the first two variables are required, and the second two are optional. Because only one of the two required variables is populated, the query will not run until the user enters a Business Area.

3.3.2 Manual Input Flexibility

There are five basic types of variables that take manual input from users, each with a different degree of flexibility for entering values:

- **Single Value:** Users can enter a maximum of one value.

- **Multiple Single Values:** Users can enter any number of individual values or hierarchy nodes, one at a time. Exclusions are not allowed.

- **Interval:** Allows a "from" and "to" value to create a single range of values. Both a "from" and "to" value must be entered, and "between" is the only logical operator allowed.

- **Selection Option:** Allows the user to enter any number of single values, ranges, logical operators (greater than, less than, etc.), exclusions, and pattern matching. This is the most flexible type of variable, but you cannot combine a selection option variable with a hard-coded restriction.

- **Precalculated Value Set:** allows you to select a precalculated value set that has already been created using the BEx Broadcaster tool (covered later in the book), essentially using the output of another query as the input to the variable in this query.

Figure 3.4 shows an example of how these different variable types look after they are filled out. In BW 7, the only way to distinguish between these variable types is to click the box on the right side of the variable, bringing up a Select Value screen. The Select Value screen will automatically provide the appropriate functionality based on the type of variable. Because some values are already populated in Figure 3.4, you can see that the Individual Cost Centers variable is a selection option, as it contains a single value (10100), a range (20000 - 25000), and an exclusion (!20100).

In older versions of BW, the visual differences between these variable types were readily apparent on the variable screen itself. This often led to intimidating variable screens when several selection option variables were included, as more interface elements were included directly on the variable screen. Since BW 7 moved this functionality into the Select Value screen, the variable screen itself is somewhat simpler, but it is still important to choose the type of variable carefully. It may be tempting to just make every variable a Selection Option, but this may not make sense in all cases — for example, when using a variable associated with a hierarchy, Single Value or Multiple Single Value is probably a better choice. The

Select Value screen for Selection Option variables is also the most complex, which can negatively impact end user productivity, especially among casual users.

Another setting that impacts manual input variables is the Ready for Input option. When this option is checked (the default setting), the variable will appear in the variable screen. If it is unchecked, the variable will not be displayed in the variable screen and it cannot be changed by the user at query runtime, so the default value of the variable will be used. Be careful with this feature when using a required variable with no default value: if you uncheck Ready for Input for this variable, the query will never run, because there is no way for the user to enter the missing value.

Variables can be associated with characteristic values, hierarchies, text descriptions, or formulas. There are also different variable processing options: so far we have discussed only Manual Input variables. Replacement Path variables use the output of another query or characteristic variable as an automatic input into a text description or formula in the query. SAP provides a number of existing SAP Exit variables with delivered business content — these variables use prewritten code to automatically populate data such as the current fiscal month. You also have the ability to write your own code to populate data using a Customer Exit variable. Finally, Authorization variables are automatically populated based on the end user's level of authorization for that characteristic (maintained in Transaction RSSM).

3.3.3 Creating Your Own Manual Input Variables

Now that you have more background information about manual input variables, we can walk through the variable creation process. We'll start by creating a variable based on the Business Area characteristic.

Procedure 3.2: Query-Level Variable Characteristic Restriction

1. Right-click the Business Area characteristic and select Restrict.
2. Locate any hard-coded value restrictions on the right side of the dialog box, and double-click each one to remove them.
3. Pull down the Show menu and select Variables.
4. Make sure Characteristic Value Variable is selected in the Type dropdown, then click the first icon next to the dropdown to create a new variable (to edit an existing variable, select the variable and click the second icon).

5. In the Change Variable screen (see Figure 3.5) enter a Description and Technical Name for your new variable. Keep *User Experience Tip 3.1* (regarding variable naming conventions) in mind when entering your description, as it will be displayed on the variable screen — in this case, we'll enter Business Area (Required) as a description.

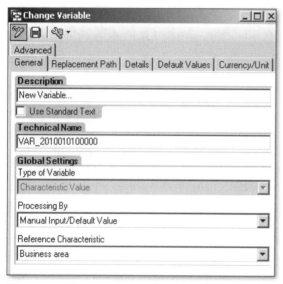

Figure 3.5 Change Variable Screen, General Tab

6. Because this variable is associated with a characteristic, the Type of Variable cannot be changed from Characteristic Value. The processing type for this variable will remain Manual Input.

7. Click the DETAILS tab to view more settings (see Figure 3.6). This is where we can change the manual input flexibility options discussed in the previous section, we'll stick with SINGLE VALUE for this variable.

8. The second dropdown under the DETAILS tab controls whether or not the user is required to enter a value: change this dropdown from OPTIONAL to Mandatory

9. Click the DEFAULT VALUES tab. For now, we will leave the default value for this variable blank, but click the Change Default Values button and note how you are only allowed to select a single Business Area; click cancel to back out of the default value selection. This behavior is controlled by the SINGLE VALUE option selected in step 6.

10. Make sure Variable is Ready for Input is checked — if it's unchecked, the variable will not appear in the variable screen.

11. Click the OK button, confirm the Description and Technical Name, then click OK again.

12. The new variable will appear on the left side of the characteristic Select Values screen, double-click the new variable to move it over to the right side, then click OK.

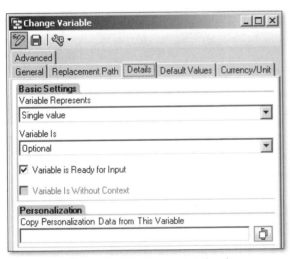

Figure 3.6 Change Variable Screen, Details Tab

You will now see the variable appear under the characteristic in the query; you may have to click the plus sign next to the characteristic to see it. Note that because this variable is mandatory and has no default value, the variable screen will appear and the user must enter a Business Area before the query can be run.

Exercise 3.1: Reproduce the Sample Variable Screen in Figure 3.4

As an exercise, try reproducing the sample variable screen in Figure 3.4. You'll need to add the cost center, company code, and fiscal year characteristics to the query under either Characteristic Restrictions or Default Values. Then, you'll create an optional selection options variable for cost center, an optional multiple single values variable for company code, and a required interval variable for fiscal year with default values of 2009 - 2010.

You can run the query by clicking the Execute button (the fifth icon in the Query Designer toolbar) — the variable screen will appear, but the query will not contain any data because we haven't set up the key figures yet.

User Experience Tip 3.3: Sorting Variables on the Variable Screen

One way to make the variable screen less daunting for casual users is to organize it using criteria that make sense for your business. A common practice is to list required variables first, especially required variables without default values. You can further sort variables by grouping them by function, such as including all of the variables for organizational unit characteristics together (i.e., business area, company code, cost center), followed by a group of time characteristics such as fiscal year and posting period.

To change the order of variables on the variable screen, click the Query menu at the top of the Query Designer window, and select Properties. On the right side of the window under the Properties pane, click the Variable Sequence tab. On this tab, you can select individual variables and click the up or down arrows to arrange them.

If you haven't done so already, you may want to save your query. Click the disk icon (the third icon in the toolbar) on the main Query Designer screen, assign the query a technical name and description, and click OK to save the query in your Favorites.

3.3.4 Hierarchies and Hierarchy Variables

It is common for SAP implementations to utilize hierarchies as a means of organizing certain master data characteristics into a hierarchical format. The creation and maintenance of master data hierarchies is beyond the scope of this book, but we will examine how hierarchies are utilized in Query Designer, including hard-coded hierarchy restrictions, variables for both hierarchy nodes, and variables for hierarchies themselves.

Because hierarchies are often built for Cost Centers, we will use the Cost Center characteristic as an example for how to include hard-coded restrictions based on hierarchies. There are two settings relating to hierarchies we need to be concerned with: the hierarchy used for the hard-coded restriction, and the hierarchy used for the characteristic itself. We'll start by setting up the restriction.

Procedure 3.3: Query-Level Fixed Restriction Based on Hierarchy

1. If you haven't already done so, add the Cost Center characteristic to either Characteristic Restrictions or Default Values in Query Designer.

2. Right-click Cost Center and select Restrict.

3. Change the Show dropdown menu to Single Values.

4. Change the Hierarchy dropdown menu to reflect a cost center hierarchy you have already created. You can click the Wrench icon in the top right to show technical names if necessary.

5. The hierarchy itself will appear in the left-hand pane. Expand the hierarchy and add any number of hierarchy nodes to the right side by double-clicking the nodes or selecting them and clicking the right arrow.

6. If you've already added the Individual Cost Centers selection option variable from a previous section, remove it by double-clicking the variable from the right side.

7. Click OK.

You have now created hard-coded restrictions for hierarchy nodes based on the hierarchy you selected. Note that step 6 was necessary because selection option variables cannot be combined with a hard-coded restriction in the same characteristic. The next step is to assign a display hierarchy to the characteristic itself.

Procedure 3.4: Assign Display Hierarchy to Characteristic

1. Click Cost Center in the Query Designer screen once.

2. Look at the far right of the Query Designer screen and confirm that the properties for Cost Center are displayed (see Figure 3.7).

3. Click the Hierarchy tab.

4. Near the top of the Hierarchy tab, you will see Press Button for Hierarchy Selection under the Selected Hierarchy heading. Follow this advice and click the button on the right side of this field.

5. Make sure Hierarchy Name is selected, click the dropdown list, and select a hierarchy.

6. Click OK, and note that the Activate Hierarchy Display checkbox is automatically checked. The icon for Cost Center in Query Designer will also change to reflect the hierarchy assignment.

7. Adjust any additional hierarchy parameters as needed, such as the default expansion level or sorting options (see Section 3.5.2, Characteristic Properties, for more information).

The display hierarchy assigned to the characteristic is often the same hierarchy used to set up the hard-coded restriction, but the two can be different if necessary.

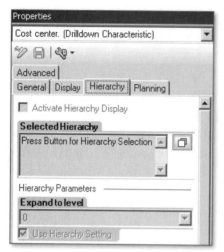

Figure 3.7 Properties of Characteristic with Hierarchy

You may have noticed in step 5 that you have the option of setting up a Hierarchy Variable — this type of variable allows a user to choose which display hierarchy to use for a characteristic at query runtime. To create a Hierarchy Variable, continue from step 5, but instead of selecting a hierarchy, click the Hierarchy Variables radio button and click the button on the right of the field. Click the Create New Variable button in the resulting dialog box, and step through the variable creation process from Section 3.3.3, Creating Your Own Manual Input Variables. Hierarchy Variables must be single value, but they can be optional or mandatory. They can also be assigned a default value. Note that a characteristic with a Hierarchy Variable must appear in the Default Values pane of the Filter tab in Query Designer; if it is in the Characteristic Restrictions section, the user *will not be prompted* to select a hierarchy.

In addition to a variable that prompts the user to select which hierarchy will be displayed, you can also create variables that allow the user to add restrictions based on the structure within a hierarchy. The procedure to add a hierarchy node variable follows.

Procedure 3.5: Query-Level Variable Restriction Based on Hierarchy

1. If you haven't already done so, add the Cost Center characteristic to either Characteristic Restrictions or Default Values in Query Designer.

2. Right-click Cost Center and select Restrict.

3. Remove any existing variables or hard-coded values from the right side by double-clicking them.

4. Change the Show dropdown menu to Variables.

5. Change the Type dropdown menu to Hierarchy Node Variables.

6. At the bottom of the screen, find the Variable Hierarchy section, and click the box to the right of the field to select which hierarchy to use for your new variable. You can either hard-code a specific hierarchy, or use a hierarchy variable so the user can select both which hierarchy to use for the restriction and which nodes in the hierarchy to restrict on.

7. Click the first button next to the Type dropdown menu to create a new variable based on the hierarchy you selected in the previous step.

8. Enter a description and technical name. You may wish to include the word "Hierarchy" or "Node" in the description to distinguish this variable from a nonhierarchy variable.

9. Click the Details tab for additional settings.

10. Choose whether to allow the user to enter only one hierarchy node (single value) or multiple hierarchy nodes (multiple single values).

11. Choose whether to make the variable mandatory or optional.

12. Click the Default Values tab and select a default hierarchy node, if needed.

13. Click OK and save the variable.

14. Drag the new variable over to the right pane and click OK.

In the main Query Designer screen, you will see the new variable under the Cost Center characteristic, and it will have the traditional Variable icon along with the Hierarchy icon to indicate that it is a hierarchy node variable.

3.4   Building a Query Layout

We will now shift gears from setting up restrictions with hard-coded values and dynamic variables to putting together a query layout to display data in rows and columns. The tools to build layouts can be found on the Rows/Columns tab of Query Designer.

3.4.1 An Overview of the Rows/Columns Tab

There are four sections within the Rows/Columns tab in Query Designer. The Free Characteristics section contains characteristics that are not displayed in the initial query layout, but can be displayed by the user at query runtime by utilizing the drilldown or drill across functionality. The Rows and Columns sections represent the initial view of the query, and items added to these two sections are displayed on the left side or the top of the query, respectively. While Free Characteristics can only contain individual characteristics, the Rows and Columns sections can contain individual characteristics or a Structure consisting of one or more Selections or Formulas. The last section is a Preview of what the query will look like.

You can add characteristics to Free Characteristics, Rows, or Columns the same way they are added to the Characteristic Restrictions or Default Values sections from the Filter tab: by dragging the characteristics from the InfoProvider pane. If a characteristic is added to the Free Characteristics section, it will not be displayed in the query's initial view, but it will be available to the user under the Free Characteristics section of the query navigation area. If it is added to the Rows section, the characteristic will be displayed on the left side of the query in the initial view, and any characteristic added to Columns is shown at the top of the query's initial view.

3.4.2 Creating a Simple Structure

While it is possible to create a query with only characteristics in Rows and Columns, such a query would only be able to show master data. To show transaction data (from Key Figures), a Structure must be created. There are two types of structures: a Key Figure Structure is, surprisingly enough, a structure that contains key figures. The other type of structure, a Characteristic Structure, cannot contain key figures. A query can have a maximum of two structures, only one of which can be a Key Figure Structure.

But what exactly is a structure? The (relatively) short answer: a structure is a collection of Selections — items containing one or more restrictions on characteristics or key figures — and Formulas, which can use a number of different operators to derive values from other query components. Structures provide an incredible amount of flexibility: the items we created earlier on the Filter tab provided query-level restrictions on characteristics, but each element of a structure can be set up to restrict data based on any number of characteristics at the individual line level.

Structures are very easy to create. In fact, if you drag a key figure from the Info-Provider tab to either the Rows or Columns pane, Query Designer will automatically create a new structure called Key Figures, containing a single key figure. This key figure is really a Selection that has not yet been set up with any characteristic restrictions. Because this new selection contains a key figure, the structure is now your query's one and only Key Figure Structure. Let's create a Key Figure Structure with a few selections for a simple financial report that shows actual and plan transaction data.

Procedure 3.6: Create Selections with Fixed Restrictions

1. Expand Key Figures in the InfoProvider pane on the left, and drag the Amount key figure to the Columns pane on the right. A new structure called Key Figures will be created, with a new selection containing Amount.

2. Double-click the Amount selection under the Key Figures structure to open the CHANGE SELECTION window (see Figure 3.8).

3. Change the Description at the top to read "Actual."

4. Expand Dimensions on the left side of the window. In SAP, actual and plan transaction data are typically segregated by Value Type. Find Value Type under the relevant InfoProvider dimension and drag it over to the right side. For now, do not expand Value Type in the list on the left side.

5. Right-click Value Type on the right side pane and click Restrict.

6. Move Actual from the left side to the right side by either double-clicking it or selecting it and clicking the right arrow button, then click OK.

7. Click OK one more time to save the current selection.

8. Now that we have created the Actual selection, we can move on to the Plan selection. Right-click the Key Figures structure in the Columns pane and click New Selection.

9. A new empty selection will be created. Double-click this new selection to open the Change Selection screen.

10. Change the description to Plan.

11. Because you created this empty selection from scratch, you'll need to manually add the Amount key figure. Locate it on the left side under Key Figures and drag it to the right pane.

12. This time we'll use a shortcut to add the Value Type restriction. Locate Value Type under Dimensions on the left side pane, and click the plus sign next to Value Type to expand it.

13. Click the plus sign next to Characteristic Values to show all of the potential values for Value Type.

14. Drag Plan from the left side pane to the right side pane. Value Type will automatically be created on the right side with Plan as a restriction.

15. Click OK to return to the main Query Designer screen.

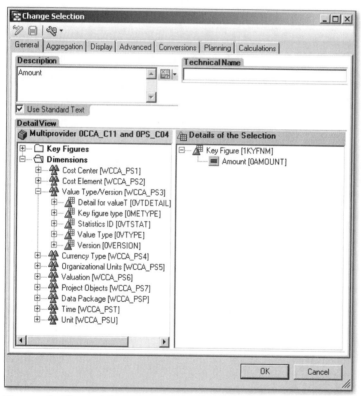

Figure 3.8 Change Selection Screen

You will now see two selections under the Key Figures structure: Plan and Actual. If you'd rather have Actual first, you can drag the Actual selection up until you see a black line between Key Figures and Plan. Be careful not to release the mouse button if the Plan selection is highlighted, otherwise you will end up with nested selections — hierarchical views within structures will be covered later in the book.

Now that we have two selections, we can create a Formula that calculates a new value using these two selections. A commonly used calculation is a variance, which is Plan — Actual. Let's go ahead and create a formula for variance.

Procedure 3.7: Create a Simple Formula Using Existing Selections

1. Right-click the Key Figures structure in the Columns pane and click New Formula.

2. A new empty formula will be created. Double-click this new formula to open the CHANGE FORMULA screen (see Figure 3.9).

3. Delete the existing DESCRIPTION at the top. Type "Variance," press ⌈Enter⌉, and type "(Plan – Actual)." This will create a two-line column header in the query view.

4. In the AVAILABLE OPERANDS pane at the bottom left of the screen, expand KEY FIGURES and double-click PLAN. This will insert the Plan selection into the DETAIL VIEW section of the screen

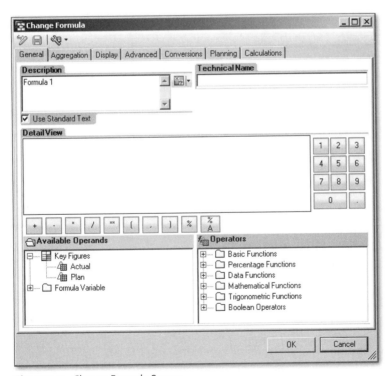

Figure 3.9 Change Formula Screen

5. A number of operators are available at the bottom right of the screen, but basic mathematical functions are found in a toolbar just above Available Operands. Locate this toolbar and click the minus sign (-).

6. Double-click Actual under the Available Operands pane.

7. The Detail View section should now read Plan −Actual. Click the OK button to return to the main Query Designer screen.

You will now see Variance (Plan − Actual) as the first entry under the Key Figures structure. To move this formula to the end, drag it down until you see a black line under Plan. Again, ensure that Plan is not highlighted when you release the mouse button.

User Experience Tip 3.4: Explain Formulas in Column Headers

It is a good practice to explain your formulas directly in column headers whenever possible, especially for casual users. Obviously, a complex formula may not be easily summarized, and you should be mindful of column widths, but if it's possible to clarify the gist of a formula with a few extra words, that's well worth the extra use of screen real estate.

This tip is of particular value when a specific term has different meanings to different people in your organization. For example, some groups may use a Plan − Actual calculation for Variance, while others may use Actual − Plan.

You can go back and edit existing selections or formulas at any time, and selections may contain any number of characteristic restrictions. It is common for plan data to be further segregated into different plan versions using the Version characteristic, so let's revisit the Plan selection and add a new restriction for Version. While we're at it, let's allow the user to select which version they want to see by using a variable instead of a hard-coded restriction.

Procedure 3.8: Including Line-Level Variable Restrictions in a Selection

1. Double-click the Plan selection under the Key Figure structure in Columns to show the Change Selection screen.

2. Locate Version under the relevant dimension on the left side and drag it to the right side of the window.

3. Double-click Version from the right side of the window.

4. Click the Show dropdown at the top and select Variables.

5. If you have a Version variable already created (or activated from business content), drag it over to the right side. If not, click the Create New Variable button and step through the process of creating a new version variable, ideally mandatory and single value.

6. Click OK to return to the Change Selection screen.

7. Confirm that the new variable appears correctly under Version, and click OK.

The user will now be prompted to select a plan version at the variable screen before running the query. If we had not included this variable (or a hard-coded restriction), and data existed on your InfoProvider under multiple versions, the Plan column would have shown a sum of all of those versions, which is probably not what your users want to see. It is critical to carefully examine the data in your InfoProviders to ensure you have the correct restrictions on your key figures.

Now that we have a simple structure in place, let's start adding tools to allow users to analyze the data at higher levels of detail.

3.4.3   Adding Characteristics as Drilldowns

The real power of an analytical reporting system comes from the ability to easily drill down into data with increasingly finer granularity. Query Designer provides this functionality with the Free Characteristics, Rows, and Columns panes, as discussed earlier in this chapter.

If you check the Preview pane in Query Designer, you will see that the query created in the previous section consists of one row with three columns. Because we have not provided any options for drilling down on characteristics, the data shown will be at the highest level possible — the only restrictions other than those in the Key Figures structure are at the query level, based on those created earlier in the Characteristic Restrictions and Default Values sections. Let's remedy this situation by adding a few characteristics to the Rows and Columns so they display in the initial query view.

Looking at a financial report as an example, it is common to show higher-level characteristics broken down by lower-level (more detailed) characteristics as "drilldowns." Let's add Company Code, a high-level characteristic, to the Rows column by dragging it over from the InfoProvider pane. Unlike items within a structure, you cannot add restrictions to individual characteristics here; the only options are adding query-level restrictions in Characteristic Restrictions or Default Values under the Filter tab, or creating a structure and adding line-level restrictions within a selection.

Now let's add Cost Center to the Rows section by dragging it from the InfoProvider pane. Make sure to drop Cost Center under the existing Company Code characteristic. Checking the Preview pane, we can see that this query will now show Actual, Plan, and Variance data broken down by company code first, then by cost center.

If you'd like to add a characteristic's display attributes, you can do so by expanding the characteristic on the InfoProvider pane and expanding the Attributes folder. All of the characteristic's display attributes will be listed, and you can drag them over to the characteristic on the right side. The attribute will appear under the characteristic. If you try to drag an attribute to the right side without first adding the characteristic, Query Designer will automatically include the characteristic.

It is also common to add a timeframe drilldown to the query — without such a drilldown, the query will show the sum of all data populated in the InfoProvider from the current year, future years (for plan data), and past years, based on query-level timeframe restrictions. Time characteristics are often added to the Columns section of the query, so let's drag Fiscal Year from the InfoProvider pane over to the Columns section, and drop it in the small space between the Columns header and the Key Figures structure. Technically, this is considered a "drill across" because the characteristic is in the columns of the query, but I prefer using the terms "drilldown" or "breakout." When it is necessary to distinguish them, you can add "in the rows" or "in the columns" to either term.

As you can see from the Preview pane, the top of the query will show a breakout of fiscal years, followed by the Actual, Plan, and Variance values for each year. In terms of the end user's view of the query, the structure is treated as just another characteristic.

Recall that restrictions cannot be added to individual characteristics in the Rows/Columns tab of Query Designer. If you completed Exercise 3.1 earlier in the chapter, you already have a Fiscal Year Range variable attached to the Fiscal Year characteristic at a query level, meaning that the user will be prompted to select a range of years to restrict data for the entire query. You can click the Filter tab at the bottom to see this variable; it will appear under Fiscal Year in either Characteristic Restrictions or Default Values. When you add a characteristic anywhere in the Rows/Columns tab, it will automatically add an entry for the characteristic under Default Values in the Filters tab. This entry will initially be empty, but you can add hard-coded restrictions, add a variable, or leave it without any restrictions.

We've added entries into the Rows and Columns, so let's add a few characteristics to the Free Characteristics pane. Look in the InfoProvider pane on the left side of the Query Designer window, and drag Business Area, Cost Element, and Posting Period to Free Characteristics. Notice that the Preview section does not change, as the items in Free Characteristics are not displayed in the initial query view, but users have the option of adding these characteristics to either the rows or the columns ("drilling down") at query runtime.

The Rows/Columns tab of the Query Designer screen should now look something like Figure 3.10. Now that we have a more filled-out query, let's return to the Key Figures structure to examine how text variables can be used to dynamically label components of a structure.

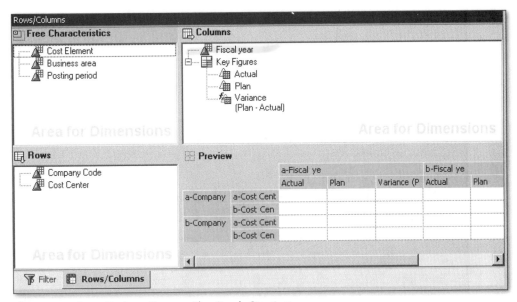

Figure 3.10 Query Designer Screen with a Simple Structure

3.4.4 Dynamic Labeling with Text Variables

Looking back at the Plan selection we created in the last section, you'll notice that the contents of the selection will change depending on which plan version the user selects when they run the query. However, the current description of the selection does not tell the user which plan version is being displayed. Luckily, this is easily remedied by using a text variable. Let's create a text variable that displays the contents of the Version variable.

Procedure 3.9: Create a New Text Variable

1. From the Rows/Columns tab, locate the Key Figures structure under Columns and double-click Plan.

2. Click once in the Description field after Plan, and hit enter to create a new line.

3. Click the dropdown next to the Variables icon to right of the description field, and select New Variable.

4. We will now create a Replacement Path text variable that will display the contents of the Version attribute. On the General tab, enter a technical name and a relevant description such as "Version – Key." Although the end user will never see this description, it will still be useful to anyone who utilizes this variable in the future.

5. Click the Processing By dropdown and select Replacement Path.

6. A new dropdown labeled Reference Characteristic will appear: this is where the text variable will get its displayed value from. Select Version from this list.

7. Click the Replacement Path tab, and make sure the Replace Variable With dropdown has InfoObject selected. You can also replace the text variable with the value from another variable, but we'll stick with InfoObject for now.

8. There are several options in the Replace With dropdown. We'll go over these options later, for now select Key.

9. The Use Interval option lets you select the first value in a range, the last value, or the difference between the two. Because Version is not a range in this case, we will leave From Value selected.

10. The Offset Setting is not useful in this situation, so we'll leave it empty. This setting is discussed in more detail later.

11. Click the OK button to create the text variable.

The new text variable will now appear on the second line of the Description field, displayed as the technical name of the variable with ampersands on either side, like this: &ZVARNAME&. In the future, you can add this text variable to other descriptions of structure components by clicking the dropdown next to the Variables button on the right side of the description field and clicking Entry of Variables, or just clicking on the Variables button itself.

Because we selected Key in step 8 earlier, the user will see the key value associated with the selected version under Plan in the column header. Other options include the external key value or the text description (Label in the Replace With dropdown). You can also select an attribute value (another dropdown appears to select which attribute of the characteristic to use, if any) or a hierarchy attribute, but these two options are only useful in formula variables, which are discussed later.

A common use of text variables is to indicate which timeframe is being viewed when timeframe selections are dynamic. Our next exercise will involve removing our existing query-level fiscal year variable restriction and adding a line-level restriction into the Key Figures structure. We will then add appropriate text variables to indicate which year is being displayed. We will also use this opportunity to look at the time-oriented variables SAP provides with business content, and variable offset functionality.

Procedure 3.10: Applying an SAP Exit Variable and Text Variable to a Selection (Fiscal Year)

1. To remove the query-level fiscal year variable restriction, switch to the Filter tab at the bottom of Query Designer, expand Fiscal Year, right-click on the variable you created, and select Remove. You can also left-click the variable and press the Delete key on your keyboard.

2. Switch back to the Rows/Columns tab.

3. Because we will be filtering on Fiscal Year within the Key Figures structure, there's no need for a separate Fiscal Year drilldown. Right-click Fiscal Year in the Columns and select Remove.

4. Double-click the Actual selection under the Key Figures structure.

5. Look on the left side of the window under Dimensions, locate Fiscal Year, and drag it to the right side.

6. Right-click Fiscal Year on the right side and select Restrict.

7. Change the Show dropdown box to Variables.

8. If you've activated the necessary business content, you will see a number of existing variables here. Look for Current Fiscal Year (SAP Exit) [0FYEAR]. This variable is provided by SAP and automatically returns the current fiscal year. You can select this variable and click the Edit Variable button at the top to examine the variable settings: notice that on the General tab the Processing By setting is SAP exit, and on the Details tab the Ready for Input box is

not checked, meaning that the user will not be able to change the value of the variable at query runtime.

9. Drag this variable over to the right side of the screen and click OK. Notice that the Current Fiscal Year variable now appears under Fiscal Year.

10. Click in the Description field at the top left, just after the word Actual, press Enter, and click the Variable button to the right of the field.

11. Locate the SAP-provided text variable Text variable replaced by 0FISCYEAR [0T_FYEAR] and double-click it. You will see &0T_FYEAR& on the second line of the description.

12. Click OK to return to the Query Designer screen and confirm that the Actual selection has changed to Actual &0T_FYEAR&.

When the query is run, the Fiscal Year characteristic will automatically be replaced by the current year, and the description of the Actual column will display that year. In order for a text variable to function correctly, it must refer to a single value. If no value is found for the characteristic or if there are multiple single values, the text variable will output its technical name instead of a value. For example, if we set up a hard-coded restriction on fiscal year for the single values of 2009 and 2010, the name of the column will appear as Actual &0T_FYEAR&. However, if we set up a value range restriction instead of multiple single values, the text variable will show the first value in the range, the last value, or the difference between the two, according to the settings in step 9 of Procedure 3.9.

Note that we've added the current fiscal year restriction to the Actual selection, but not to Plan. To avoid the Plan column showing data from all fiscal years — because we removed the query-level fiscal year variable restriction — we'll need to run through Procedure 3.10 one more time to apply the current fiscal year variable and the text variable to the selection. The Plan selection already contains a text variable, but a single selection can support any number of text variables, again assuming each text variable references a characteristic with a unique value in the query.

Let's not forget about the Variance formula we created earlier — formulas can also use text variables. Double-click Variance and add the fiscal year text variable to the description. As a shortcut, if you already know the technical name of the text variable (in this case, 0T_FYEAR) you can type it directly into the description field as long as it is between two ampersands: &0T_FYEAR&. The name of the text variable will be automatically highlighted as soon as you type the final ampersand.

User Experience Tip 3.5: Automatically Populate Current Year or Not?

Even though SAP provides an exit variable that automatically populates the current year, you may find that it makes more sense for your users if the current year is not automatically populated, especially at the beginning of the new year (calendar year or fiscal year). If you create a variable for calendar year or fiscal year on your own, you would have to manually maintain the default value, but you can choose when to change the default value to the current year. In our experience, for the first week or two of the year, most users would rather see the full prior year rather than the nearly empty current year. Later in the book, we will see additional options for creating more flexible timeframe selections that will help alleviate this issue.

Another useful setting involving text variables is the Offset Setting, found on the Replacement Path tab of the Change Variable screen. You can see this setting by editing an existing text variable: click on the text variable's technical name in the Description field of the Change Selection or Change Formula screen, then click the dropdown triangle next to the Variables icon to the right of the Description field and select Change Variable. The two entries under the Offset Setting section of the Replacement Path tab, Offset Start and Offset Length, control where the text variable starts displaying data and how many characters it displayed.

Let's use the Fiscal Year variable as an example. If the text variable is set up to show the External Characteristic Value Key of the Fiscal Year characteristic, and the Fiscal Year characteristic is compounded with Fiscal Year Variant, the text variable would display something like K4/2010, where K4 is the fiscal year variant. Because the end user probably isn't all that interested in the fiscal year variant, you'll want to set the Offset Start value at 3, so the text variable starts *after* the third character. The Offset Length would be 4 to display the four-digit year. Alternatively, if you wanted to display the two-digit year, the Offset Start would be 5 and the Offset Length would be 2.

3.4.5 Using Variable Offsets and Ranges

In some cases, you may want to have a column in your query to show current year data and a column that shows prior year data. While it is possible to implement this by creating a separate fiscal year variable for the prior year column, the second variable requires additional input from the end user. Luckily, SAP has provided a way to automatically offset the value of a variable within a specific selection. This is a separate concept from the text variable offset discussed before, as this variable offset affects that actual value of the variable. It also only works with variables based on time characteristics.

Let's set up a new selection in the Key Figures structure to show Actual data for the prior year, based on the fiscal year variable. Because this new selection will be very similar to the existing Actual selection, we can take a shortcut by copying and pasting: right-click the Actual selection in the Key Figures structure, click Copy, then right-click the Actual selection again and click Paste. This will insert a copy of the Actual selection just after the original. Alternatively, you can click an existing selection, press ⌷Ctrl⌷ + ⌷C⌷ to copy the selection, and press ⌷Ctrl⌷ + ⌷V⌷ to paste the copy. The new copies of the selection will have the same description, so if the original selection is included in a formula, be sure not to change the original. We will now set up the variable offset.

Procedure 3.11: Offset the Value of an Existing Variable

1. Double-click the new Actual selection under the Key Figures structure you just pasted to edit it. We will now change the fiscal year variable to show the prior year instead of the current year.

2. Right-click Fiscal Year and select Restrict to open the Select Values screen.

3. Confirm that there is already a fiscal year variable on the right side, and left-click the variable once to select it.

4. Click the − + icon (the third icon to the right of Chosen Selection at the top of the right side). This will open the Set Variable Offset window.

5. Because we are looking for the year prior to the one in the existing fiscal year variable, enter -1 in the Variable Offset Value field and click OK.

6. Confirm that the variable under Fiscal Year now has a -1 at the end of its description to indicate the offset.

7. If you wish, you can change the description to read "Prior Year Actual" or "PY Actual" followed by the text variable. Note that the text variable does not have to be changed, as it automatically uses the value in the variable after the offset has been applied.

8. Click OK to return to the Query Designer screen.

The new selection for prior year actual is now complete. Next, we'll look at an example that combines the concepts of text variables and variable offsets with value range restrictions: creating a new selection to show the previous three months of actual data (not including the current month). To create this restriction, we'll need to use a new time characteristic: Fiscal Year/Period (OFISCPER).

Procedure 3.12: Use Variable Offsets within a Value Range

1. Copy and paste the existing Actual selection to create a new duplicate selection, and double-click the new selection.
2. Locate Fiscal Year/Period on the left side of the screen under the relevant dimension, and drag it to the right side.
3. Double-click Fiscal Year/Period on the right side.
4. Click the Show dropdown menu at the top and select Value Ranges.

We will now set up a range that restricts values from four months before the current month to the one immediately before the current month. For example, if the current month is July, this range will run from April through June.

1. Make sure Between is selected in the first dropdown box, and click the button next to the second dropdown box to open the Select Values screen for the From value of the range.
2. Click the Show menu and select Variables.
3. Find the variable Current Fiscal Year/Period (SAP Exit) [OFPER] in the list, click on it, and press OK. This variable is provided by SAP in business content, and it uses the Date_to_Period_Convert function module to return the current fiscal month and year.
4. Click the button next to the third dropdown box and repeat steps 6 and 7 above. The Current Fiscal Year/Period (SAP Exit) variable should now appear in both dropdown boxes on the left side.
5. Click the right arrow button to move this range over to the right side.
6. As it stands now, the range will only select the current month, as we have not entered offsets yet. To enter variable offsets, right-click the range on the right side and select Set Offset for Variable.
7. The Set Variable Offset dialog box will now appear twice in succession: the first box is for the "from" value, the second is for the "to" value. In the first box, enter -4 and click OK. Enter -1 in the second box, and click OK again.
8. Confirm that the right side of the screen now says CURRENT FISCAL YEAR/PERIOD (SAP EXIT) – 4 – CURRENT FISCAL YEAR PERIOD (SAP EXIT) – 1, as seen in Figure 3.11, and click OK to return to the Change Selection screen.

Because the new Fiscal Year/Period range already includes Fiscal Year as a restriction, let's remove the existing Fiscal Year entry from the right side of this selection by clicking Fiscal Year and pressing the Delete key on your keyboard. Leaving this additional restriction would cause issues near the beginning of the year: for example, in February 2010, the Fiscal Year/Period Range would include January 2010, December 2009, and November 2009. If this selection was restricted to only fiscal year 2010, data for the previous December and November would not appear, as selection restrictions are processed on an AND basis rather than OR.

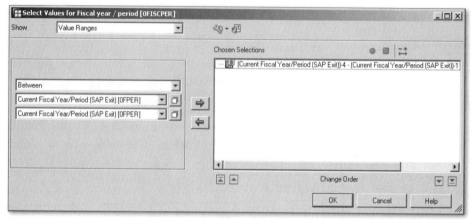

Figure 3.11 Fiscal Year/Period Value Range with Variables

This new selection will now automatically show the previous three months of actual data, not including the current month. You can label this selection something like "Actual - Trailing 3 Months," but it's more straightforward to include the actual months in the description. We can do this by using text variables SAP has included in business content.

Procedure 3.13: Use Text Variables with a Variable Value Range

1. In the Change Selection screen, delete the existing text variable in the Description field and position the cursor on the second line of the field.

2. Click the Variables icon to the right side of the Description field to add an existing text variable.

3. We will need two variables here: one to show the "from" value of the range, and one to show the "to" value. Luckily, SAP has provided variables for both. If technical names are not already shown, click the Wrench icon at the top right until they are displayed.

4. Locate Text Variable Replaced by 0FISCPER [0T_FPERF] in the list, click the variable once, then click the Edit Variable button at the top right. Click the Replacement Path tab and confirm that the Use Interval setting is From Value, then click OK.

5. Locate Text Variable Replaced by 0FISCPER [0T_FPERF] in the list again, click the variable once, and click OK. &0T_FPERF& should appear in the description under Actual.

6. Make sure the cursor is positioned just after the new text variable, type "to," then click the variable icon on the right side of the Description field again.

7. Repeat steps 4 and 5 for Text Variable Replaced by 0FISCPER [0T_FPERT], this time confirming that the Use Interval setting is To Value. Once step 5 is complete, both text variables will appear in the selection description.

8. Make sure there is a space between "to" and both text variables, and click OK to return to the Query Designer screen.

When the query is run, this new selection will now display both the "from" and the "to" values of the fiscal year/period interval: for example, Actual 11/2009 to 01/2010. Once all of these changes have been made, the Rows/COLUMNS tab of Query Designer should look something like Figure 3.12.

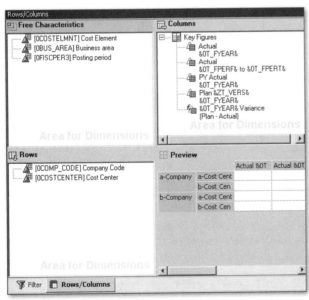

Figure 3.12 Query Designer Screen: Structure with Text Variables

Next we will explore the different properties that can be set for the query as a whole, and for individual query components.

3.5 Properties for Queries and Query Components

The Properties pane on the right side of the Query Designer screen offers many options for customizing the behavior of your query. There are two ways to select an item so its properties are displayed: you can click on the item (or the area), or you can select from the dropdown box at the top of the pane. You can also `Shift` + click or `Ctrl` + click on multiple items in Query Designer to make contiguous or noncontiguous selections, respectively, allowing you to change properties on multiple items at once.

We'll start by examining the properties of the query itself: to see the query's properties, you can either select the first item in the dropdown box (containing the name or technical of the query), or click the Query menu and select Properties.

3.5.1 Query Properties

There are seven tabs containing properties for the query as a whole; we'll start by examining the options on the General tab (see Table 3.1).

Description	Name of the query as seen by end users, can include text variables
Technical Name	Unique identifier given to a query, cannot be changed after query creation
InfoProvider	Technical name of the InfoProvider the query is assigned to, cannot be changed after query creation
Key Date	Determines the date to use when reading time-dependent data, defaults to the current date, can be populated with a fixed value or a variable based on 0CALDAY

Table 3.1 Properties of Query: General Tab

At the bottom of the General tab, the username of the person who created the query is shown, along with the username of the person who last modified the query and when they modified it.

The next tab, Variable Sequence, was discussed in Section 3.3.3. It can be used to modify the order of the variables as they appear on the variable screen.

The settings in the Display tab only affect output in BEx analyzer, the Excel interface for running queries (see Table 3.2). For queries run on the Web, the properties of the Analysis web item in WAD must be changed. Both BEx analyzer and WAD will be discussed later in the book.

Adjust Formatting after Refreshing	Checked by default, this setting will reapply formatting when refreshing a query within the BEx analyzer Excel interface.
Hide Repeated Key Values	Checked by default, this setting will only show the first value when multiple contiguous rows have the same value. See Figure 3.13 for an illustration.
Display Scaling Factors for Key Figures	When checked, this setting displays an additional line in the query output below each column heading indicating the scaling factor for that column. Scaling factor is set in the properties of Key Figure structure components.
Document Links	These three checkboxes control the display of three different types of BI documents. InfoProvider Data documents are displayed on individual cells, and are used to comment on transaction data, i.e., actual dollars spent for a specific cost center during a certain month. Master Data documents are attached to characteristics such as business area or plan version. Metadata documents are at the query level. BI documents are discussed in more detail later in the book.

Table 3.2   Properties of Query: Display Tab

Hide Repeated Key Values: Checked				Hide Repeated Key Values: Unchecked		
Cost Center	**Cost Element**	**Actual**		**Cost Center**	**Cost Element**	**Actual**
100	500	$200		100	500	$200
100	510	$500			510	$500
100	600	$150			600	$150
100	630	$750			630	$750
101	600	$300		101	600	$300
102	600	$800		102	600	$800
102	630	$800			630	$800
103	610	$250		103	610	$250
103	600	$250			600	$250
103	650	$900			650	$900

Figure 3.13   Hide Repeated Key Values Setting

Unlike the Display tab, the rest of the tabs affect query output via both the BEx analyzer Excel interface and queries run on the Web. The Rows/Columns tab includes a preview at the bottom of the window to show the impact of changing settings (see Table 3.3).

Result Position: Rows, Columns	Controls where summarized results rows and columns (typically highlighted in yellow) appear in the query: either above or below existing rows, and to the left or right of existing columns. Default settings show results at the bottom right of existing data.
Suppress Zeros	The default setting, Do Not Suppress, shows all data in the query, even if the data in a row or column is all zero. Changing this setting to Active will hide a row or column if its total adds up to zero, even if individual cells in the row or column are nonzero. The Active (All Values = 0) setting will only hide a row or column if all of the data in the row or column is zero. See User Experience Tip 3.5 for more information.
Effect on	Controls how zero suppression is applied: either only on rows, only on columns, or both rows and columns. For example, if you always want the same set of columns shown, even if one or more of the columns contains no data, you'll want to either disable zero suppression entirely (using the previous setting) or apply the suppression to rows only.

Table 3.3 Properties of Query: Rows/Columns Tab

User Experience Tip 3.6: Watch Out for Active Zero Suppression

Be very careful when using the Active setting for Suppress Zeros, especially when dealing with financial reports with month-by-month breakdowns. For example, offsetting postings may occur within a cost center during the year. If the total for the year adds up to zero and Suppress Zeros is set to Active, that line of data may disappear from the query, depending on which characteristics are active drilldowns. It is safer to use the Active (All Values = 0) setting, which will still show the line containing offsetting postings, even if the total is zero.

Display of +/- Signs	Allows you to change how negative values are displayed, with a minus sign before the number, a minus sign after the number, or the number in parentheses.
Zero Value Display	Not to be confused with Suppress Zeros, this option controls how cells with a value of zero are displayed in the query. Zero values can be shown with the currency or unit (for example, 0 HRS or EUR 0.00), without the currency/unit, as an empty cell, or as a text string.

Table 3.4 Properties of Query: Value Display Tab

The Value Display tab, shown after the Rows/Columns tab, contains settings that can change how negative and zero values are displayed. The next tab, Planning, contains a single checkbox that controls whether or not a query starts in "change mode." This setting is only active for input-ready queries created for BI Integrated Planning.

Finally, the Advanced tab has an option that enables external reporting tools to access the query via the Object Linking and Embedding Database (OLE DB) for Online Analytical Processing (OLAP) interface.

This concludes the properties available for the query as a whole. If you click the dropdown box at the top of the Properties pane, you will see a hierarchy of all of the query components, many of which have their own properties. We'll examine characteristic properties next: expand SHEET (Page), then Rows (Area), and click Cost Center.

3.5.2 Characteristic Properties

Each characteristic has five tabs of settings in its Properties pane. Looking at the General tab for the Cost Center characteristic, you can see the same Description and Technical Name fields available in the query properties section. Changing the description of a characteristic here in the query may come in handy if different user populations have different names for a specific characteristic.

Next, we'll take a look at the Display tab, which contains a number of useful settings for changing how characteristic values appear in the query (see Table 3.5). For these settings, you have the option to check the Use Characteristic Setting checkbox, which will use the settings maintained in the RSD1 maintenance screen for the relevant InfoObject.

Value Display: Display As	Controls how the characteristic value is displayed: you can show only the key value, only the text value, or both the key and the text (the latter options are only available if text values are maintained for the characteristic). You can also choose No Display to hide the characteristic value — for example, if you have Currency as an active drilldown, displaying the characteristic value may be redundant if the currency is already shown on the key figure.
Text View	If you are showing the text value of the characteristic, this option allows you to show Standard text (default value, uses shortest available text), short text, medium text, or long text. Only text lengths that have been maintained in the characteristic are available on this menu.
Sorting: Sort Characteristic	Allows you to sort the characteristic values displayed in the query. The default value uses the order specified in the query definition, sorting by characteristic key if no order specified. Other options include sorting by the values of the characteristic itself, or by an attribute of the characteristic.
Sort by/Sort Direction	Control whether to use the key or text value of the characteristic or attribute, and whether to sort ascending or descending.
Results Rows	There are three options for displaying results rows. The Always Display option will show a results row after each characteristic value displayed in the query, even if there is only one row for that value. Display If More Than One Value will not show a results row if there is only one row for a characteristic value, but it will display the results row for multiple values. The Always Suppress option will never show a results row.

Table 3.5   Properties of Characteristic: Display Tab

User Experience Tip 3.7: Results Row Overload

Superfluous results rows can be distracting, so pay close attention to the Results Rows setting for each characteristic, even those that are not drilled down by default. The Always Display option in particular can potentially lead to the display of non-value-added information. Enabling zero suppression in the query can also lead to the unexpected display of results rows when the Display If More Than One Value option is selected.

We've already introduced the Hierarchy tab in Section 3.3.4, Hierarchies and Hierarchy Variables, when going over the procedure for assigning a display hierarchy to a characteristic, but there are a few additional options on this tab (see Table 3.6). As with the Display tab, you have the option here to use default values maintained in the RSD1 InfoObject maintenance screen by checking the Use Hierarchy Setting checkboxes.

Activate Hierarchy Display	Toggles between displaying the characteristic values according to the display hierarchy selected and displaying the values as a flat list. Grayed out if no display hierarchy is selected.
Selected Hierarchy	Selects a display hierarchy for the characteristic. See Procedure 3.4 in Section 3.3.4 for instructions on how to select a display hierarchy.
Expand to Level	Controls the level the hierarchy will display by default when the characteristic is an active drilldown.
Position of Lower-Level Nodes	You can choose whether to show child nodes above or below their parent node. The default setting is "below," which will show the highest level node at the top or left and the overall result at the bottom or right. The "above" setting flips this around.
Values of Posted Nodes	Controls whether values posted to a hierarchy node are displayed or hidden. Values posted to a node are displayed as an additional entry directly under the node, while the node itself continues to display the aggregated total of all child nodes (including the value posted to the node).
Nodes with Only One Lover-Level Node	This setting allows you to hide hierarchy nodes that only have a single child node, to avoid cluttering up the query with potentially non-value-added information. See Figure 3.14 for an illustration. If a node with only a single child node is already collapsed, when expanded it will be replaced with the next child node that contains multiple values. For example, let's say this option is set to HIDE and the HIERARCHY TOP node in Figure 3.14 is collapsed by default. When the user expands this node, it will automatically be replaced by the THIRD LEVEL A node.
Sorting	Controls whether the order of the values in the hierarchy is according to the order defined in the hierarchy itself (the default value), or by the characteristic value's key or text.

Table 3.6 Properties of Characteristic: Hierarchy Tab

Nodes with Only One Lower-Level Value: Always Show			Nodes with Only One Lower-Level Value: Hide		
▼ Hierarchy Top			▼ Third Level A		
▼ Second Level A			Posted Value 1		
▼ Third Level A			Posted Value 2		
Posted Value 1					
Posted Value 2					

Figure 3.14 Nodes with Only One Lower-Level Value

The next tab, Planning, contains settings that are only valid for queries built for the BI Integrated Planning component. However, the Advanced tab contains a few interesting options (see Table 3.7).

Access Type for Result Values	Allows you to choose how you want characteristic values displayed in the query. If you select Posted Values, the default setting, characteristic values will only appear in the query if there is corresponding transaction data. The Characteristic Relationships option will display data if a relevant characteristic relationship has been created in the BI Integrated Planning module. Finally, choose Master Data if you want all values for this characteristic to be displayed, even values without posted transaction data.
Filter Value Selection During Query Execution	When a user filters on a characteristic, this setting controls the values displayed in the filter list. The Only Posted Values in Navigation setting will only display the values shown based on existing query filters and variable selections. You can also set the filter box to only display values contained in the InfoProvider, display all values in the master data table, or restrict data based on characteristic relationships from BI Integrated Planning.
Refresh Variables	A recent addition to the Advanced tab, this setting is useful if an exit variable associated with this characteristic is being used in the query. If an exit variable is not populating the contents of the variable correctly, try changing this setting to Refresh As Designed instead of the default Refresh Dynamically.

Table 3.7 Properties of Characteristic: Advanced Tab

You can also change properties of display attributes, but the available options are much more limited. Only the General tab and the Value Display settings on the Display tab are available.

3.5.3 Rows and Columns Area Properties

Properties are also available for the Rows and Columns areas, accessible through the dropdown menu at the top of the Properties pane or by switching to the Rows/Columns tab and clicking the Rows heading or the Columns heading in Query Designer.

There is only one option available in the properties for either the Rows area or the Columns area: DISPLAY AS HIERARCHY. If this option is activated, all of the active drilldowns in either the Rows or the Columns section will be shown in a hierarchical format. This type of hierarchical view can be very useful for users who need to selectively drill down on an ad hoc basis to see detailed data in a pseudo-hierarchy across several different characteristics.

Figure 3.15 illustrates the impact of this setting. You'll notice that the rows section of the report is much narrower in the hierarchical view, as the characteristics are nested within a single column. This format is ideal for a summary level report, which can be included as a component in a high-level dashboard.

Display As Hierarchy: Inactive					Display as Hierarchy: Active (in Rows area)	
Cost Center	Cost Element	Actual			Cost Center	Actual
100	500	$200			▼ 100	$1,600
	510	$500			500	$200
	600	$150			510	$500
	630	$750			600	$150
101	600	$300			630	$750
102	600	$800			▼ 101	$300
	630	$800			600	$300
103	610	$250			▼ 102	$1,600
	600	$250			600	$800
	650	$900			630	$800
					▼ 103	$1,400
					610	$250
					600	$250
					650	$900

Figure 3.15 Displaying Rows as a Hierarchy

You can control the default expansion level of the hierarchy with the Expand To option. The characteristic you select in the dropdown menu will be the lowest expanded level of the hierarchy when the report is run. Looking at the example in Figure 3.15, selecting Cost Center in the Expand To dropdown menu will only show the four cost centers, collapsed by default. Users would be able to expand each individual cost center to see data at the cost element level of detail.

When enabling the DISPLAY AS HIERARCHY setting for either rows or columns (or both), note that all of the items in the rows or columns pane are automatically included in the hierarchy. However, only the first characteristic or structure is labeled at the top of the first column of the report, so it is important to utilize training or inline documentation (more on this later) when running reports with hierarchical rows or columns.

It is possible to include characteristics with their own display hierarchies in the hierarchical view of the rows or columns. If the characteristic with the display hierarchy is not the last item in rows or columns, the user would need to expand to the lowest level of the characteristic's hierarchy to uncover the next characteristic.

Using Figure 3.15 as an example again, if the Cost Center hierarchy were enabled, Display as Hierarchy was enabled in the rows, and Expand To was set to Cost Center, the user would only see the Cost Center hierarchy by default (expanded according to the Hierarchy tab properties from Section 3.5.2). The user would then have to expand the Cost Center hierarchy to its lowest level, at which point one more expansion would reveal the Cost Element characteristic. However, if Expand To was set to Cost Element, the Cost Center hierarchy would be again expanded to its default level, with Cost Element displayed as the next level.

As you can see, enabling the hierarchical view of rows or columns can be a powerful tool, but it also has the potential for confusing users, especially those who are used to dealing with the traditional nonhierarchical view of rows or columns. Adding the display hierarchies of individual characteristics into the mix allows for the creation of a hybrid hierarchy that incorporates several different characteristics, but again this can cause usability issues if users are not aware of the structure of the query.

3.5.4 Structure Properties

Now let's use the dropdown menu at the top of the properties pane to select the Key Figures structure by expanding SHEET (Page) and Columns (Area). You can also just click the Key Figures structure in the Columns section of the Rows/Columns tab in Query Designer.

As with the characteristic properties, the General tab for structure properties allows you to change the Description and the Technical Name of the structure. By default, a Key Figure structure will be labeled Key Figures. We usually end up renaming this structure to Columns, because from the user's perspective it typically controls which columns are available in the report.

The technical name of the structure is only used when the structure is saved as a reusable object or when the structure is accessed from an external interface. Saving structures as reusable objects will be covered later in the book. For now, you can leave the technical name blank.

The Display tab offers just one setting, related to zero suppression. When the checkbox Structure as Group is checked, and zero suppression is enabled in the query properties, the structure will only be suppressed if all of the selections and formulas within the structure are zero. If this box is unchecked, individual selections and formulas within the structure will be suppressed if they only contain zeros.

As an example, let's say a query structure contains one selection for Actual data (which contains data) and one for Plan data (which has not yet been populated). If Structure as Group is enabled, the user will see both the Actual and Plan columns in the query, even though the Plan column will be empty. If the setting is disabled, the user would only see the Actual column.

Note that there is no distinction between a selection that is hidden due to zero suppression and one that is hidden based on a filter value on the structure. For this reason, you may want to be careful when unchecking the Structure as Group checkbox in the structure properties if you want users to be aware that a specific column in the query is not populated with data.

3.5.5 Selection and Formula Properties

Several more properties are available for the components of structures: selections and formulas. Click one of the selections in the Key Figures structure, and take a look at the General tab in the Properties pane.

The General tab allows you to change the description of the selection, including adding text variables. This is the same functionality available in the Change

Selection screen. You can also add a technical name to the selection, which is useful when accessing the selection from an external interface (such as OLE DB for OLAP). The Edit button at the bottom is another way to access the Change Selections screen.

The Aggregation tab allows you to change the exception aggregation settings, which are only applicable to formulas and calculated key figures (covered later in the book). The default setting of Use Standard Aggregation means that data is aggregated to the displayed level in the query before the formula is calculated. If you select another option from this menu, you must select a reference characteristic. Data will then be aggregated by this reference characteristic before the formula is calculated.

Several additional options are available on the Display tab, as outlined in Table 3.8.

Hide	Controls whether the selection or formula is displayed in the structure. The default value, Always Show, means that the selection or formula is displayed by default, but can still be hidden by filtering on the structure. Other options include Always Hide, which is hidden by default and cannot be shown by filtering on the structure, or Hide (Can Be Shown), which is also hidden by default but can be shown by the user through the structure filter.
Highlight	The default value, Normal Display, shows data normally. The Highlighted Display option highlights the selection or formula based on the style used in BEx analyzer.
Number of Decimal Places	Controls how many digits are shown after the decimal place, from zero (0) to nine (0.000000000).
Scaling Factor	Can be used to scale the displayed value up, anywhere from a factor of 1 (default value, leaves the value unchanged) to a factor of one billion. For example, if the selection value is 34,500, and the scaling factor is 1000, the query would display 34 if zero decimal places are shown or 34.5 if one decimal place is shown. The scaling factor in use is displayed just under the selection heading, assuming Display Scaling Factors for Key Figures is checked in the Display tab of query properties.

Table 3.8 Properties of Selection/Formula: Display Tab

Sign Change	Selecting the Reverse Sign option here will switch the sign on the displayed value from + to − and vice versa. This option does not affect the value of the selection or formula; it only changes the displayed value, so the original value will be used if included in any other formulas.
Status of Node	This option applies to structure components that are nested to form hierarchies within the structure — a parent node can be expanded or collapsed by default. Nested structure components are discussed in detail later in the book.

Table 3.8 Properties of Selection/Formula: Display Tab (Cont.)

The Advanced tab changes depending on whether we are looking at the properties of a selection or a formula. With a selection, the Constant Selection option is available. When checked, the Constant Selection box will make sure that selection is not affected by any other filters or variable selections in the query. A common example involves showing Actual and Plan data: if plan data is defined on a yearly basis, the value for the entire year is often stored in period 12. If you restrict the plan selection to period 12 and mark it as a constant selection, you will always see the plan data from period 12 regardless of any filters on the posting period.

The properties of a formula (or a calculated key figure, discussed later) will show an option for Formula Collision instead of Constant Selection. Later in the book, we will show how to create multiple structures in Query Designer. In instances where one structure includes a formula with multiplication or division and the other structure has a formula with addition or subtraction, the cell where these two formulas intersect is said to have a formula collision. In these cases, you can tell the query to use one formula over the other to ensure a consistent result, because due to mathematical order of operations the result may be different depending on which formula is evaluated. The Eliminate Formula Collision dropdown can be set to Use Result of This Formula, in which case the formula with the properties window open will be evaluated at the intersection cell. Alternatively, you can select Use Result of Competing Formula, which will use the formula from the other structure.

The next tab, Conversions, includes settings dealing with the conversion of currency and units. The first Conversion Type dropdown menu — for currency translation — is populated with the translation types created in Transaction RSCUR in your BI system. Once you select a currency conversion type, you can pick a target currency, or use a 0CURRENCY variable to allow the user to select a target currency. The next option is for unit conversion, and the conversion types here are populated from Transaction RSUOM in your BI system. As with currency translation, you can also select a fixed target unit from the dropdown menu or create a 0UNIT variable.

The Planning tab deals with settings specific to the BI Integrated Planning component. The options on this tab are disabled unless you have a planning query.

Finally, we have the Calculations tab. The settings on this tab can have a significant impact on how data is displayed in your query. The Calculate Results As dropdown box provides several options for how to determine the correct value for the results rows in the query. Normally, the results row will simply be a sum of the preceding rows, but you can use this setting to change the results row to a number of different possible calculations, including minimum value, maximum value, average, average of nonzero values, first value, last value, or a count of all values. One particularly useful option here — if you have set a scaling factor — is Summation of Rounded Values, which will add values after rounding has taken place. The default summation behavior will add values before rounding, which may lead to a discrepancy between the displayed values and the result. Note that the Calculate Results As setting has no effect on a characteristic with a display hierarchy shown.

The next dropdown box, Calculate Single Values As, allows you to control how the values in individual data cells are calculated. In addition to options such as minimum value, maximum value, moving average, or count (based on the characteristic displayed), you can also normalize the values to reflect a percentage of the characteristic result (Normalize According to Next Group Level Result), the Overall Result of the query, or the query result without taking into account filters set at runtime (Unrestricted Overall Result). Additional options exist to display values as a rank or Olympic rank.

The Cumulated checkbox will calculate the value of a cell by adding all of the previous cells within the characteristic (above or to the left), effectively creating a running total. The Also Apply to Results checkbox will apply the calculation method selected above to the results rows of the query.

Calculation Direction allows you to change how the query handles calculating results. A common example is a month-by-month breakout of financial data along the columns with a characteristic drilled down in the rows – results are calculated top to bottom first, then left to right. If you'd like a month-by-month running total, you would need to check the Cumulated checkbox and change the Calculation Direction to Calculate Along the Columns. The running total would then appear as the results row for each month.

Finally, the Use Precalculated Value checkbox applies to selections that contain a restricted key figure, a reusable component that will be discussed later in the book. With this box checked, the properties in the Calculations tab will be derived from the properties of the restricted key figure.

3.6   Summary: Query-Building Basics

In this chapter, we discussed the basic concepts necessary to build a BW query. Your first step was sourcing the data from an InfoProvider. Next, you set up hard-coded query-level restrictions in the Characteristic Restrictions and Default Values sections of Query Designer. Dynamic restrictions in the form of variables were introduced in the next section, along with the concept of hierarchies.

Once the query-level restrictions were in place, the next step involved populating the query layout. The process for creating a new Key Figure structure was introduced, allowing transaction data to appear in the query via selections and formulas. Drilldown capabilities were then added via characteristics drilled down by default in the Rows and Columns, and optional available drilldowns in the Free Characteristics.

Text variables were then introduced, allowing for dynamic labeling based on variable entries. The next topic involved setting offset values for variables and including variables in ranges.

Finally, we explored the properties available for the query itself and the query components. The properties pane for characteristics, the rows and columns areas, structures, selections, and formulas were discussed.

There are some more features available in Query Designer that were not discussed in this chapter, including multiple structures, the cell editor, exceptions and conditions, nesting selections, and reusable query objects. These features will be discussed later in the book, but first we will move on to the different methods available for running BW Queries.

As one of the major user-facing components of your business intelligence (BI) system, the query runtime interface must help your users do their job and minimize roadblocks.

4   Running Queries on the Web: Business Explorer (BEx) Web Analyzer

The best query design in the world won't do much good if users can't run the query successfully. SAP provides two main avenues for executing BI queries: on the Web, using an SAP-delivered web template or a template of your own making; or via the BEx analyzer Excel interface.

We'll begin our discussion by looking at the query runtime environment on the Web, also known as BEx Web analyzer. In the BW 7 Query Designer, when you click the Query menu and select Execute, the query will launch within your BI portal environment using a default web template. SAP includes the 0ANALYSIS_ PATTERN as the default web template for running queries on the Web, but this template can be changed. For now, let's examine the features of SAP's default web runtime environment for BI queries.

4.1   The Variable Screen: Personalization and Variants

Because the variable screen is often the first item that appears when running a query, we might as well cover it first. We briefly discussed the variable screen in Chapter 3, Section 3, Variables. For a more in-depth analysis of the features available in the variable screen, we will be using a different example query, this time relating to headcount reporting. Based on the skills you gained in Chapter 3, Building Effective Queries: The Basics of Query Designer, you should be able to construct this example query yourself. However, if you wish to follow along with the actual versus plan query created in the previous chapter, feel free to do so, as the same concepts will still apply.

Figure 4.1 shows the default variable screen with no default values. Note that there is one required variable without a default value, so the variable screen will always display first when running this report. However, even if there were no required variables, the variable screen would still automatically display first when executing a query from Query Designer: this is because Query Designer includes the VARI-ABLE_SCREEN=X parameter in the URL. When you run the query directly from your portal environment instead of from Query Designer, the variable screen will behave normally.

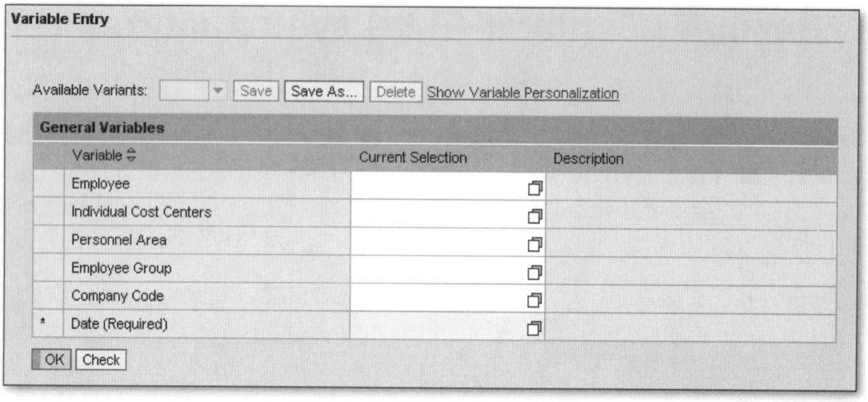

Variable Entry

Available Variants: [ ] ▼ [Save] [Save As...] [Delete] Show Variable Personalization

General Variables		
Variable ⇕	Current Selection	Description
Employee	⊡	
Individual Cost Centers	⊡	
Personnel Area	⊡	
Employee Group	⊡	
Company Code	⊡	
* Date (Required)	⊡	

[OK] [Check]

Figure 4.1 The Variable Screen

As discussed before, the value help screen for each variable will differ, depending on whether the variable allows a single value selection, multiple single values, an interval, or a selection option (multiple values and ranges with different logical operators).

Some groups of users will always end up filling out one or more variables with the same value whenever they run reports. For example, a cost center manager may only be interested in data pertaining to his cost center, or an executive responsible for a particular subsidiary may always want to restrict data to a certain company code. SAP provides a tool called *variable personalization* that allows users to "set and forget" a variable — when the user fills out the variable with a specific value, they can "personalize" it so SAP will remember that value for *any* query using that variable.

Click the SHOW VARIABLE PERSONALIZATION link at the top right of the variable screen. A new PERSONALIZED VARIABLES section will appear below the main GENERAL VARIABLES block. To "personalize" a variable, fill out a value for the variable and click the single down arrow button. Let's fill out a value for COMPANY CODE and add it to the PERSONALIZED VARIABLES section. Figure 4.2 shows the state of the variable screen after a variable has been personalized.

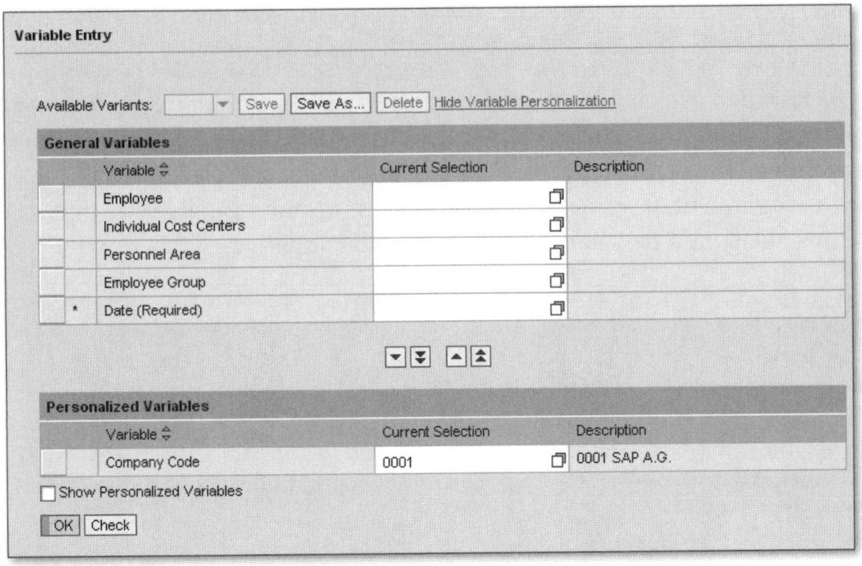

Figure 4.2 Variable Screen with Personalized Variable

If you click OK, the COMPANY CODE variable will now be hidden when running any query containing that variable, not just the current query. When you go back to the variable screen (or the variable screen of any query containing a personalized variable) BW 7 will notify you that one or more variables are personalized. You can click the Show Variable Personalization button again to view your personalized variables.

Change the value of a personalized variable works the same way as changing a non-personalized variable, you just need to click Show Variable Personalization and modify the value. The new value is immediately personalized.

At the bottom of the PERSONALIZED VARIABLES section, there is a SHOW PERSONALIZED VARIABLES checkbox. If you check this box, personalized variables will appear with the rest of the variables in the variable screen, even if the personalized variables section is hidden. With this setting enabled, there is no distinction between personalized and nonpersonalized variables in the variable screen, unless you click SHOW VARIABLE PERSONALIZATION.

To "depersonalize" a variable, click SHOW VARIABLE PERSONALIZATION, select the personalized variable, and click the first up arrow. The variable will now appear in the GENERAL VARIABLES block instead of under PERSONALIZED VARIABLES. Depersonalizing the variable will not clear the value for this run of the query, but future query executions will no longer use the personalized value. When you depersonalize a variable, it is depersonalized for all queries at once.

If you ever need to personalize or depersonalize all variables on the variable screen, you can click the double down arrow or double up arrow respectively. Note that it is possible to personalize variables without entering a value – this may be useful for users who will never need to deal with one or more variables, as they can personalize them with no values to hide them and simplify the variable screen.

> **User Experience Tip 4.1: Know When to Train Users to Personalize**
>
> Variable personalization can be a great feature, but make sure it is targeted to appropriate user populations. While BW 7 is better than previous versions about letting users know when they have a personalized variable, if you set up a query to bypass the variable screen, the user does not have a chance to review personalized variable values unless they go back to the variable screen after the report has been run. If a user often needs to look at different company codes, variable personalization on company code is probably not going to work well. Because you don't have control over when your users will personalize variables, this feature needs to be covered in user training.
>
> This is especially important if multiple queries share the same variables. "Set and forget" works well in this case, as long as users are aware that their variable personalization applies across multiple queries.

> **User Experience Tip 4.2: Oops, I Forgot I Personalized This Before**
>
> If you cover variable personalization when running training classes related to BW queries, always make sure to depersonalize the variable after you personalize it. Otherwise, in your next training session you may inadvertently end up working with only a subset of available data.

Another method of saving variable values involves using a query variant. A query variant will save all of the variable values in a specific query (including personalized variables) as either a global variant or a user-specific variant. To save a variant, fill out your variables first, then click the Save As button at the top. If the Save As User Variant checkbox is checked, the variant will only be available to that user. If unchecked, the query variant will be global and available to all users, and the system will prompt for a unique technical name. Global variants can only be created by users with the S_RS_PARAM authorization object maintained.

To apply a previously saved variant, simply select the variant from the dropdown box at the top of the variable screen. This will override all existing values in the variable screen, including any personalized variables. To make changes to an existing variant, you can select it, make the necessary changes, and click the Save button. You can also delete a variant by selecting it and clicking Delete.

Because you're probably tired of staring at the variable screen by now, let's fill out the variables (select variable values so the query will return some data) and click OK to run the query.

4.2   Query Analysis with Drag-and-Drop Navigation

The main query analysis screen of SAP's default web template (seen in Figure 4.3) contains three main parts: a header with a toolbar, a navigation pane on the left side, and an analysis grid showing the query's data. BW 7, unlike previous versions, allows you to navigate the query by dragging and dropping elements from the navigation pane and the analysis grid.

You'll note that the analysis grid only shows a limited amount of data per screen. You can use the three down arrow buttons at the bottom of the analysis grid to scroll down one line, scroll down one page, and jump to the end of the data, respectively. The three right arrow buttons at the bottom right will let you scroll to the right in much the same way.

The example query shows headcount by month, drilled down to the cost center and the individual employee level. Let's say we only want to see a summarized headcount at the cost center level instead of individual employees. We can remove the EMPLOYEE drilldown via drag and drop two different ways: the first method involves dragging the EMPLOYEE header from the analysis grid to an empty spot below FREE CHARACTERISTICS in the navigation pane (or an empty space outside the analysis grid). Alternatively, you can drag the Employee entry in the navigation pane from the rows to an empty spot under FREE CHARACTERISTICS.

If you make a mistake, you can right-click on any cell in the analysis grid to view the context menu, point to Back, and select Back One Navigation Step or Back to Start. You can also go back to Query Designer and execute the query again.

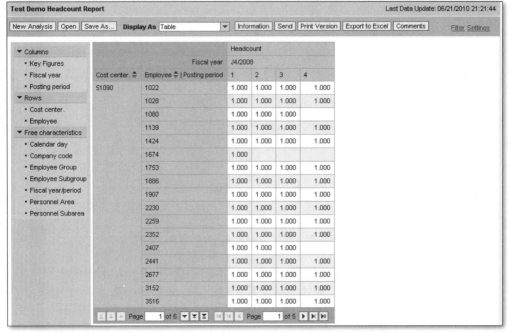

Figure 4.3 Query Analysis Screen

Be careful where you drop the Employee header: if you are pointing to another characteristic when you release the mouse button, the Employee drilldown will be swapped with the target characteristic. The cursor will change depending on which action will be taken, see Figure 4.4 for a description of the different cursors and what they mean.

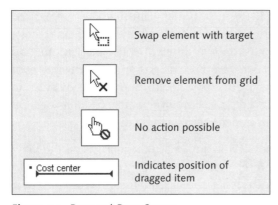

Figure 4.4 Drag-and-Drop Cursors

As an example, let's try swapping one of the drilled down characteristics. If you drag the COST CENTER header (from either the analysis grid or from the Rows section of the navigation pane) onto COMPANY CODE under FREE CHARACTERISTICS in the navigation pane, COST CENTER will be removed from the report and replaced with COMPANY CODE. The report should now only contain Company Code in the rows.

You can also change the order of structure elements by dragging and dropping. This example query only has one structure element (HEADCOUNT), but in the query from the previous chapter you would be able to drag the Actual column to the right of the Plan column to change the order.

In addition to swapping individual characteristics, you can also swap entire sections of the navigation pane. For example, if you drag the COLUMNS header onto the Rows header, all of the characteristics within columns and rows will be swapped. You can also drag the FREE CHARACTERISTICS header onto the ROWS or COLUMNS header to add all available drilldowns at the same time to the rows or columns. Finally, dragging the Rows or COLUMNS header onto the FREE CHARACTERISTICS header will remove all characteristics drilled down in the rows or columns.

You can also add characteristics as new drilldowns. The easiest way to do this is by dragging the characteristic from the FREE CHARACTERISTICS section of the navigation pane up to the Rows section (or the COLUMNS section if you want to drill across). Again, you should be careful where you release the mouse button — if another characteristic is selected, you will execute a swap instead of adding a new drilldown. Instead, you should aim for the white space above or below an existing characteristic. A black line will appear to indicate the position of the new drilldown, as seen in Figure 4.4.

An alternative method of adding a new drilldown is to drag the characteristic from the navigation pane to the analysis grid. With this method, aim for the vertical line that separates the characteristics in the grid — as with the previous method, you will see a black line (vertical this time) to indicate where the characteristic will be placed.

Let's add COST CENTER as a drilldown, this time after COMPANY CODE. You can use either method discussed previously. Once COST CENTER has been drilled down, remove COMPANY CODE. You should now see a list of cost centers similar to the one shown in Figure 4.5.

We will now use drag-and-drop functionality to simultaneously add a new drilldown and filter on existing data. This is accomplished by dragging a characteristic from the navigation pane onto an existing characteristic *value* in the report rows or columns (as opposed to the characteristic header) or an individual cell in the analysis grid.

Using Figure 4.5 as an example, if you drag the EMPLOYEE characteristic onto the 51194 value under COST CENTER, the report will return a list of all employees within cost center 51194 during all months visible in the columns. EMPLOYEE will be automatically added as a drilldown, COST CENTER will be removed, and a filter on COST CENTER will be set up. Alternatively, if you drag the EMPLOYEE characteristic onto the 2 value next to POSTING PERIOD, it will only show headcount data for February (assuming a January - December fiscal calendar), but the EMPLOYEE characteristic will now be drilled across in the columns, and COST CENTER will still be an active drilldown in the rows.

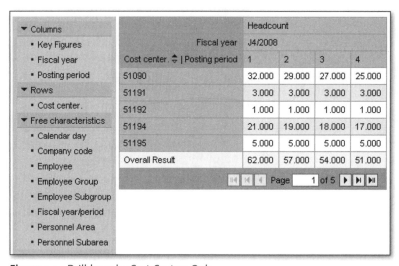

Figure 4.5 Drilldown by Cost Centers Only

If you instead drag the Employee drilldown onto one of the data cells in the grid, it will remove all existing drilldowns in the rows and columns, leaving only the new Employee drilldown in the rows and the structure (in this case, HEADCOUNT) in the columns. Filters will be automatically set up for all previously visible characteristics based on the position of the data cell. For example, if you drag EMPLOYEE onto the 19.000 value in the fourth row of the second column, you will see a list of all employees in cost center 51194 during the second posting period.

You can also navigate the query using context menu commands; the context menu will be covered in a later section of the chapter.

To see which filter values have been set up, you can click the Filter link on the right side of the header at the top of the screen. Click this link now to open the filter screen.

4.3 Setting Filter Values

Figure 4.6 shows an example of the filter section, accessible from the Filter link on the right side of the header. All characteristics in the query are shown here, along with all structures. In this example, KEY FIGURES represents the structure, and if the query has multiple elements in the structure you can filter on one or more of them.

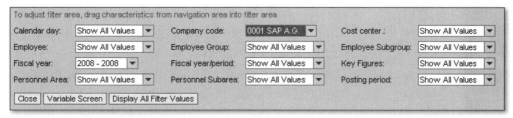

Figure 4.6 Filter Screen in Web Runtime Environment

To set up a new filter, you can click the dropdown menu next to the characteristic and select Edit. A new window will open, allowing you to select values for the characteristic. The select value window is the same one used for a Selection Option variable, so you have the maximum amount of flexibility in terms of choosing a single value, multiple single values, and ranges using different logical operators. The default view of the select value window, as seen in Figure 4.7, will allow you to select one or more single values by clicking the values on the left side and moving them to the right side with the Add button.

The ability to search by key or text is available by clicking the SHOW VIEW dropdown and selecting Search. You can also directly enter characteristic values using the Enter a value field at the bottom left of the window. Once a value has been added to the right side, you can choose to specifically exclude the value by clicking the red button above the Description header.

Figure 4.7 Select Value Box for Filter, Single Values View

To add one or more value ranges using logical operators, click the SHOW TOOL dropdown menu and select Value ranges. This interface, as seen in Figure 4.8, will allow you to create value ranges using operators such as between, greater than (greater), and less than (lower). Once you've created a value range, don't forget to click the Add button to move it to the right side.

The example shown in Figure 4.8 reflects a value range combined with an excluded single value (the red equal sign indicates that it is excluded). You can have any number of ranges and single values in the filter. As a shortcut, you can directly enter values in the Enter a range field. The direct entry syntax for the restrictions shown in Figure 4.8 is 1 – 6; !3. Make sure to include spaces before and after the dash, and after the semicolon to indicate there are multiple values.

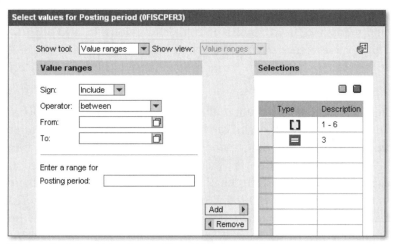

Figure 4.8 Select Value Box for Filter, Value Ranges View

If you change the filter value for a characteristic with an active hierarchy, the select values box will show a hierarchical view, where you can add multiple hierarchy nodes or characteristic values within the hierarchy. You can still switch back to the Single values tool to add individual characteristic values without using the hierarchy.

The icon at the top right of the window will display a number of properties specific to the select value screen. The General tab allows you to display key, text, or both key and text characteristic values, and you can also choose the Member Access Mode: to show all characteristic values from the mater data table, only values within the InfoProvider, or only the values shown in the query's current navigational state.

If the characteristic has display attributes, the Attributes tab allows you to choose which attributes to display in the select value screen, and how you want to display them (key, text, or both). If the characteristic has an active hierarchy, the Hierarchy tab has options for access mode (similar to the General tab), and settings for how you want the hierarchy nodes to be displayed.

The Sorting tab lets you modify the sort direction, and it will let you sort by the characteristic itself (Default) or by a display attribute. To select the display attribute to use for sorting, select Members in the Sort by dropdown, then select the attribute in the new dropdown box that appears. You can also select how you want to sort by attribute (key or text).

79

When you're finished changing settings, click the OK button to return to the select values screen, and then click OK to confirm your filter selections. Instead of Show All Values, the filter value you've selected will be displayed next to the characteristic. To remove the filter, pull down the menu next to the characteristic and select Clear.

Restrictions made in the query design under the Default Values section will appear in the filter section at query runtime, and can be removed just like a regular filter setting. However, remember from the previous chapter that restrictions set up in the Characteristic Restrictions section of Query Designer cannot be changed at runtime, and as such will not appear in the filter section. You can see a complete list of all filter values by clicking the Display All Filter Values button. Characteristic Restrictions will appear under Static Filters, while other restrictions show up under Dynamic Filters or Variables.

The Variable Screen button at the bottom of the filters section provides another way to return to the variable screen. Values entered on the variable screen also appear as filters and can be changed either in the filters section or the variable screen.

Another way of setting up a single filter value is to drag the value from the data cell in the analysis grid onto the filter area. Pay close attention to the cursor: if you drag the value onto an existing characteristic in the filter section and you see the "remove element" cursor (see Figure 4.4), that value will be *excluded* from the query, and you will see the value preceded by an exclamation point in the filter value of the relevant characteristic. However, if you drag the value to an empty space in the filter section and you see the "swap element" cursor, that value will be included in the filter for the relevant characteristic. Note that the latter will overwrite any previous filter values for the characteristic.

When you are finished setting up filters, click the Close button. Note that filters are applied to the report immediately after you click the OK button in the select values box.

4.4 Changing Query Settings at Runtime

You may have noticed the Settings link next to the Filter link at the top right of the query header. Let's click that link and explore some of the runtime settings available. These are primarily high-level settings that deal with the query or the analysis grid as a whole; later in the chapter we will take a look at lower-level settings for characteristics, data cells, and so on.

Unlike the Filters section, you must click the Apply button at the bottom of each tab to save the changes to settings on that tab. We'll start by looking at the TABLE tab, as seen in Figure 4.9.

The first option under LAYOUT allows you to enable or disable alternating row colors in the analysis grid. The next item, EXCEPTION VISUALIZATION, controls how exceptions are displayed on the screen. You can show exceptions by color, symbol, or with both a symbol and text. Color-blind users will find this setting especially useful if they use exceptions in reports.

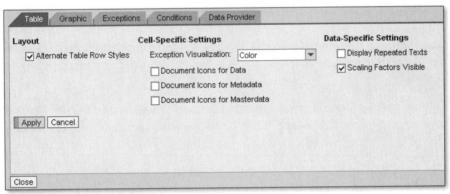

Figure 4.9 Runtime Query Settings: Table Tab

Next, you will find the same three checkboxes found on the Display tab of query properties in Query Designer dealing with BI documents. See Chapter 3, Section 3.5.1, Query Properties, for more information about these properties. The last two DATA-SPECIFIC SETTINGS are also similar to checkboxes found in the query properties Display tab. When unchecked, the DISPLAY REPEATED TEXTS option only shows the first value when multiple contiguous rows have the same value. See Figure 3.13 in Chapter 3 for an illustration. The SCALING FACTORS VISIBLE checkbox controls whether or not an additional line is shown below each column heading indicating the scaling factor of that column.

The GRAPHIC tab contains settings pertaining to graphs and charts. The DATA PROVIDER tab, as seen in Figure 4.10, has four groups of options. The DATA FORMATTING options include a setting to control where results rows are displayed in the query. There are also two checkboxes that enable a hierarchical view of columns and rows — see Chapter 3, Section 3.5.3, Rows and Columns Area Properties, for more information and an illustration of this setting.

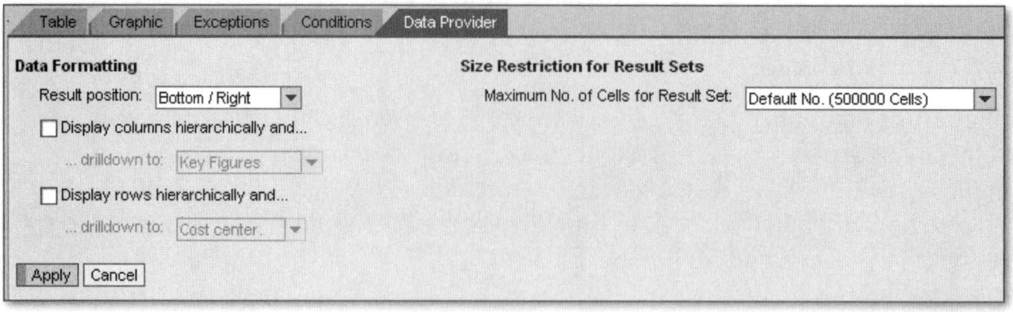

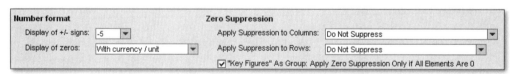

Figure 4.10 Runtime Query Settings: Data Provider Tab

The next setting allows the user to restrict the maximum number of rows available in the query. For performance reasons it is not recommended that users adjust this value.

The continuation of the DATA PROVIDER tab is shown in Figure 4.11. The NUMBER FORMAT settings allow the user to control how negative signs and cells containing a value of zero are displayed.

Finally, the ZERO SUPPRESSION features in this tab are identical to those discussed in the previous chapter. See the discussion of the Rows/Columns tab in Chapter 3, Section 3.5.1, for more information about zero suppression, and Chapter 3, Section 3.5.4, Structure Properties, for an explanation of the "KEY FIGURES" AS GROUP setting.

Figure 4.11 Runtime Query Settings: Data Provider Tab Continued

4.5   Opening and Saving Queries at Runtime

Looking to the left of the Filter and Settings links, you will see a toolbar consisting of a series of buttons. These buttons are part of SAP's delivered 0ANALYSIS_PATTERN web template, and we'll see how to modify the toolbar in later chapters.

For now, let's go over the functionality of the New Analysis, Open, and Save As buttons.

Unlike previous versions, the default web template in BW 7 allows you to run additional queries directly from the template at runtime. When you click the New Analysis button, you will be prompted to select a new query to run using the default web template. You can search for a query, look in your history, open a query from your favorites, select a query from one of your assigned roles, or inspect the queries available within InfoProviders (based on your authorization).

The New Analysis button also allows you to open previously created query views by changing the Type dropdown to View. You can even create a new query running directly off an InfoProvider by selecting InfoProvider from the Type dropdown. The result is similar to using Transaction LISTCUBE in your Business Warehouse (BW) system: all key figures in the InfoProvider are displayed, and you can add additional drilldowns as needed from the Free Characteristics section of the navigation pane.

Unlike the New Analysis button, which allows users to "start from scratch" by loading a query from the BW server, the OPEN button displays BI web applications that have been previously saved to your portal environment in one of three areas: Favorites, My Portfolio, and BEx Portfolio (see Table 4.1).

Favorites	Accessible only to a single user, saved web application appears in Portal Favorites iView (basic list of links) within Detailed Navigation section of BI portal.
	Knowledge Management (KM) path in the portal: userhome/<userid>/favorites
My Portfolio	Accessible only to a single user, saved web application appears in My Portfolio iView (KM navigation iView using Broadcasting layout), available from BEx portal role.
	KM path in the portal: BIuserhome/<userid>/Personal BEx Documents
BEx Portfolio	Accessible to multiple users, saved web application appears in BEx Portfolio iView (KM navigation iView using Broadcasting layout), available from BEx portal role.
	KM path in portal: /documents/Public Documents

Table 4.1 Saved BI Web Application Repositories in the Portal Environment

Each repository exists within the KM infrastructure built into the portal environment. The key differences between the repositories are the intended audience (single user versus multiple users) and the presentation style of the resulting list of saved web applications (basic list versus rich KM layout). The rich KM layout includes features such as the ability to rate entries, attach notes, search, create folders, send a link via email, and provide feedback directly to the owner. These differences are summarized in Table 4.2.

	Intended audience	Presentation style
Favorites	Single user	Basic list of links
My Portfolio	Single user	Rich KM layout
BEx Portfolio	Multiple users	Rich KM layout

Table 4.2   Key Feature Matrix of BI Web Application Repositories

The third button on the toolbar, Save As…, allows you to save the navigation state of the current web application as a document in one of the three repositories mentioned previously.

Users of previous BW versions may be used to using bookmarks and web template personalization to save the navigation state of BW reports run on the Web. Both concepts are still around in BW 7, and they will be discussed later in the book.

You can also still save the state of a web application as a query view; this is done using the Save View command on the context menu (covered later in this chapter). Note that query views saved in this manner only exist on the BW server and cannot be included in a BI web application repository on the portal. However, you can open a query view using the New Analysis button and use the Save As button to save it on the portal.

4.6   The Rest of the Toolbar

There are several additional options available on the rest of the toolbar included in the default web template. The first option after Save As is a dropdown menu that allows you to switch between viewing only the analysis grid, only a graphical representation of the data, or both. The type of graphical representation is determined by the Graphic properties, which are accessible by clicking the Settings link on the right side of the toolbar and selecting the Graphics tab.

Options in the Graphics tab include the type of chart shown (bar, pie, area, and many more), the type and position of the legend, and manual descriptions of the different axes. You can also elect to swap display axes, hide or show the query result as a value on the chart, and hide or show expanded hierarchy nodes.

The next button on the toolbar, Information, shows several useful pieces of information about the query, including the query technical name, InfoProvider information, who last changed the query and when, and the name of the web template. This screen also shows static filters, dynamic filters, and variables, the same information found in the Display All Filter Values screen discussed in Section 4.3, Setting Filter Values. The second tab in the Information screen, Query Documentation, displays the BI documents associated with this query from the KM repository on your portal system.

The Send button opens the Broadcasting Wizard, which uses the BEx Broadcaster tool to send the current navigation state of your query to others via email. In step 1 of the wizard, you can choose to send data as a link to the online report, or in MHTML (MIME HTML — essentially an HTML email message), XML, HTML, or PDF format. In step 2, you enter your recipient email addresses, subject line, and the body of the email. If you'd like to send the email right away, click the Execute button at the bottom right of the step 2 dialog box. To continue on to steps 3 and 4, which allow you to schedule the email to be sent in the future or periodically, click the Continue button.

The Print Version button could very well have been called "Export to PDF." This button will bring up the Export Dialog screen, with a number of options to format the print-friendly output of the query. Scaling functionality is built into this dialog box, and you can scale the query output to the page width, fit it to the entire page, or print it in a poster format. You can also adjust margins, change page sizes, and add custom headers and footers. Clicking the OK button in this dialog box will open a PDF file showing the current navigational state of your query.

Next, we have the Export to Excel button. This button, surprisingly enough, exports the current navigational state of the query to a Microsoft Excel file, and prompts you to open or save the file.

All of the export options under the last three buttons are offline data dumps, with the exception of the Send button's option to email a link to the online report.

Finally, the Comments button displays BI documents in your portal's KM repository that are associated with the current InfoProvider. You can add a new plain text comment, add a formatted text document, or upload your own document. The resulting documents are automatically added to the KM repository.

We've now covered all of the buttons and links available on the default web template toolbar. You may have noticed that the top line of the header includes the query name on the left and a "last data update" date and time on the right. The "last data update" information indicates the last time data was loaded into the query's InfoProvider.

4.7 The Context Menu

In addition to the buttons on the toolbar, there are several more functions available in the right-click context menu. The default web template can be modified to add or remove functions to the context menu, but for now we will go over the default functionality available.

4.7.1 Back

One of the most useful functions in the BEx Web analyzer is the Back feature. Later in the book we will see how to add a Back button to the toolbar, but for now we will make do with the two options available in the context menu: Back One Navigation Step and Back to Start. Because the browser's back button does not function correctly in BEx Web analyzer, the Back One Navigation Step option takes its place. If you select Back to Start, you will go back to the default navigation state of the query. Be careful when selecting Back to Start, because there is no way to undo this function. The Back options are available when right-clicking anywhere in the navigation pane or analysis grid.

If you have jump targets set up via the Report-to-Report Interface (RRI) in Transaction RSBBS, these jump targets will appear under the Goto menu just after Back.

4.7.2 Filter

The Filter items in the context menu provide shortcuts to the functionality available in the Filter screen discussed in Section 4.3. The item you right-click on to bring up the context menu is referred to as "in-context."

Keep Filter Value	Available only on characteristic values.
	Removes the in-context characteristic from the rows or columns, and sets up a filter for only the characteristic value selected.
Keep Filter Value on Axis	Available only on characteristic values.
	Keeps the in-context characteristic drilled down in the rows or columns, and sets up a filter for only the characteristic value selected.
Filter and Drill Down By	Available only on characteristic values, requires the selection of another characteristic from the submenu.
	Removes the in-context characteristic from the rows or columns, sets up a filter for only the characteristic value selected, and adds the selected characteristic as a new drilldown.
Select Filter Value	Available on characteristic headers and characteristic values. Opens the Select Values screen for the in-context characteristic, see Section 4.3 for more information.
Remove Filter Value	Available on characteristic headers and characteristic values with active filters only. Removes all values from the active filter on the in-context characteristic. Will also remove filter values set up in the Default Values section of Query Designer, but does not affect filter values in Characteristic Restrictions.
Variable Screen	Available on characteristic headers and characteristic values. Opens the variable screen. More information is available in Section 4.1, The Variable Screen: Personalization and Variants.

Table 4.3 Context Menu: Filter

By modifying the web template, you can show another item in the context menu under Filter that lets you manage conditions. An option to manage exceptions can also be shown in the main context menu.

4.7.3 Change Drilldown

The Change Drilldown functions (listed in Table 4.4) are also shortcuts that provide some of the same drag-and-drop functionality discussed in Section 4.2, Query Analysis with Drag-and-Drop Navigation.

Drill Down By (from characteristic header)	When called by right-clicking on a characteristic header, the Drill Down By item displays either Horizontal or Vertical, allowing you to move the in-context characteristic from the rows to the columns or vice versa.
Drill Down By (from characteristic value)	When called by right-clicking on a characteristic value, the Drill Down By item requires the selection of another characteristic, which is added as a new drilldown just after the in-context characteristic.
Swap with	Available on characteristic headers and characteristic values, requires the selection of another characteristic from the submenu. Swaps the position of the in-context characteristic and the selected characteristic. If the selected characteristic is not currently drilled down, the in-context characteristic will be removed from the rows or columns and replaced with the selected characteristic.
Remove Drilldown	Available on characteristic headers and characteristic values. Removes the in-context characteristic from the rows or columns.
Swap Axes	Available anywhere in the analysis grid or navigation pane. Moves all characteristics and structures from the rows to the columns and vice versa.

Table 4.4 Context Menu: Change Drilldown

4.7.4 Hierarchy

There are three functions (listed in Table 4.5) in the context menu that deal exclusively with hierarchies, and are only available when right-clicking on a characteristic with an assigned display hierarchy. See Chapter 3, Section 3.3.4, Hierarchies and Hierarchy Variables, for details on assigning display hierarchies to characteristics.

Hierarchy Active	Available on characteristic headers and characteristic values with assigned display hierarchies. When checked, the in-context characteristic is displayed according to the assigned hierarchy. When unchecked, the characteristic values are displayed as a flat list. Selecting this item toggles between these two states.

Table 4.5 Context Menu: Hierarchy

Hierarchy Node Expanded	Available on characteristic values with *active* display hierarchies only. When checked, the in-context hierarchy node is expanded to show the next level. When unchecked, the hierarchy node is collapsed. Selecting this item toggles between these two states.
Expand Hierarchy	Available on characteristic headers and characteristic values with *active* display hierarchies only, requires the selection of a hierarchy level in submenu. When checked, the *entire* in-context hierarchy is expanded to the selected level.

Table 4.5 Context Menu: Hierarchy (Cont.)

4.7.5 Broadcast and Export

The next group of functions, Broadcast and Export, provides some of the functionality from toolbar buttons, and a few options only available from the context menu. All of the options under Broadcast and Export (see Table 4.6) are available when right-clicking anywhere in the navigation pane or analysis grid.

Broadcast by Email	Available anywhere in the analysis grid or navigation pane. Opens the same Broadcasting Wizard available from the Send button in the toolbar, allowing you to send your web application via email in a number of different formats. See Section 4.6, The Rest of the Toolbar, for more information.
Broadcast to Portal	Available anywhere in the analysis grid or navigation pane. Opens a similar Broadcasting Wizard as the one available from the Send button, except this wizard allows you to save your web application to a KM folder on your portal. The default option is to save the web application to My Portfolio (KM path Bluserhome/<userid>/Personal BEx Documents), but you can select any other folder within the KM repository.
Broadcast to Printer	Available anywhere in the analysis grid or navigation pane. Opens a Broadcasting Wizard that helps you send your web application to a network printer in either PS/PCL or PDF format.

Table 4.6 Context Menu: Broadcast and Export

Export to Excel	Available anywhere in the analysis grid or navigation pane.
	Just like the Export to Excel button on the toolbar (see Section 4.6), this menu item will export the current navigation state of your web application as a Microsoft Excel file.
Export to CSV	Available anywhere in the analysis grid or navigation pane.
	Exports the current navigation state of your web application as a comma separated values (CSV) formatted file. The default separator is a semicolon (";"), but you can change this in Transaction SPRO on your BI system, via the following menu path: SAP REFERENCE IMG • SAP NETWEAVER •BUSINESS INTELLIGENCE •LINKS TO OTHER SOURCE SYSTEMS • CONNECTION BETWEEN FLAT FILE AND BI SYSTEM • SET OPTIONS FOR UPLOADING FLAT FILES • SET FIELD SEPARATOR FOR CSV FILE.
Bookmark	Available anywhere in the analysis grid or navigation pane.
	Creates a specific URL that refers to the current navigation state of your web application and offers to add the URL to your browser's favorites. Unlike the functionality offered by the Save As button on the toolbar, this option does not create any new KM documents in the portal.

Table 4.6 Context Menu: Broadcast and Export (Cont.)

Note that there is a hidden context menu item under Broadcast and Export that lets you export query data to a format specific to Microsoft Excel 2000, in case there are compatibility issues with the traditional Export to Excel feature.

4.7.6   Save View/Personalize Web App

There are two additional hidden items within the main context menu: Save View allows you to save a query view to your BW server, where it can be opened from the New Analysis button, and Personalize Web Application saves the current navigational state as the new default state for your web application. After personalizing your web application, it will appear in the personalized state every time you run it from that point forward. To undo this, select the Delete Personalization option under Personalize Web Application.

These hidden context menu items can be enabled by modifying the web template with Web application designer (WAD), as shown later in the book.

> **User Experience Tip 4.3: Should You Enable the Personalize Web Application Feature?**
>
> Given the number of methods available to save the navigational state of your query discussed in Section 4.5, Opening and Saving Queries at Runtime, you may want to think twice before enabling the Personalize Web Application feature. Unlike variable personalization, there is no indication to the user that the current web application has been personalized, so users might think they are seeing one set of data when in fact they are only seeing a subset of that data. It may be safer to have your users create bookmarks or save navigation states to their favorites using the Save As button.

4.7.7 Properties

The next item, Properties, allows you to change settings for a characteristic, data cells within a specific structure, all data cells for all structures, or an axis (rows or columns).

The characteristic properties available here are similar to those found in Query Designer (see Chapter 3, Section 3.5.2, Characteristic Properties, for more information), with the notable addition of the Attributes tab, which allows you to add any number of display attributes to the analysis grid. The characteristic properties box is slightly different when a structure is selected — here you can set zero suppression options for the structure, as seen in Chapter 3, Section 3.5.4, Structure Properties.

The properties for data cells and all data cells are the same, and they have the same effect if the query has a single structure. If there are multiple structures, changing the properties of data cells will only affect the cells within the in-context structure, while the properties of all data cells apply to both structures. The options here are similar to those found in the selection and formula properties in Query Designer, as explained in Chapter 3, Section 3.5.5, Selection and Formula Properties.

Axis properties in BEx Web analyzer include options found in Query Designer query properties (Chapter 3, Section 3.5.1, Query Properties) and the Rows and Columns Areas (Chapter 3, Section 3.5.3): zero suppression settings, the position of overall results rows, and the option to view the row or column hierarchically.

4.7.8   Calculations and Translations

The options under the Calculations and Translations submenu include more of the items available in the selection and formula properties in Query Designer (Chapter 3, Section 3.5.5). You can change the way single values or results are calculated, and you can enable the cumulative display of data.

However, the most interesting item here is the option to create a new local formula by selecting Formulas, then New Formula. As seen in Figure 4.12, a web-based version of the FORMULA BUILDER screen will appear, allowing users to build a new formula based on the existing selections and formulas in the structures combined with a number of available operators. Formulas created this way will disappear once the user closes their session, but saving the web application using the Save As button will preserve the local formulas. Existing formulas that have been created in Query Designer cannot be edited using this tool; you can only create new ad hoc formulas.

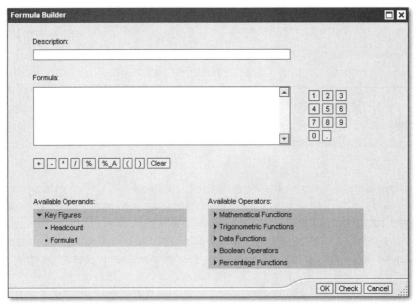

Figure 4.12   Web-Based Formula Builder

User Experience Tip 4.4: Spread the Word about Local Formulas in Web Reports

In previous versions of BW, a common user complaint was the inability to add custom calculations directly in BW reports run on the Web, a gap that caused many users to use the BEx analyzer Excel interface over the Web. SAP has added this functionality in BW 7, but because it's still buried in the context menu for structures, it's up to you to publicize this feature to your users. Allowing power users to create custom formulas as needed and saving those formulas in a shared BEx Portfolio may significantly reduce the need to create large numbers of queries.

4.7.9 Documents

The items under the Documents submenu allow you to display or create BI documents (stored in the portal KM repository) attached to the characteristic or cell. There are three types of BI documents:

- Metadata (type META), associated with query structures or characteristics
- Master data (type MAST), associated with characteristic values
- InfoProvider data (type TRAN), associated with individual data cells

To show a list of BI documents associated with a query element, right-click on the element and select Documents, then Display Documents. There are also options to create plain text comments or formatted text comments on query structures, characteristics, or data cells, and an option to upload a document attached to the in-context query element.

When you create or upload a new document, make sure to select the BI tab and enter the relevant document type. Don't forget to click the Save button before you click OK, you may need to scroll down using the inner scroll bar to see the Save button in the New Document dialog box.

4.7.10 Sort

Bringing up the Sort item on the context menu from a structure element (selection or formula) will give you the option to sort all data within that selection or formula in ascending or descending order. If you open the context menu from a characteristic or characteristic value, you will have the option to sort by that characteristic, ascending or descending by key or text.

4.8   Summary: BEx Web Analyzer

In this chapter, we walked through most of the functionality available in SAP's default BW 7 web template, known as BEx Web analyzer. BW 7 has a number of useful tools available to users running web reports, including variable personalization, drag-and-drop query analysis, filters, and the ability to save existing analyses for later. Some additional functionality, such as a "back" feature and the ability to create local formulas (Section 4.7.8, Calculations and Translations), is only available in the context menu — at least in the default web template.

In a future chapter, we will take a look under the hood of SAP's default web template and make a few modifications along the way to increase user productivity. Before we do that, though, let's take a look at the BEx analyzer tool, which allows users to run BW queries through an Excel interface.

Like it or not, Excel is an integral tool for ad hoc analysis in most businesses — especially in Finance departments — so delivering a robust business intelligence (BI) solution that integrates with Excel may be just as important as your web-based analytics.

5 Running Queries in Excel: Business Explorer (BEx) Analyzer

In addition to running queries on the Web, users can run Business Warehouse BW reports directly in Microsoft Excel using SAP's BEx analyzer tool. BEx analyzer is an Excel add-in that must be installed on the user's computer along with the SAP front-end software. Excel workbooks with the BEx analyzer add-in running can include embedded BW 7 reports that are based on live data from the BW system.

BEx analyzer has two modes: Analysis mode, which is used for navigating queries and displaying data, and Design mode, which includes a toolset for adding new functionality and interface elements to a workbook. In this chapter, we will be looking at the Analysis mode.

Because BEx analyzer requires software to be installed on the client PC, it is a good practice to make sure users need BEx analyzer before they are granted access to it. Most of the functionality available in BEx analyzer is also present in BEx Web analyzer (see Chapter 4, Running Queries on the Web: Business Explorer Web analyzer), but users who are more familiar with Excel's interface may resist switching to a web-based tool.

That said, there are certainly valid reasons to roll out BEx analyzer to users — in some companies, Excel may be the life blood of business and financial analytics. In these situations, it makes sense to include BEx analyzer as an available tool to allow analysts to integrate BW reports into other Excel workbooks.

However, you may want to have a long-term goal in mind that involves transitioning the analytics process from individuals with their own Excel workbooks to a centralized web-based center for reporting, including easily configurable dashboards. Later in the book we will see how to build web applications that can improve users' productivity.

5.1 Starting BEx Analyzer

Before we can take a look at the features of BEx analyzer, we first have to launch it. There are a few ways of accessing BEx analyzer once it has been installed: it can be launched from Windows, from the BW 7 GUI, or from the SAP Portal.

To open BEx analyzer from Windows, you can click the Start Menu, then navigate to PROGRAMS • BUSINESS EXPLORER • ANALYZER. Excel will open, and BEx analyzer will be loaded in the Add-Ins tab (assuming Excel 2007 or higher). If you click on the ADD-INS tab, you will see the BEx ANALYZER toolbars, as seen in Figure 5.1. In the screenshot in Figure 5.1, the bottom two rows are BEx ANALYZER toolbars, and the top toolbar belongs to SNAGIT, another Excel add-in.

Most of the functionality will be grayed out at this point — because we opened BEx analyzer from Windows, we are not yet connected to an SAP BW system. If you try to open a query at this point by clicking the Open button (the first icon on the second BEx analyzer toolbar), you will be prompted to connect to a system first.

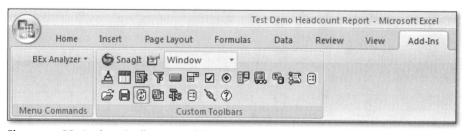

Figure 5.1 BEx Analyzer Toolbar in Excel 2007

Another method of launching BEx analyzer involves opening it from the BW 7 GUI. You'll first have to log in to your BW 7 system via the SAP logon pad. Once you are logged in, run Transaction RRMX to automatically launch Excel with the BEx analyzer add-in. If Excel is already open, the BEx analyzer add-in will be loaded in-place, meaning embedded BW 7 functionality will be available on the currently open workbook. Excel will automatically be connected to the system you used to run Transaction RRMX.

You can also use Transaction RRMXP to launch BEx analyzer from your BW 7 GUI. Transaction RRMXP does not immediately launch Excel with the BEx analyzer add-in — it brings you to a selection screen where you can choose either a workbook that has been saved on the BW server (more on this later) or an existing BW query. Once you've selected a workbook or a query, clicking the green checkmark will open the chosen workbook or query with Excel using BEx analyzer.

The final method of launching BEx analyzer involves the SAP Portal. The portal allows you to create iViews (small applications) that can run a transaction on a specific system. Creating an iView to run Transaction RRMXP on your BW 7 system will launch Excel with the BEx analyzer toolset, just as if you had run the transaction manually. The advantage to using the portal is Single Sign-On (SSO) — if your landscape is configured correctly, your users will not have to enter their BW 7 credentials to run a query in Excel with BEx analyzer.

You can also create iViews in the portal that launch specific workbooks with BEx analyzer, this is possible by using Transaction RRMXP described previously. Launch BEx analyzer now, using whichever method you prefer, and click the Open button (the first icon on the second BEx analyzer toolbar). If you opened BEx analyzer directly from Windows, you will be prompted to log in to your BW system. Otherwise, you will proceed directly to the open screen. Now we're ready to run a query in Excel — let's select the sample headcount query we used in Chapter 4.

5.2 The Variable Screen: Excel Flavor

Whenever a query is run with BEx analyzer in a new workbook, the variable screen will always be displayed first, as long as variables exist that are "ready for input" (see Chapter 3, Section 3.3.2, Manual Input Flexibility, for more information). If an existing workbook with an embedded query is opened with BEx analyzer, the variable screen will also be displayed unless the Refresh Workbook on Open property is unchecked (workbook-specific properties are discussed later in the book). If this property is unchecked, the variable screen will only display if there are required variables with no default values, the same behavior seen in BEx Web analyzer.

The functionality available in the variable screen in BEx analyzer is virtually identical to the BEx Web analyzer version, but the interface looks a little different. Because we already looked at the basic functionality of the variable screen in Chapter 4, Section 4.1, The Variable Screen: Personalization and Variants, we'll just take a look at the differences between the Excel interface and BEx Web analyzer.

Figure 5.2 shows the Excel version of the variable screen. Compare this with the web version of the variable screen shown in Figure 4.1 from the previous chapter. You'll notice that the options for saving variants are still available, albeit in icon form. When saving a variant, the CREATE NEW VARIANT screen appears, as seen in Figure 5.3. Unchecking the SAVE AS USER VARIANT checkbox will save the variant as a global variant, accessible to all users. Global variants require a unique technical name before they can be saved.

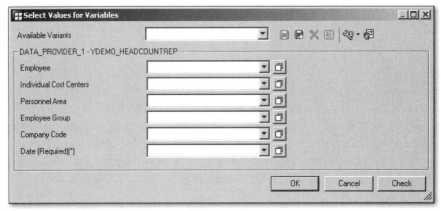

Figure 5.2 Variable Screen in BEx Analyzer (Excel)

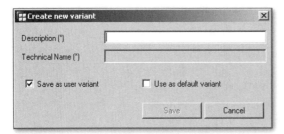

Figure 5.3 Create New Variant Screen in BEx Analyzer

The USE AS DEFAULT VARIANT checkbox is an example of functionality available exclusively in BEx analyzer — if you check this box when saving a variant, that variant will be loaded as the default set of variable values whenever you run the query.

After saving a variant, you will be back at the main variable screen. Let's look at the fourth icon at the top of the screen: Properties. This icon — grayed out in Figure 5.2 — becomes active when a variant is selected in the AVAILABLE VARIANTS dropdown box. Clicking this icon brings up the Edit variant screen, which allows you to modify the name of the variant and the Use as default variant option for the variant. It does not allow you to change user-level variants to global variants or vice versa.

Neither the default variant option nor the edit variant screens are available in BEx Web analyzer. However, variable personalization provides functionality similar to that of the default variant option. To rename a variant in BEx Web analyzer, you would need to save the existing variant as a new variant with a new name.

As we will see later, BEx analyzer workbooks can contain multiple embedded queries, and all variables associated with the queries in a workbook will appear on the variable screen. If there is only a single embedded query in the workbook (as would be the case in a new workbook), the variable variant will be associated with the query. If there are multiple embedded queries in a workbook, and the workbook is saved on the server, the variant will be associated with the workbook. We will see an example of how to save a workbook to the server later in the chapter.

The fifth icon in the main variable screen, which looks like a wrench, allows users to switch between seeing the technical names and descriptions of variables, variants, and workbook DataProviders (discussed later in the chapter). It is rare that users would need to see the technical names for any of these items, and the default option is to see descriptions only. This option is not available in BEx Web analyzer.

The final icon controls variable personalization. While BEx Web analyzer displays a new section within the main variable window to handle personalization (see Figure 4.2), BEx analyzer opens a new window that allows you to set personalized values for one or more variables, as seen in Figure 5.4.

To personalize a variable with a specific value, you can enter that value on the variable screen before opening the PERSONALIZE VARIABLES window so the value appears on the left side. Then, select the variable on the left side and click the right arrow button to move it to the right side. Alternatively, you can modify the value directly in the PERSONALIZE VARIABLES window by adding the variable to the right side, selecting it, and clicking the MODIFY SELECTIONS button at the bottom.

As with the main variable screen, the wrench icon at the top right allows users to toggle the display of technical names. There is also a checkbox that controls whether or not personalized variables are displayed on the variable screen. Unlike in BEx Web analyzer, in BEx analyzer there is *no indication* that a variable is personalized or that personalized variables may be hidden.

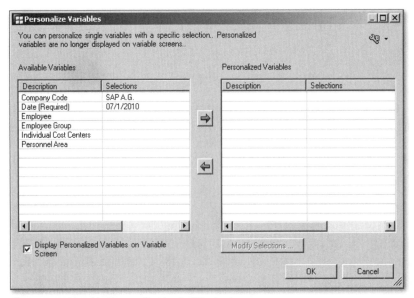

Figure 5.4 Variable Personalization in BEx Analyzer

User Experience Tip 5.1: Pitfalls with Personalized Variables and BEx Analyzer

It is highly recommended to keep the DISPLAY PERSONALIZED VARIABLES ON VARIABLE SCREEN option checked, because BEx analyzer does not notify users that personalized variables may be hidden. This is especially important if the user runs reports on both BEx Web analyzer and BEx analyzer, as any variables personalized in a web report will also be personalized in the Excel interface, and vice versa.

The rest of the variable screen is identical to the variable screen in BEx Web analyzer. Let's click OK on the variable screen to see how our query looks in the BEx analyzer Excel interface.

5.3 Query Navigation in BEx Analyzer

Figure 5.5 shows a screenshot of a sample query run in BEx analyzer using Excel 2007. Below the title of the report, you can see the author of the query and the date and time data was last refreshed in the InfoProvider.

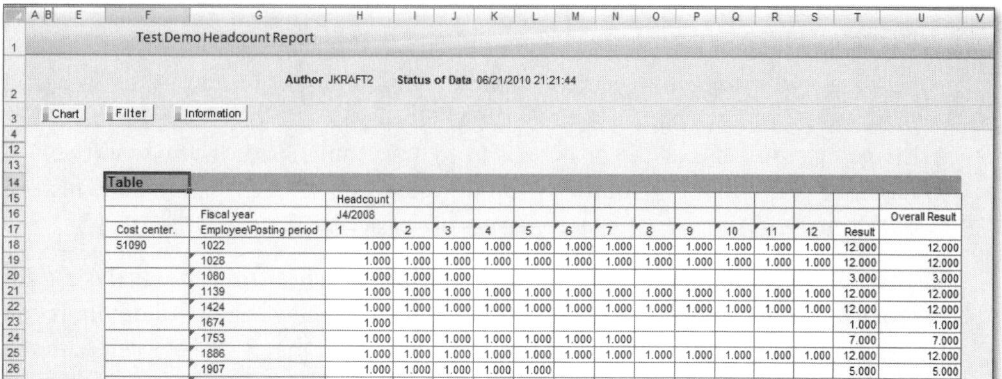

Cost center.	Fiscal year / Employee\Posting period	Headcount J4/2008 1	2	3	4	5	6	7	8	9	10	11	12	Result	Overall Result
51090	1022	1.000	1.000	1.000	1.000	1.000	1.000	1.000	1.000	1.000	1.000	1.000	1.000	12.000	12.000
	1028	1.000	1.000	1.000	1.000	1.000	1.000	1.000	1.000	1.000	1.000	1.000	1.000	12.000	12.000
	1080	1.000	1.000	1.000										3.000	3.000
	1139	1.000	1.000	1.000	1.000	1.000	1.000	1.000	1.000	1.000	1.000	1.000	1.000	12.000	12.000
	1424	1.000	1.000	1.000	1.000	1.000	1.000	1.000	1.000	1.000	1.000	1.000	1.000	12.000	12.000
	1674	1.000												1.000	1.000
	1753	1.000	1.000	1.000	1.000	1.000	1.000	1.000						7.000	7.000
	1886	1.000	1.000	1.000	1.000	1.000	1.000	1.000	1.000	1.000	1.000	1.000	1.000	12.000	12.000
	1907	1.000	1.000	1.000	1.000	1.000								5.000	5.000
	2230	1.000	1.000	1.000	1.000	1.000	1.000	1.000	1.000	1.000	1.000	1.000	1.000	12.000	12.000

Figure 5.5 Query Output in BEx Analyzer

The toolbar included with the default BEx analyzer workbook includes three buttons: CHART, FILTER, and INFORMATION. The CHART button toggles between displaying data in table form and graphical form — when the chart is displayed, the — button is labeled "Table."

The FILTER button displays a navigation pane to the left of the analysis grid, similar to the navigation pane in BEx Web analyzer (see Chapter 4, Section 4.2, Query Analysis with Drag-and-Drop Navigation). Unlike the navigation pane on the Web, the Excel version of the navigation pane does not have separate sections for rows, columns, and free characteristics — all characteristics and structures are presented in a single list.

The last button in the toolbar, INFORMATION, displays metadata pertaining to the query such as the user who last changed the query, when it was last changed, the technical name of the query, and when the query was last refreshed by the user.

Now let's take a look at a few different methods for navigating queries in BEx analyzer.

5.3.1 Drag-and-Drop Navigation

As with BEx Web analyzer, the BEx analyzer Excel interface allows users to navigate queries using drag and drop. However, the relative lack of visual cues in the Excel interface makes some drag-and-drop functionality a bit more difficult to master.

Dragging Characteristics

Let's start with something simple: removing a drilldown. To do this, simply drag the heading of any characteristic (such as Fiscal year or Cost center) from either the navigation pane or the analysis grid to any empty space in the workbook. It might be easier to focus your users on dragging from the navigation pane instead of the analysis grid, as the characteristics are easier to identify.

There is also a limitation when dragging characteristics from the analysis grid: looking at Figure 5.5, let's say we want to remove Employee as a drilldown. If you try to select the Employee characteristic, you will find that it shares a cell with the Posting Period characteristic. Dragging the combined EMPLOYEE/POSTING PERIOD cell to an empty space in the workbook will remove Posting Period, not Employee. Therefore, we need to drag the Employee characteristic from the navigation pane to remove it. The resulting analysis grid can be seen in Figure 5.6, along with the navigation pane.

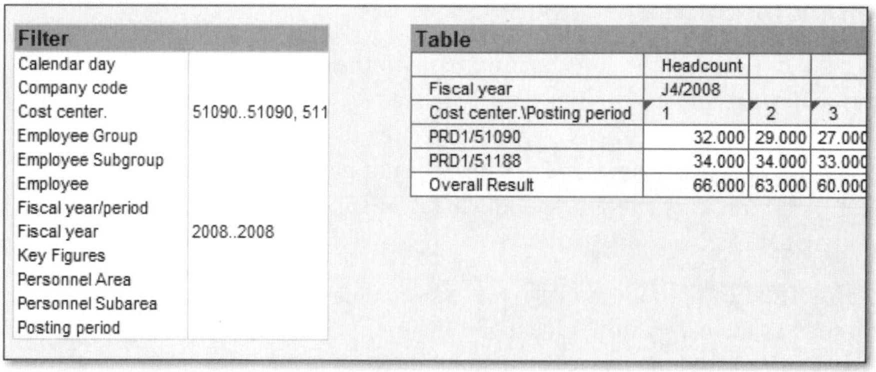

Filter	
Calendar day	
Company code	
Cost center.	51090..51090, 511
Employee Group	
Employee Subgroup	
Employee	
Fiscal year/period	
Fiscal year	2008..2008
Key Figures	
Personnel Area	
Personnel Subarea	
Posting period	

Table			
	Headcount		
Fiscal year	J4/2008		
Cost center.\Posting period	1	2	3
PRD1/51090	32.000	29.000	27.00
PRD1/51188	34.000	34.000	33.00
Overall Result	66.000	63.000	60.00

Figure 5.6 BEx Analyzer Navigation Pane and Analysis Grid

Dragging a characteristic to another characteristic (either in the analysis grid or the navigation pane) will swap the two characteristics. If you want to add a characteristic as a new drilldown, you would drag that characteristic from the navigation pane to a *characteristic value* or structure element on the analysis grid. The new drilldown will appear to the right — or below, if in the columns — of the target characteristic or structure.

For example, if you wanted to add EMPLOYEE as a drilldown again just after COST CENTER, you would drag EMPLOYEE from the navigation pane to either of the values of COST CENTER displayed in the navigation grid (51090 or 51188). This differs from the BEx Web analyzer interface, where you would drag the new characteristic to the vertical line to the right of the Cost Center characteristic. Note that you cannot add a new drilldown to the left of the first characteristic: you would need to perform a swap first, and then add the original drilldown after the new one.

Dragging Characteristic Values

You can also use drag-and-drop navigation to set filter values. This is accomplished by dragging characteristic values to one of two locations: the navigation pane or an empty space in the workbook.

If you drag a characteristic value to anywhere on the navigation pane (you don't have to drop it on the relevant characteristic), BEx analyzer will set up a filter that only includes that characteristic value. Any previous filter on that characteristic will be overwritten.

However, if you drag a characteristic value to an empty space in the workbook, a new filter will be created that *excludes* that value. This action will *not* overwrite the existing filter on the characteristic; the exclusion will just be added to the filter.

Figure 5.7 illustrates some of the different cursors that appear when using drag-and-drop functionality in BEx analyzer, along with a description of what the cursor means.

If you'd prefer that users avoid drag-and-drop functionality in BEx analyzer, it can be disabled in workbook settings, as we will see later in the chapter.

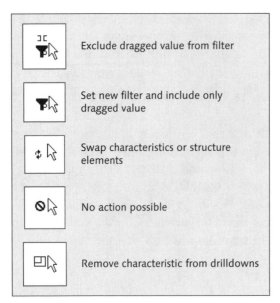

Figure 5.7 BEx Analyzer Drag-and-drop Cursors

User Experience Tip 5.2: Drag and Drop in BEx Analyzer and User Expectations of Excel

While drag and drop in BEx analyzer may provide some useful shortcuts, all of the functionality it provides is also available via other interface elements. You may get negative feedback from users who are familiar with dragging in Excel to select cells, as the BEx analyzer drag-and-drop feature will override the default Excel dragging behavior. If you do get this type of feedback, you may want to consider unchecking the Allow Drag and Drop checkbox in the Workbook Settings of the default workbook. We will discuss how to make this modification later in the chapter.

5.3.2 Double-Click Navigation and Direct Filter Entry

One of the easiest ways to perform simple navigation tasks in BEx analyzer is by double-clicking different components of the query. Table 5.1 illustrates what happens when you double-click specific types of cells in the navigation pane or analysis grid.

Query Element	Double-Click Action
Characteristic in navigation pane	Characteristic added as new drilldown after the last characteristic drilled down in the rows.
Structure in navigation pane	Prompt for the creation of a new local formula for that structure (see Chapter 4, Section 4.7.8, Calculations and Translations, for more information).
Filter value or empty cell in navigation pane	Display the Select Values dialog box to set a filter value for the characteristic or structure.
Characteristic in analysis grid	Removes characteristic from active drilldowns.
Results row in analysis grid	Removes the characteristic associated with the results row from active drilldowns.
Characteristic value in analysis grid	Sets up a filter to only include the double-clicked value. Overwrites existing filters for the relevant characteristic.
Structure element in analysis grid	Sets up a filter on the structure to only show the double-clicked element. Overwrites existing filters for the structure.
Any data cell in the analysis grid	Shows the Query Properties dialog box.

Table 5.1 Types of Cells in the Navigation Pane or Analysis Grid

You can also directly enter filter values in the navigation pane by simply typing the value and pressing ⌷Tab⌷ or ⌷Enter⌷. If the value exists in master data for that characteristic, the filter will be applied immediately.

5.3.3 Navigational State in Query Properties

Another useful tool for navigating a BEx analyzer query is found in the Query Properties dialog box, accessible by right-clicking any cell in the query and selecting Query Properties, or by double-clicking any data cell. The first tab, NAVIGATIONAL STATE, is an overview of the different characteristics and structures present in the query. The NAVIGATIONAL STATE window is shown in Figure 5.8.

Similar to the navigation pane in BEx Web analyzer, the BEx analyzer NAVIGATIONAL STATE window differentiates between characteristics and structures that are currently drilled down in the rows or columns, and free characteristics that are not active drilldowns.

You can move characteristics and structures by dragging and dropping them, or by using the arrows between each section of the window. You can also easily change the order of characteristics via drag and drop or by using the CHANGE ORDER buttons at the bottom of each section. The wrench icon at the bottom left of the screen will toggle the display of technical names for characteristics and structures.

You can also right-click any of the characteristics in the NAVIGATIONAL STATE window to change properties such as displaying key/text values or toggling results rows. You can even set up filters from this window by right-clicking a characteristic or structure and clicking Select Filter Value.

This is an exclusive feature to BEx analyzer, as the NAVIGATIONAL STATE window does not exist in BEx Web analyzer.

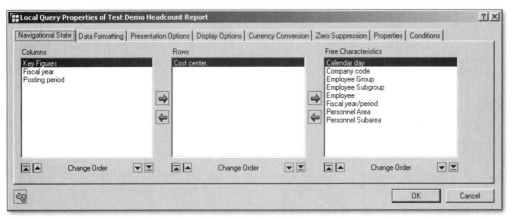

Figure 5.8 BEx Analyzer Query Properties — Navigational State

---

User Experience Tip 5.3: The Navigational State Window is a Power User's Best Friend

Do not overlook the utility of the navigational state window described previously. It allows advanced BW users to quickly reconfigure the active drilldowns in a query without having to wait for the query to refresh each time. If a user is not sure of the impact of adding and removing drilldowns, this tool may not be as appropriate, as it does not provide any feedback until all changes have been confirmed with the OK button. However, it is recommended to promote this tool to BEx analyzer power users to enhance their productivity.

5.3.4   Context Menu Navigational Tools

BEx analyzer's context menu contains a number of useful options for navigation, some of which are not available elsewhere in the BEx analyzer interface. This section will briefly describe context menu functionality, but because most of the items are similar to those in the BEx Web analyzer context menu, see Chapter 4, Section 4.7, The Context Menu, for more details.

The same Back One Navigation Step and Back to Start functions are available in BEx analyzer, their functionality is self-explanatory.

Convert to Formula

The next option, Convert to Formula, converts the entire analysis grid into "Formula Mode." Formula Mode essentially decouples the data supplied by the BW system from the design and formatting features of BEx analyzer, so data is loaded on a cell-by-cell basis, but formatting is controlled by Excel. This feature is discussed in greater detail later in the book.

Filters, Drilldowns, and Hierarchy

The options relating to filters and drilldowns are all identical to the BEx Web analyzer context menu as discussed in Chapter 4, Sections 4.7.2, Filter, and 4.7.3, Change Drilldown. The Hierarchy options are also similar to Chapter 4, Section 4.7.4, Hierarchy, except that you cannot activate or deactivate hierarchies directly from the context menu in BEx analyzer.

Properties and Goto

The items related to properties, query properties, conditions, and exceptions will be discussed later in the chapter. The Goto option is also available if jump targets are set up. There are also a number of functions related to input-ready cells used for BI integrated planning.

Drill Across Worksheets

The context menu has another item exclusive to BEx analyzer that enables you to "Drill Across Worksheets," a function that automatically creates new Excel worksheets based on the values of a characteristic. If you right-click a characteristic in the navigation pane that is not an active drilldown, the option Add Drilldown According to <Characteristic> in New Worksheets may be available. If the characteristic is currently drilled down in the rows or columns, the characteristic has a filter value consisting of anything other than single values, or there is an active display hierarchy, this menu item will not appear.

When you select the Add Drilldown According to <Characteristic> in New Worksheets option for a specific characteristic, BEx analyzer will create one new worksheet for each single value in the characteristic. For example, if you remove the Cost Center drilldown from our headcount report example and you set up a filter on Cost Center to include four single cost centers, using the Drill Across Worksheets function will create four additional worksheets in the current workbook, each one filtered on a single cost center. All four worksheets will contain copies of the embedded query on the original worksheet, and each one can be navigated independently.

While it is possible to use the Drill Across Worksheets function on a characteristic without a filter value, you should be aware of how many values the characteristic contains. BEx analyzer will create up to 200 additional worksheets with this function, but any more than a dozen or two may prove unmanageable and will drastically increase how long this function takes to execute.

5.4   Properties in BEx Analyzer

The properties for queries, characteristics, and data cells in the BEx analyzer interface differ from those available in BEx Web analyzer, although there is some overlap. Let's take a look at query properties first, accessible by right-clicking on any cell in the analysis grid or navigation pane and selecting Query Properties.

5.4.1   Query Properties

The first tab in the Query Properties window, Navigation State, was discussed in Section 5.3.3, Navigational State in Query Properties. The Navigation State tab provides an easy way to rearrange the active drilldowns in the query, and set filters and properties.

Data Formatting is the second tab, and it allows the user to switch between Multidimensional View and Tabular View. Multidimensional View is the standard view of BW queries, and it allows for the addition and removal of characteristics as drilldowns. The Tabular View shows all active drilldowns specified in the query design along a single dimension. You cannot add or remove drilldowns in Tabular View, but you can rearrange the order drilldowns appear along the single dimension.

Two other options in this tab exist under Multidimensional View: Display Columns Hierarchically and Display Rows Hierarchically. These functions will display all of the characteristics in either the columns or the rows (or both) in a hierarchical format, expanded by default to the specified characteristic. See Chapter 3, Section 3.5.3, Rows and Columns Area Properties, for more information.

The next tab, Presentation Options, controls the position of results rows, the display of + and – signs, and how zero values are displayed. The Display Options tab allows users to toggle the display of scaling factors, BI documents, and repeated values. These options are similar to those found in the Query Designer query properties, as discussed in Chapter 3, Section 3.5.1, Query Properties.

The Currency Conversion tab allows users to select whether to disable currency conversion, use the conversion specified in Query Designer, or specify a custom currency conversion. Zero Suppression settings for the query, covered in section 3.5.1, are in the next tab.

The Properties tab displays information about the query, including who created it, who last changed it, and when it was last changed. Finally, the Conditions tab displays a list of all conditions set up on the query.

5.4.2 Characteristic Properties

You can also access a number of options for characteristics and structures by right-clicking any characteristic or characteristic value in the analysis grid or navigation pane and selecting Properties.

Every characteristic will have a General tab in its properties box, with options to change how the characteristic values are displayed in the query. Most of the options here are identical to those in Query Designer, so you can refer to Chapter 3, Section 3.5.2, Characteristic Properties, for more information.

One notable addition in BEx analyzer is the Access Type for Result Values setting, which controls when data rows are generated for the characteristic. The default access type, Posted Values, will only generate a data row for a characteristic value if transaction data exists for that value. If you select Characteristic Relationships, only those values specified in the characteristic relationships section of the BI Integrated Planning workbench will be displayed. Finally, the Master Data setting will display all characteristic values, even if there is no transaction data associated with those values.

The Attributes tab in the characteristic properties box will only display if the characteristic has display attributes. This tab enables the user to show display attributes after the characteristic on the query in any order. Right-clicking any attribute will let you set the display properties for that attribute, where you can choose whether to display the key or text and the type of text displayed.

The Hierarchy tab is only shown if at least one hierarchy exists for the characteristic. You can select a hierarchy from the dropdown menu at the top, and activate it with a checkbox. If a hierarchy has been selected, you can set the properties of the characteristics and the hierarchy nodes separately by right-clicking each item in the section below the Activate Hierarchy checkbox. As in the Attributes tab, you can choose to display the key or text and the type of text for the characteristic values themselves and the higher level nodes of the hierarchy.

5.4.3 Data Cell Properties

Right-clicking an individual data cell in the analysis grid and selecting properties will bring up a different group of settings, all of which we have seen before. See Chapter 3, Section 3.5.5, Selection and Formula Properties, for an outline of the properties for selections and formulas in Query Designer. The properties for a data cell will apply to all of the cells under the in-context structure element (selection or formulas).

In the Number Format tab, you can change the scaling factor, number of decimal places, and whether or not you want the data to be "highlighted." In BEx analyzer, highlighted data is assigned the Excel style *SAPBEXstdDataEmph*. In Excel 2007, you can modify this style by clicking the Cell Styles button on the Home tab (in the main Excel interface, not BEx analyzer), right-click SAPBEXstdDataEmph, and select Modify.

The Calculations tab controls how results and single values are calculated, and the Sorting tab lets users sort data either ascending or descending. The options on both these tabs are discussed in greater detail in Chapter3, Section 3.5.5.

5.5 The BEx Analyzer Analysis Toolbar

You may have noticed that we started this chapter by using the Open functionality of the BEx analyzer toolbar to launch a query (see Figure 5.9). Let's go back and take a closer look at the different functions available.

Figure 5.9 BEx Analyzer Toolbar

The screenshot from the beginning of the chapter is reproduced here for your convenience. The top row of buttons belongs to SNAGIT, a different Excel add-in. Depending on how and when you launch BEx analyzer, its toolbars may appear above or below other Excel add-ins.

The middle row is the BEx ANALYZER Design toolbar, and it deals primarily with design mode, which allows you to customize the interface of your workbook. Design mode will be discussed later in the book. The last row in the screenshot is the BEx ANALYZER Analysis toolbar. We'll begin by explaining this toolbar's functionality.

5.5.1 Open and Save

The first icon in the Analysis toolbar, Open, allows you to run a query or a workbook from the BW server. We've already seen how the Open Query option will open a specific query, embed it in a workbook, and run it. The Open Workbook option will run a workbook that has been previously saved on the BI server.

So how exactly do we save a workbook on the BW server? This is accomplished by clicking the second icon on the Analysis toolbar and selecting Save Workbook As. You will be prompted to save your workbook into your BW Favorites folder or into an existing role on the BW server. The Save Workbook function will save any changes to an existing workbook on the BW server without changing the workbook's name.

The Assign Workbook to Role option provides another way to add an existing workbook to a BW role. This option brings up an Add to Folder dialog box, which allows you to create or delete folders within BW roles and assign the current workbook to a role, assuming you have the correct authorization.

When you use the Save Workbook option, all of the items within the workbook are saved on the BW server, including the navigation pane, analysis grid(s), and any custom elements you may have created in Design mode (more on design mode later in the book). If you want to save just the navigation state of a single analysis grid, you can do this by selecting the analysis grid and using the Save View function from the Save button on the toolbar. This will create a query view reflecting the current navigation state of the selected analysis grid, which can be saved under your BW favorites or BW roles.

User Experience Tip 5.4: BEx Analyzer Save versus Excel Save

Note that saving a workbook on the BW server using the BEx analyzer save functionality is a completely different function from using Excel's save feature to save a workbook on the local PC. The processes and culture of your user population will dictate which feature is used more frequently, but if a specific set of workbooks will be used by a number of BEx analyzer users, it is recommended to store them on the BW server in a role.

It is important to make the distinction between these two save features clear in training classes. It is easy to get out of sync if both save features are used — for example, a user could open a workbook from the server, make some design changes, save the workbook locally on their PC (without saving it on the BW server), and email the changed workbook to colleagues.

5.5.2   Automatic Refresh

The third button is a toggle button that controls when the workbook is refreshed. In its default state, the workbook is refreshed automatically with live data whenever you make a change to the query's navigational state. This includes adding or removing drilldowns, changing filters, or modifying query properties.

When the workbook is in automatic refresh mode, there is a square around the button, and the button's tooltip will say Pause Automatic Refresh. If you click the button in this mode, automatic refresh will be disabled. Any navigational changes made in this mode will not be reflected in the workbook until you click the refresh button again. As an example, let's say our example headcount query is only drilled down to Cost Center in the rows. If you wanted to add Employee Group, Employee Subgroup, and Employee as drilldowns, you would have to wait for the query to refresh after you add each characteristic. However, if you disable automatic refresh, you can double-click each characteristic in the navigation pane to add them as new drilldowns. However, because automatic refresh is paused, you won't see the results until you click the Refresh button again.

When automatic refresh is disabled, drag-and-drop functionality will not work, so all changes must be made by double-clicking the navigation pane, using the context menu, or via the Navigational State tab of the Query Properties window.

> **User Experience Tip 5.5: Why Can't I Make Changes to My Query?**
>
> It's easy to disable automatic refresh by accident, so it's a good idea to check the refresh setting if users report trouble in BEx analyzer. In practice, if users want to make multiple changes to the query navigation state quickly, it might be preferable to push the Navigational State tool discussed in Chapter 3, Section 5.3.3, instead of the automatic refresh feature.

5.5.3 Change Variable Values

The fourth button in the Analysis toolbar will bring up the query's variable screen. For more information on the BEx analyzer variable screen, see Section 5.2, The Variable Screen: Excel Flavor. The variable screen called from this button is functionally identical to the one that appears when the query is run in BEx analyzer.

5.5.4 Tools

Next in the Analysis toolbar we have the Tools button, which brings up a submenu of its own. The first item in the submenu, Create New Query, will open BEx Query Designer, which was discussed at length in Chapter 3, Building Effective Business Warehouse Queries: The Basics of Query Designer.

The Query Designer window opened with this menu item will have two additional buttons in the toolbar. The first button, a green checkmark, will exit Query Designer and run the query you just created in Excel, starting in the cell that was selected when you chose the Create New Query menu option. The second button, a red X, will also close Query Designer, but it will cancel the query creation process. Note that when you select Create New Query, you cannot perform any action in the main Excel window until you finish in Query Designer and select one of these two buttons.

If you have an existing query selected in your workbook, another menu item will appear in the Tools menu: Edit Query. This option will also open the Query Designer window, but it will open the selected query for editing. The same green checkmark and red X icons will be shown in the Query Designer toolbar, and again you must select one of these options to return to the main Excel window.

The BEx Broadcaster option on the Tools menu is normally grayed out — it is only active if you open a workbook that's been stored on the BW server (see Section 5.5.1, Open and Save, for more information). Selecting this option will open your web browser and connect you to the BEx Broadcaster tool on your BW portal, with the current workbook selected. From here, you can precalculate and distribute the workbook automatically to a list of email recipients or to your portal.

If you use the BI Integrated Planning component, the Planning Modeler tool is accessible through an item in the Tools menu. BI Integrated Planning functionality is not covered in this book.

The next item, BEx report designer, launches the report designer tool. A later chapter will have more information about this tool, which allows you to generate formatted reports.

The BEx Web analyzer menu item will launch the currently selected query in your web browser using the default web template. The features of BEx Web analyzer are covered in Chapter 4.

The last item in the Tools menu, Copy Sheet, is available starting in SAP NetWeaver 7.0 Enhancement Package 1. When you select this item, the current worksheet will be copied to a new worksheet within the current workbook. The new worksheet will have all of the functionality available on the original worksheet, and navigation of the query or queries embedded in the new worksheet will be independent from the original worksheet.

5.5.5 Global Settings

Now let's take a look at the Global Settings dialog box, available by clicking the sixth icon in the Analysis toolbar. The options in Global Settings apply to the BEx analyzer application as a whole, rather than individual workbooks. Make sure you click the correct icon on the Analysis toolbar, there is another identical icon at the end of the Design toolbar that shows the Workbook Setting dialog box (discussed later).

Behavior Tab

Most of the options in the GLOBAL SETTINGS dialog box are found in the BEHAVIOR tab, shown in Figure 5.10. The first item, MAXIMUM NUMBER OF OBJECTS IN LOCAL

HISTORY, can be used to enable the display of recently opened queries and workbooks under the Open icon in the BEx analyzer toolbar. The default value of zero disables the display of recent items. If you set the value to any number greater than zero, recently opened queries and workbooks will display at the bottom of the Open menu, under the Open Workbook item. For example, if you set this value to 5, the last 5 queries or workbooks that were opened in BEx analyzer will be accessible via items in the Open menu.

Note that BEx analyzer only starts keeping track of recently opened items *after* you enable this option by changing it to a nonzero value, so recently opened items will only start populating when you open another query or workbook. Workbooks opened locally from the user's PC are not included in this menu; only workbooks opened from the BW server are tracked.

The second option is also related to the local history displayed in the Open menu — if DISPLAY SYSTEM NAME IN LOCAL HISTORY is checked, the system name associated with each query and workbook opened is displayed in the Open menu.

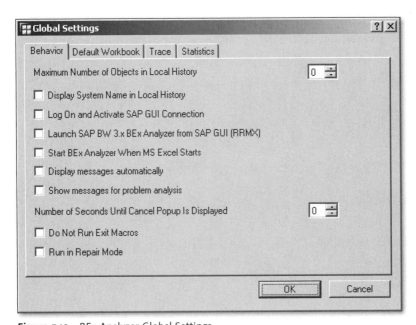

Figure 5.10 BEx Analyzer Global Settings

User Experience Tip 5.6: Enable Local History!

There's really no reason not to enable the local history option for active BEx analyzer users who run multiple queries and workbooks. For users who will only be running queries in one production system, the Display System Name option is not necessary. It may be useful for your BI development team though, because they often run queries in multiple systems.

The Log On and Activate SAP GUI Connection function controls the display of transport messages from the BW server. If this option is checked, transport prompts may appear when you save workbooks if the standard transport system is active.

As seen in Section 5.1, Starting BEx analyzer, Transaction RRMX on your BW system can be used to launch BEx analyzer. In a BW 7 system, Transaction RRMX will launch the 7.0 version of BEx analyzer. Users can change this behavior by checking the Launch SAP BW 3.x BEx analyzer from SAP GUI (RRMX) checkbox. When checked, Transaction RRMX will instead launch the 3.x version of BEx analyzer. This behavior can be changed globally for all users on a BW system by executing Transaction RRMX_CUST and selecting the Always Start 3.x Version option. The selection in Global Settings takes precedence over the Transaction RRMX_CUST setting.

If your users primarily use Excel with BEx analyzer loaded, the next option might be useful. When checked, the Start BEx analyzer When MS Excel Starts item will load the BEx analyzer add-in. However, add-in functionality will not be activated until the user starts BEx analyzer using one of the methods in Section 5.1.

Depending on your patch level, the remaining settings in the dialog box may be worded differently. The Display Messages Automatically and Show Messages for Problem Analysis checkboxes are useful when debugging problems with workbooks, but they should probably remain off for most users to avoid confusion.

The Number of Seconds Until Cancel Popup Is Displayed setting allows you to change how long BEx analyzer waits before popping up a dialog box allowing the user to cancel the current action. The default value of zero means that the cancel popup will never be displayed. This sounds like a great idea in theory, but clicking the cancel button can often cause an error that will result in BEx analyzer disconnecting from the BW server.

If the current workbook contains macros defined in the Workbook Settings dialog box (covered later in the book), the Do Not Run Exit Macros will disable the execution of those macros for troubleshooting purposes.

Finally, the Run in Repair Mode option will automatically delete unused objects in workbooks each time you open them. SAP Note 1160093 has more information on this option.

Default Workbook Tab

This tab lets you change the default workbook opened when a user runs a query with BEx analyzer. Later in the book we will see how to modify workbooks to include branding, additional design elements, and other custom features.

To set a new default workbook, the workbook must first be saved on the BW server. Once you open the saved workbook from the server, the Use Current button on the Default Workbook tab of Global Settings will be enabled. Click this button to set the open workbook as the new default workbook for the current user. You can also set the default workbook to the default value set on the BW server, or you can revert back to the SAP-provided default workbook.

Trace Tab

If you're experiencing a technical issue with BEx analyzer, the Trace tab allows you to record a log of everything BEx analyzer does. The activity log is stored in your system's temporary folder, but after you start the trace by checking the Record Trace box, you can click Display Trace to view the file. Make sure to save the contents of the trace file before you uncheck the Record Trace box, because the trace will be deleted.

Statistics Tab

The Statistics tab can be useful for tracking workbook performance. If you check the Collect Statistics box in the Statistics tab, BEx analyzer will start recording a number of different statistics the next time you connect to the BW system. You can view these statistics in a separate workbook by clicking the Display Statistics button.

5.6   Summary: Running BW Queries in Excel

In this chapter, we looked at the functionality offered in BEx analyzer's analysis mode. We learned the different methods that can be used to start BEx analyzer, and discussed the differences between the variable screen in Excel and on the Web. We also examined the four main ways to navigate queries in BEx analyzer:

drag and drop, double-clicking the navigation pane, the navigational state dialog box in Query Properties, and the context menu.

Next, we looked at the differences between the properties available in BEx analyzer and BEx Web analyzer. The functionality available on the Analysis toolbar was explained, including the differences between saving workbooks on the BW server and using the Excel save function on the local PC.

Now that you are comfortable running BW queries in Excel with BEx analyzer's Analysis mode, it's time to move on to Design mode, where we make significant changes to the functionality available in your workbook.

When the default Excel workbook template doesn't quite do the job, Business Explorer (BEx) analyzer design mode and its plethora of customization options can save the day.

6 Developing Workbooks with BEx Analyzer Design Mode

In BEx analyzer design mode, SAP has provided a comprehensive toolset for customizing BI workbooks through the addition of several different types of interface elements.

The toolbar for design mode is shown in Figure 6.1. In this chapter, we will discover how you can use the tools in design mode to tailor workbooks with custom controls, branding, and multiple embedded queries.

Figure 6.1 Design Mode Toolbar in BEx Analyzer

6.1 Welcome to Design Mode!

You can use BEx analyzer in either analysis mode or design mode. When you first run a query in BEx analyzer, you will be in analysis mode, and data will be visible in the embedded query. To manually switch to design mode, click the first button in the design mode toolbar.

Note that clicking any other button in the toolbar will automatically switch BEx analyzer to design mode. Looking back at our sample headcount query, Figure 6.2 shows what the design mode looks like with the navigation pane displayed.

You can see that different icons represent the various interface elements (or "design items") in the workbook itself: the navigation pane and analysis grid elements are at the bottom, while the top section of the workbook contains several text elements.

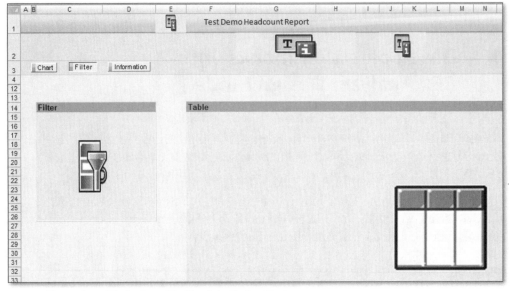

Figure 6.2   BEx Analyzer Workbook in Design Mode

You'll also notice that the large icons on the interface elements themselves correspond to the small icons in the toolbar. We will go through the functionality of the design mode toolbar in the following sections.

The design toolbar is also accessible by clicking BEx ANALYZER on the left side of the toolbar (see Figure 6.1) and pointing to Design Toolbar in the resulting menu. You will see a list of all of the toolbar functions, and an informational list of all of the design items created in the workbook.

In design mode, if you left-click on an item in the workbook, the properties for that item will be displayed. If you right-click an item in the workbook, you will see a border appear around the item with eight handles that can be used to change the size of the item, and a ninth green handle at the top that can be used to rotate the item.

To move an item, you need to right-click it first to get the border to appear, and then you can drag the item. Later in the chapter we will look at how to exactly specify the location of the item by cell. To delete an item, right-click the item once and press Delete. You can also right-click the item, then right-click again to bring up a context menu that lets you delete the item or set the properties.

When you are finished in design mode, you can click the first button in the design mode toolbar again to switch back to analysis mode. Let's stay in design mode for now as we delve into the process of adding additional analysis grids to the workbook.

6.2 DataProviders and Analysis Grids

As we've seen in previous chapters, the main interface element in most Business Warehouse (BW) reports is the analysis grid, which shows structures, drilled down characteristics, and key figures as defined in Query Designer. When you run a query in BEx analyzer, the default workbook provided by SAP includes a single analysis grid designed to show data from that query.

In this section, we will look at how to create additional analysis grids in the workbook, but before we start let's examine the DataProvider concept in the context of BEx analyzer.

6.2.1 DataProviders

Not to be confused with an InfoProvider, a DataProvider is an object that gathers data from a source on the Business Intelligence (BI) server and feeds it to interface elements in a BEx analyzer workbook. The source for the DataProvider is typically a query or a query view, but you can also connect a DataProvider directly to an InfoProvider such as an InfoCube or InfoObject. See Figure 6.3 for a graphical overview of the DataProvider concept.

Most interface elements in a BEx analyzer workbook must be associated with one and only one DataProvider, but a single DataProvider often feeds data to multiple items in the workbook. For example, in the default BEx analyzer workbook, there is a single DataProvider that grabs data from a query. This DataProvider then feeds a list of characteristics, structures, and filter values to the navigation pane, formats the analysis grid according to the query design, and fills in data for characteristic values and key figures.

A single BEx analyzer workbook can have multiple DataProviders. An additional DataProvider can connect to different queries to show data from a different Info-

Provider, or the new DataProvider can connect to the same query as an existing DataProvider.

The relationship between DataProviders and queries is similar to that of queries and query views. While a query view represents a snapshot of the current navigational state of a query (including filters, drilldowns, variables, and property settings), a DataProvider is an additional abstraction layer, removing the need to interface BEx analyzer elements to communicate directly with queries.

Multiple DataProviders within a BEx analyzer workbook are independent of one another, even if the DataProviders are connected to the same query — just as two query views from the same query can be independently navigated if opened side by side. Furthermore, all interface elements connected with a single DataProvider are linked, so a navigation change made in one interface element will be reflected in the other elements, as long as they use the same DataProvider.

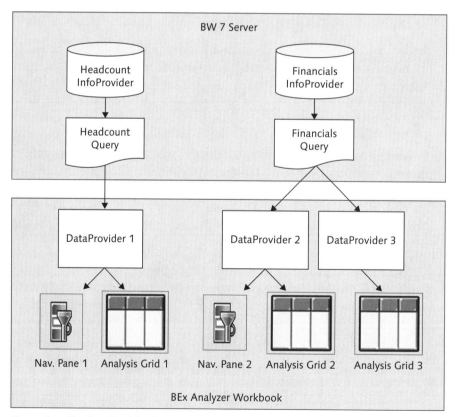

Figure 6.3 The DataProvider Concept

For example, in Figure 6.3, you can see that the FINANCIALS QUERY is associated with two different DataProviders. DATAPROVIDER 2 is connected to NAV. PANE 2 and ANALYSIS GRID 2, while DATAPROVIDER 3 is connected to ANALYSIS GRID 3. Query navigation performed in NAV. PANE 2 will affect ANALYSIS GRID 2, but not ANALYSIS GRID 3. Because DATAPROVIDER 3 does not have its own navigation pane, the only way to change the navigation state in ANALYSIS GRID 3 is via the analysis grid context menu or drag-and- drop navigation within the analysis grid.

To summarize, you need to create one DataProvider and one set of interface elements for each independently navigable set of data in your BEx analyzer workbook. The most important interface element is the analysis grid.

6.2.2 Analysis Grid Properties

As we saw in Chapter 5, Section 5.3, Query Navigator in BEx Analyzer, the analysis grid is the primary interface element used to display data from BW queries. There are several important properties associated with analysis grids, so let's take a look at the properties window now. Make sure you're in design mode first, then left-click the main analysis grid in your workbook to open the PROPERTIES OF ANALYSIS GRID screen, shown in Figure 6.4.

DataProvider Assignment

The first item in the GENERAL tab, after the unique name of the grid, allows you to choose a DataProvider to assign to this analysis grid. Right now we only have one DataProvider to choose from, but we will see later in the chapter how we can add and assign an additional DataProvider when we look at the procedure for creating a new analysis grid.

There are two options associated with DataProviders that are only visible in the Create Data Provider screen. The Provide Results Offline checkbox will, when checked, save the current data set to the workbook so data can be viewed without connecting to the server — this option is typically used in conjunction with formula mode.

The Restore Initial Query View on Refresh checkbox controls whether or not the navigational state of the query is saved when you save the workbook. If the box is checked, the navigational state is not saved, and the default layout specified in Query Designer will be displayed when the workbook is opened. If unchecked, the navigational state will be saved with the workbook and displayed when the workbook is next opened.

Cell Range

The next field, RANGE, controls which cells the analysis grid occupies on the Excel worksheet. The analysis grid in Figure 6.4 extends from the top-left corner at cell F15 to the bottom-right corner at T20. Note that the cell references in the RANGE field are absolute, which is why they are displayed as F15 and T20.

You can change the cells in the RANGE field manually to move or resize the analysis grid. Dragging and dropping the analysis grid is another way to move it around the worksheet, and you can also right-click the analysis grid in design mode and drag one of the handles to resize it. The RANGE field will be automatically updated if you use drag and drop to move or resize the analysis grid.

The actual size of the analysis grid might be larger if the amount of data returned by the query is larger than the specified size of the analysis grid. We will see how to control this automatic expansion when we get to the CLIPPING tab later in this section.

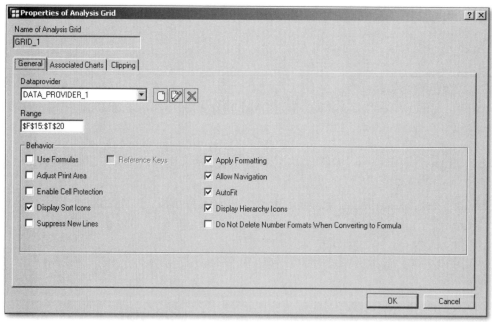

Figure 6.4 Properties of Analysis Grid (BEx Analyzer Design Mode)

User Experience Tip 6.1: Dragging Elements in BEx Analyzer Design Mode: Not as Smooth as You Think

When dragging interface elements around a BEx analyzer worksheet, you may notice that you are able to smoothly drag items around and drop them so the item's edges are not aligned with specific cells. This is an illusion: the item will automatically be pushed to the top-left of the current cell.

The drag-and-drop method for moving and resizing elements in design mode can often be a little flaky, so if precise adjustments are needed we recommend entering cell references into the RANGE field as described previously.

Formula Mode

If you check the USE FORMULAS checkbox, the analysis grid will be set to formula mode. This is the same formula mode enabled by the Convert to Formula context menu item discussed in Chapter 5, Section 5.3.4, Context Menu Navigation Tools, but using the USE FORMULAS checkbox is a little different.

When you right-click an analysis grid in analysis mode and select "Convert to Formula" from the context menu, no further navigation via BEx analyzer is possible — all data cells are converted into Excel formulas, and the context menu and drag-and-drop navigation are both disabled. You cannot undo this change, because the Convert to Formula function actually deletes the analysis grid design element when it makes the conversion.

However, when you check the USE FORMULAS checkbox in the analysis grid properties in design mode, all data cells become Excel formulas, but you can still navigate by changing filters or drilldowns via the context menu or drag-and-drop navigation. Data cells are automatically updated with new Excel formulas. You can undo this change by simply unchecking the USE FORMULAS checkbox, and data will be populated in the analysis grid by BEx analyzer rather than via an Excel formula.

If data does not appear correctly in the analysis grid after checking the USE FORMULAS checkbox, you should also check REFERENCE KEYS, which ensures formulas are uniquely specified for all cells. We will revisit formula mode again later in the book.

Adjust Print Area

When the ADJUST PRINT AREA box is checked, Excel's print area is automatically moved to the edge of the analysis grid. BEx analyzer will also repeat all characteristics drilled down in the rows on pages to the right of the first page, and all characteristics drilled down in the columns will be repeated on pages below the first page.

The action taken by this checkbox cannot be undone — if you uncheck ADJUST PRINT AREA, Excel's print area will be unchanged and drilled down characteristics will still be repeated on subsequent pages. The impact of the ADJUST PRINT AREA feature is more noticeable when in Page Layout view, accessible in Excel 2007 from the View tab.

Enable Cell Protection

Useful in reports used with BI Integrated Planning, the ENABLE CELL PROTEC-TION checkbox will lock all cells that are not "input-ready," which means they are not used to enter data for planning purposes. All input-ready cells will remain unlocked. This feature can help make sure users cannot enter data in cells that are not input-ready for planning.

Display Sort Icons

Headers for characteristics and key figure values typically display an icon that allows the user to sort values in ascending or descending order. You can hide these icons by unchecking the DISPLAY SORT ICONS checkbox.

Suppress New Lines

In BI Integrated Planning queries with input-ready fields, BEx analyzer gives users the ability to add new blank rows to enter data. Checking the SUPPRESS NEW LINES checkbox will disable this feature.

Apply Formatting

BEx analyzer automatically applies basic formatting to analysis grids — by default, characteristics and structures are displayed on a light blue background, key figure values are in white cells, and results are highlighted in yellow. If you uncheck the APPLY FORMATTING checkbox, this formatting will no longer be applied to cells within the analysis grid. This option is usually disabled for performance reasons when the format of the analysis grid is not important.

Allow Navigation

Users can navigate queries within an analysis grid by using the context menu or drag-and-drop navigation. Unchecking the ALLOW NAVIGATION checkbox will disable both the context menu and drag-and-drop navigation within the analysis grid. However, you can still change the navigation state of the analysis grid by using the navigation pane, unless the ALLOW NAVIGATION checkbox in the navigation pane has also been unchecked.

AutoFit

The AUTOFIT option, enabled by default, will automatically adjust column widths in the analysis grid to fit the content displayed. If you uncheck this option, navigation in the analysis grid will not change column widths. It is recommended to keep this option enabled to avoid wasted space or truncated content in the analysis grid.

Display Hierarchy Icons

When a display hierarchy is activated, triangle icons will appear next to hierarchy nodes to allow the user to expand or collapse specific nodes. If you uncheck the DISPLAY HIERARCHY ICONS checkbox (enabled by default) these icons will not be shown. Without these icons, context menu commands are the only way to navigate the hierarchy (see Chapter 4, Section 4.7.4, Hierarchy).

Do Not Delete Number Formats

The DO NOT DELETE NUMBER FORMATS WHEN CONVERTING TO FORMULA checkbox is unchecked by default. When unchecked, using the Convert To Formula context menu command (see Chapter 5, Section 5.3.4) will reset the formatting of all data in the analysis grid upon conversion to formula mode. For example, the number of decimal places will be automatically reset. To retain formatting, make sure this box is checked before executing the Convert To Formula command.

Associated Charts Tab

The next tab after the GENERAL tab, ASSOCIATED CHARTS, shows a list of charts in the BEx analyzer workbook. Any charts checked on this tab will be linked to the analysis grid, so the navigational state of the analysis grid will automatically be reflected on the checked chart. You can link multiple charts to a single analysis grid.

6.2.3 Clipping (Overflow Data Display)

The final tab in the PROPERTIES OF ANALYSIS GRID screen, CLIPPING, controls what happens when the size of the data set returned by a DataProvider is greater than the specified cell range of the analysis grid. The different options available are shown in Figure 6.5.

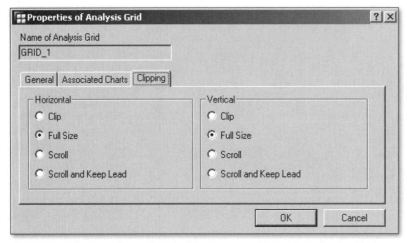

Figure 6.5 Clipping Tab, Analysis Grid Properties in BEx Analyzer Design Mode

The impact of changing these settings is best illustrated by a series of screenshots. The default setting for both horizontal (overflow columns) and vertical (overflow rows) is FULL SIZE, which will automatically expand the analysis grid until all data can be displayed, as shown in Figure 6.6.

You can see that the analysis grid stretches horizontally to column U and vertically down to row 30 to display the entire data set. If more rows were returned, the analysis grid would expand down the worksheet as far as necessary.

This setting is optimal if there are no other design elements to the right or below the analysis grid — a FULL SIZE analysis grid has the potential to cover other design elements placed to the right or below the grid, depending on the amount of data displayed.

If your workbook interface requires a set area for the analysis grid, you would need to select one of the other clipping options. Settings for horizontal and vertical overflow can be set independently.

	Test Demo Headcount Report															

		Author JKRAFT2	Status of Data 06/21/2010 21:21:44													

Chart | Filter | Information

Table

		Headcount													Overall Result
	Fiscal year	J4/2008													
Cost center.	Employee\Posting period	1	2	3	4	5	6	7	8	9	10	11	12	Result	
51090	1022	1.000	1.000	1.000	1.000	1.000	1.000	1.000	1.000	1.000	1.000	1.000	1.000	12.000	12.000
	1028	1.000	1.000	1.000	1.000	1.000	1.000	1.000	1.000	1.000	1.000	1.000	1.000	12.000	12.000
	1080	1.000	1.000	1.000										3.000	3.000
	1139	1.000	1.000	1.000	1.000	1.000	1.000	1.000	1.000	1.000	1.000	1.000	1.000	12.000	12.000
	1424	1.000	1.000	1.000	1.000	1.000	1.000	1.000	1.000	1.000	1.000	1.000	1.000	12.000	12.000
	1674	1.000												1.000	1.000
	1753	1.000	1.000	1.000	1.000	1.000	1.000	1.000						7.000	7.000
	1886	1.000	1.000	1.000	1.000	1.000	1.000	1.000	1.000	1.000	1.000	1.000	1.000	12.000	12.000
	1907	1.000	1.000	1.000	1.000	1.000								5.000	5.000
	2230	1.000	1.000	1.000	1.000	1.000	1.000	1.000	1.000	1.000	1.000	1.000	1.000	12.000	12.000
	2259	1.000	1.000	1.000	1.000	1.000	1.000	1.000	1.000	1.000	1.000	1.000	1.000	12.000	12.000
	2352	1.000	1.000	1.000	1.000	1.000	1.000	1.000	1.000	1.000	1.000	1.000	1.000	12.000	12.000
	2407	1.000	1.000	1.000										3.000	3.000

Figure 6.6 Analysis Grid with Full Size Clipping

Selecting the CLIP option for either the horizontal or vertical direction will only expand the analysis grid in that direction up to the last cell specified in the Range field on the General tab of analysis grid properties. Any data that would extend the analysis grid beyond that point is simply not displayed (or "clipped"). See Figure 6.7 for an illustration where the analysis grid's range extends to cell L23, and clipping is set to Clip for both horizontal and vertical directions.

	Test Demo Headcount Report							

		Author JKRAFT2	Status of Data 06/21/2010 21:21:44					

Chart | Filter | Information

Table

		Headcount				
	Fiscal year	J4/2008				
Cost center.	Employee\Posting period	1	2	3	4	5
51090	1022	1.000	1.000	1.000	1.000	1.000
	1028	1.000	1.000	1.000	1.000	1.000
	1080	1.000	1.000	1.000		
	1139	1.000	1.000	1.000	1.000	1.000
	1424	1.000	1.000	1.000	1.000	1.000
	1674	1.000				

Figure 6.7 Clipped Analysis Grid

129

Because the Clip option results in the display of an incomplete data set without any indication that more data is available, use this setting with caution so users don't assume they are seeing a complete report.

The SCROLL option is typically a better alternative — it truncates data the same way the Clip option does, but a scroll bar is added at the end of the analysis grid to allow the user to scroll up/down or left/right, as shown in Figure 6.8.

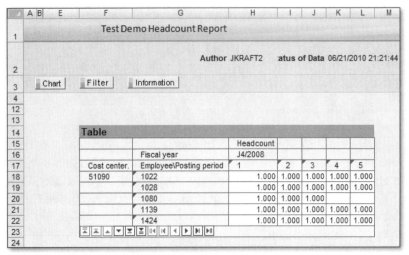

Figure 6.8 Analysis Grid with Scroll Setting

The buttons with just arrows scroll one row or column at a time, an arrow with a single line scrolls one page at a time, and arrows with two lines will jump to the very beginning or end of the data set's rows or columns.

If you scroll down or to the right using the scroll bar, you may end up with an analysis grid that looks like Figure 6.9. This is the same data set shown in Figure 6.8 after clicking the down arrow three times — you'll notice that the structure, FISCAL YEAR, and POSTING PERIOD drilldowns in the columns are no longer displayed. The entire analysis grid also looks smaller because the AutoFit option was enabled (see the previous section).

Table						
51090	1022	1.000	1.000	1.000	1.000	1.000
	1028	1.000	1.000	1.000	1.000	1.000
	1080	1.000	1.000	1.000		
	1139	1.000	1.000	1.000	1.000	1.000
	1424	1.000	1.000	1.000	1.000	1.000
	1674	1.000				
	1753	1.000	1.000	1.000	1.000	1.000
	1886	1.000	1.000	1.000	1.000	1.000

Figure 6.9 Analysis Grid Scrolled below Column Headings, Scroll Setting

To always keep drilled down characteristics displayed in the analysis grid, use the SCROLL AND KEEP LEAD setting. Figure 6.10 shows the same data set scrolled down three times, but this time you can still see the characteristics drilled down in the columns.

Table		Headcount				
	Fiscal year	J4/2008				
Cost center.	Employee\Posting period	1	2	3	4	5
	1139	1.000	1.000	1.000	1.000	1.000
	1424	1.000	1.000	1.000	1.000	1.000
	1674	1.000				
	1753	1.000	1.000	1.000	1.000	1.000
	1886	1.000	1.000	1.000	1.000	1.000

Figure 6.10 Analysis Grid Scrolled below Column Headings, Scroll and Keep Lead Setting

While the Scroll and Keep Lead setting makes it easier for users to match key figures with characteristic values when they scroll, the constant display of these characteristics means less room for key figures, so users can see fewer values at one time.

6.2.4 Adding New Analysis Grids

Now that we have an understanding of the concept of DataProviders and the different property settings for analysis grids, let's walk through the process of adding a new analysis grid for a different query on another worksheet in our existing BEx analyzer workbook.

Because the analysis grid will be showing data from a different query, we will also need to create a new DataProvider. In this case, the analysis grid will show data from the actual versus plan query we created in Chapter 3, Building Effective Business Warehouse Queries: The Basics of Query Designer.

131

**Procedure 6.1: Adding a New Analysis Grid with a
New DataProvider on a New Worksheet**

1. In a BEx analyzer workbook, click the Insert Worksheet button at the bottom of the Excel window, or click an existing blank worksheet.

2. Click a cell in the worksheet that will give you enough space to insert additional design items to the left and above the new analysis grid. Cell E7 would be a good candidate.

3. Click the Insert Analysis Grid button on the BEx analyzer design mode toolbar. BEx analyzer will automatically switch to design mode.

4. Left-click the new analysis grid item to display the properties screen.

5. Note that the analysis grid is pointing to the existing DataProvider (DATA_PROVIDER_1). Click the Create DataProvider button next to the DataProvider dropdown.

6. In the CREATE DATA PROVIDER screen (see Figure 6.11), click the ASSIGN QUERY button next to the blank field under the DataProvider name and select a query or query view to assign to the DataProvider. In this case, we will select the actual versus plan query from Chapter 3.

7. Type a relevant name for the new DataProvider. Because this DataProvider will be connected to an actual versus plan query, we can call it DP_ACTUALPLAN.

8. Confirm that the query name and cube are displayed correctly. For now, keep the PROVIDE RESULTS OFFLINE and RESTORE INITIAL QUERY VIEW ON REFRESH boxes unchecked (see the DataProvider Assignment heading of Section 6.2.2, Analysis Grid Properties, for more information), and click OK

9. Confirm that DP_ACTUALPLAN is selected under the DataProvider dropdown menu, and that the checkboxes in the Behavior section match Figure 6.4.

10. Switch to the Clipping tab and ensure that both Horizontal and Vertical are set to Full Size. Because this analysis grid has its own worksheet, we don't need to worry about clipping.

11. Click OK, and click the first button on the design toolbar to switch back to Analysis mode.

Congratulations! You've just created a second analysis grid in your BEx analyzer workbook. However, you may be seeing a Change Variable Values message in the new analysis grid instead of live data. If the query you assign to a DataProvider has required variables with no default values, BEx analyzer can't display the query until you populate those variables.

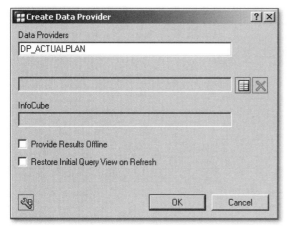

Figure 6.11 Create Data Provider Screen

Even if the change variable values message does not appear, let's click the fourth button in the analysis toolbar to open the variable screen. The variable screen will look a little different when you have multiple DataProviders in a workbook (see Figure 6.12). Because we have two DataProviders connected to two different queries in this workbook, there are three sections: one for common variables that appear in both queries, one for variables in the first DataProvider, and the last section for variables in the second DataProvider.

You'll notice that the INDIVIDUAL COST CENTERS and COMPANY CODE variables appear in the COMMON VARIABLES section — this is because both queries use the same variables. However, there are two FISCAL YEAR (REQUIRED) variables, one under each DataProvider. Why would this happen?

The answer is that the headcount query uses a Fiscal Year variable with the description FISCAL YEAR (REQUIRED), while the actual versus plan query uses another variable with the same description, but a different technical name. To correct this issue, you can open Query Designer directly to check the technical names of the variables by clicking the analysis grid in either BEx analyzer mode, clicking the TOOLS icon (the fifth icon in the analysis toolbar), and selecting Edit Query. Once both queries are pointing to the same Fiscal Year variable, that variable will appear in the COMMON VARIABLES section.

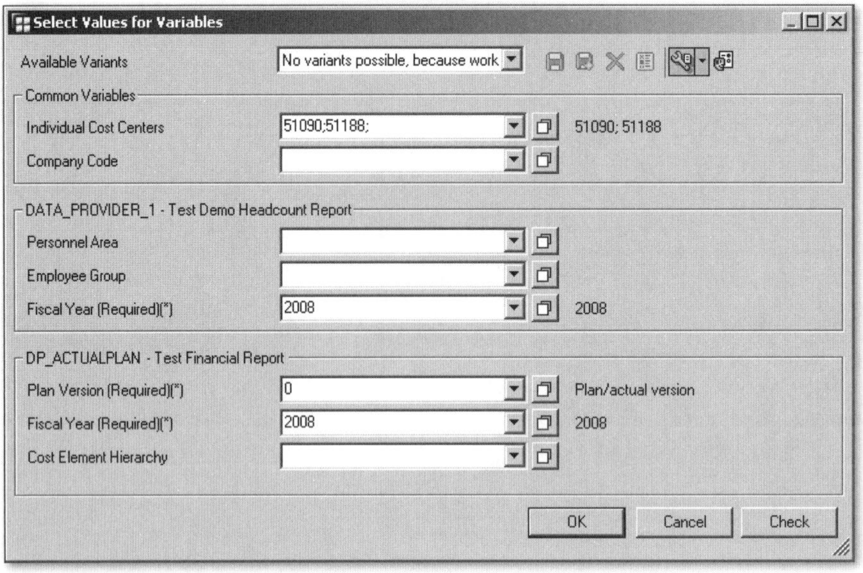

Figure 6.12   BEx Analyzer Variable Screen with Multiple DataProviders

You might think that intentionally pointing to two different variables could be a good way to ensure that users can independently set variables for different queries within a single workbook, but we will see later that the Workbook Settings option in the design mode toolbar has a setting on the Variables tab called Display Duplicate Variables Only Once. This setting is checked by default. However, if you uncheck it, variables will always appear under each DataProvider, even if more than one query uses the same variable.

The resulting query would look something like Figure 6.13. The worksheet may look a bit empty, but later in the chapter we will start adding additional items to fill out the top and left sections of the worksheet.

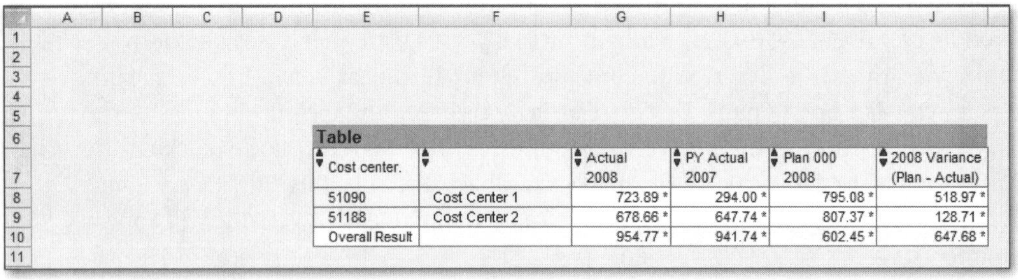

Figure 6.13   New Analysis Grid on New Worksheet

6.3   Navigation Panes

After the analysis grid, the next most important design element in a BEx analyzer query is probably the navigation pane. Chapter 5, Section 5.3, Query Navigation in BEx analyzer, explained how to use the navigation pane to change the navigational state of an analysis grid, but here we will look at how to add a new navigation pane to an existing BEx analyzer workbook.

You may have noticed that the new analysis grid we created in Section 6.2.4, Adding New Analysis Grids, does not have a navigation pane — this does not prevent the user from navigating the new analysis grid (for example, users could navigate via the context menu), but it does limit the options available.

Let's correct that by adding a navigation pane to the left of the new analysis grid — but before we start we'll examine the different properties of the navigation pane design item. You can open the properties box for the navigation pane on the first worksheet by making sure the navigation is displayed by clicking the Filter icon, then switching to design mode and left-clicking the navigation pane design item.

6.3.1   General Properties

The GENERAL tab, seen in Figure 6.14, has the same DATAPROVIDER assignment field as the analysis grid properties. If a navigation pane is assigned to the same DataProvider as an analysis grid, any actions taken in the navigation pane will affect the state of the analysis grid, and vice versa. As with the analysis grid, you have the ability to create, change, and delete DataProviders from the navigation pane properties box.

The navigation pane also has a cell range to specify the size of the design item. You can either enter cells directly into the RANGE field, or use drag-and-drop functionality to move and/or resize the navigation pane.

The AUTOFIT option here is slightly different from the analysis grid AutoFit setting. Later in this section we will see how to enable icon display in a navigation pane. For navigation panes without icons, AutoFit will only auto-expand the first column — because the second column can potentially contain a large amount of filter data it is not affected by AutoFit. If the navigation pane is set up to display icons, AutoFit will only apply to the first two columns (columns C and D in Figure 6.15), because the third column displays filter data.

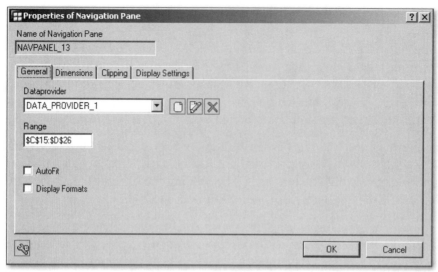

Figure 6.14 Navigation Pane Properties — General Tab

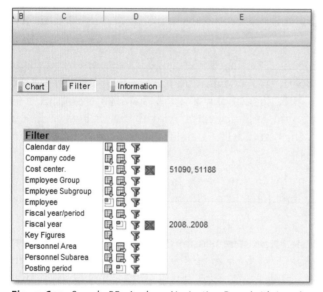

Figure 6.15 Sample BEx Analyzer Navigation Pane (with Icons)

The next checkbox, DISPLAY FORMATS, is checked by default in new navigation panes. If DISPLAY FORMATS is unchecked, BEx analyzer formatting is not applied to the navigation pane, instead relying on Excel formatting applied to the cells. If checked, the navigation pane would have borders and colored backgrounds similar to Figure 6.16, depending on your default workbook style.

Note that Figure 6.15 shows a sample navigation pane from the first worksheet of the standard BEx analyzer workbook. The DISPLAY FORMATS option on this navigation pane is unchecked, but the cells underneath the navigation pane have been formatted in Excel to have a white background with a light blue exterior border. If the DISPLAY FORMATS checkbox was enabled, the white background would not show through, and it would look more like Figure 6.16.

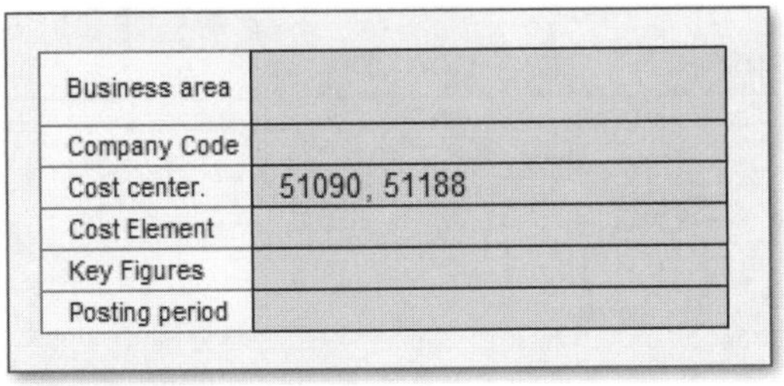

Business area	
Company Code	
Cost center.	51090, 51188
Cost Element	
Key Figures	
Posting period	

Figure 6.16   BEx Analyzer Navigation Pane with Default Formatting

6.3.2   Selecting Dimensions

The DIMENSIONS tab in the PROPERTIES NAVIGATION PANE screen allows you to select which characteristics and structures are displayed, as seen in Figure 6.17.

The AVAILABLE DIMENSIONS list on the left side includes all characteristics and structures included in the Free Characteristics, Rows, and Columns sections of the query in Query Designer. The icon on the bottom left of the dialog box toggles the display of technical names.

You can add characteristics and structures to the SELECTED DIMENSIONS list on the right side by double-clicking the item or by selecting it and clicking the right arrow button. If the SELECTED DIMENSIONS list is empty, all characteristics and structures in the AVAILABLE DIMENSIONS list will be included in the navigation pane. If the SELECTED DIMENSIONS list contains one or more items, the navigation pane will only show those items. You can reorder items in the SELECTED DIMENSIONS list via drag and drop or by using the arrow buttons at the bottom of the list.

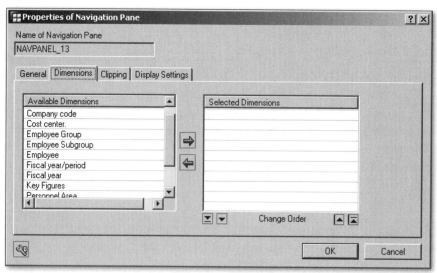

Figure 6.17 Navigation Pane Properties — Dimensions Tab

6.3.3 Navigation Pane Clipping

Clipping for navigation panes is handled in much the same way as analysis grids, except navigation panes can only expand vertically as more characteristics are added.

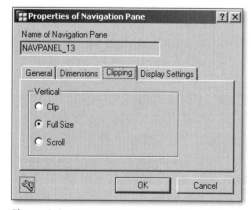

Figure 6.18 Navigation Pane Properties — Clipping Tab

If the navigation pane is set up to show all characteristics, the navigation pane can grow based on new free characteristics being added in Query Designer. The navigation pane can also grow if more characteristics are added to the Selected Dimensions list (assuming the list was not empty to begin with).

The default selection, FULL SIZE, means that the navigation pane design item will expand vertically to show all characteristics. The CLIP option will hide any new characteristics added beyond the specified cell range in the GENERAL tab, and the SCROLL option displays a small scroll bar at the bottom of the navigation pane if the cell range is not large enough to show all items.

6.3.4   Display Settings

The final tab in the navigation pane properties box includes a number of different options that control how the navigation pane is displayed (see Figure 6.19). The DISPLAY FILTER TEXTS checkbox determines whether or not the last column in the navigation pane is visible. As an example, if the navigation pane in Figure 6.16 had DISPLAY FILTER TEXTS unchecked, only the list of characteristics would be shown.

Next, we have the ALLOW NAVIGATION checkbox. As we saw in the analysis grid properties section, unchecking ALLOW NAVIGATION will disable most navigational functionality. In the case of a navigation pane, unchecking this box will disable drag-and-drop navigation (see section 5.3.1), double-click navigation and direct filter entries (see Chapter 5, Section 5.3.2), and much of the context menu (see Chapter 5, Section 5.3.4). However, right-clicking a navigation pane with ALLOW NAVIGATION unchecked will still allow users to access the Properties and Query Properties context menu items, which means that the Navigational State screen (see Chapter 5, Section 5.3.3, Navigational State in Query Properties) is still accessible.

We've already seen the results of enabling the DISPLAY ICONS feature (unchecked by default) in Figure 6.15. Each row of the navigation pane can have up to four icons: one to drill down the characteristic in the rows, one to drill down in the columns, one to select filter values for the characteristic, and one to remove filter values (if any such values are set). If a characteristic is already drilled down in the rows or columns, the relevant drill down button will be replaced by a Remove Drilldown button.

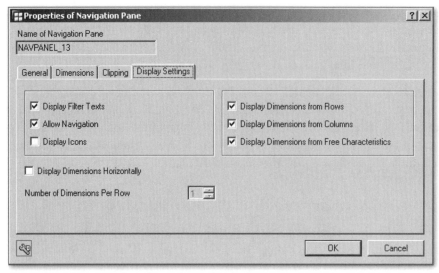

Figure 6.19 Navigation Pane Properties — Display Settings

The three checkboxes on the right side control whether or not to display characteristics and structures (dimensions) that are drilled down in the rows, drilled down in the columns, or not currently active drilldowns. The determination of what to display happens dynamically: if you are only displaying dimensions from Free Characteristics, and Cost Center is currently drilled down in the rows, it will not be displayed in the navigation pane. However, if you remove the Cost Center drilldown from the analysis grid, Cost Center will appear in the navigation pane, because it is now considered a free characteristic.

The DISPLAY DIMENSIONS HORIZONTALLY option allows you to change the orientation of the navigation pane. Instead of just being a vertical list, you can show all dimensions horizontally, or create a matrix by adjusting the maximum number of dimensions per row. When the DISPLAY DIMENSIONS HORIZONTALLY option is enabled, all clipping options are disabled, so be careful where you place a horizontally oriented navigation pane in the worksheet.

Figure 6.20 shows an example of the navigation pane in Figure 6.16 with a number of changed settings. Display Filter Texts has been unchecked, but you can still see that there is a filter on Cost Center, thanks to the Remove Filter icon. This and the other icons are showing up because the Display Icons box has been checked. Display Dimensions from Rows and Display Dimensions from Columns have both been unchecked, and in this example Cost Element and the Key Figures structure are active drilldowns, so neither is displayed here.

Finally, the Display Dimensions Horizontally option has been checked, and the Number of Dimensions Per Row option has been set to 2, resulting in a four-column-wide navigation pane (two columns for characteristic descriptions and two for icons).

Figure 6.20 Example Horizontal Navigation Pane

6.3.5 Adding New Navigation Panes

We are now ready to add a new navigation pane to our new worksheet, next to the existing analysis grid.

Procedure 6.2: Adding a New Navigation Pane

1. In the BEx analyzer workbook, click the existing worksheet with the new analysis grid.

2. Click a cell in the worksheet to the left of the analysis grid that will give you enough space to insert the navigation pane. Cell B7 would be a good candidate.

3. Click the Insert Navigation Pane button on the BEx analyzer design mode toolbar. BEx analyzer will automatically switch to design mode.

4. Left-click the new navigation pane item to display the Properties screen.

5. In the General tab, select the DP_ACTUALPLAN DataProvider. This will allow the navigation pane to control the navigational state of the analysis grid on this worksheet, which uses the same DataProvider.

6. Check the AutoFit button to ensure the columns are wide enough to display characteristic descriptions.

7. Click the Dimensions tab, for now we will leave the Selected Dimensions list empty so all characteristics and structures are displayed in the navigation pane.

8. Click the Clipping tab and make sure Full Size is selected.

9. Click the Display Settings tab and check that the settings are as shown in Figure 6.19.

10. Click OK, and click the first button on the design toolbar to switch back to Analysis mode.

You'll notice that there's no heading on the navigation pane — BEx analyzer automatically adds a heading to analysis grids, but not to navigation panes. To add the heading, you can use Excel's Format Painter tool. First, click the TABLE heading (cell E6 in our example). Then click the Format Painter — in Excel 2007 and 2010, it's located in the Home tab, the bottom-right icon in the Clipboard section on the left. Once the Format Painter is selected, drag from cell B6 to C6 to duplicate the header style. Click cell B6 and type a description such as "Navigation Pane" or "Filters."

The resulting worksheet with both the navigation pane and the analysis grid can be seen in Figure 6.21. Next up, we'll look at the List of Filters design item.

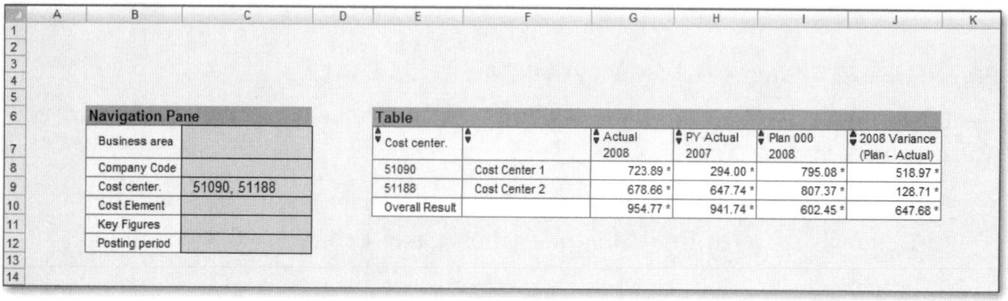

Figure 6.21 New Navigation Pane with Analysis Grid

6.3.6 List of Filters

While the List of Filters design item has its own button on the BEx analyzer design mode toolbar, it is essentially a display-only version of the navigation pane — when you bring up the context menu on a List of Filters item, the only options available are the Back and Properties commands. The properties for the List of Filters item are also very similar to the navigation pane, with a few exceptions.

The General tab of the List of Filters properties window allows you to assign a DataProvider, and specify a cell range for display, and toggle the AutoFit setting, just like a navigation pane. However, there is an additional Display Characteristic Text checkbox: when checked, the List of Filters item will display the name of the characteristic or structure next to the filter value, just as the navigation pane does. If unchecked (the default value), the item will only contain filter values, and will look like cells C7 - C12 in Figure 6.21 (the second half of the navigation pane).

The Dimensions tab here also looks almost identical to the Dimensions tab in the navigation pane properties window, the only difference is the Presentation Style dropdown menu. This dropdown allows you to display only the key value of filters, only the text value, or both in the List of Filters item. In the navigation pane, the display of key or text is controlled by characteristic properties and is always the same as the key and/or text display in the analysis grid, but this extra setting in List of Filters allows for a different display.

So, when would we use the List of Filters item in a workbook? There really aren't too many compelling reasons — the List of Filters item might be useful if you want filter values displayed in a separate area of the workbook from the navigation pane. You could also potentially use the List of Filters item in place of a navigation pane if you want to limit the amount of navigation a user can perform, but another way to accomplish this would be to uncheck the Allow Navigation checkbox in a navigation pane.

6.4   Buttons and Commands

We've seen analysis grids and navigation panes before in previous chapters — they are the primary tools for query navigation, but they offer limited customization options. Buttons, on the other hand, can be tailored to your specific needs by creating a custom command or a string of multiple commands.

These commands are documented in the BW Web Application Programming Interface (API) reference, which will be covered in detail later in the book. BEx analyzer buttons accept most Web API commands, and we will look at how to implement a few basic Web API commands in this section.

6.4.1   The Command Wizard

The procedure for adding a new button to a worksheet is very simple: select a cell above the analysis grid (cell E2 would work) and click the Insert Button icon, which is the fifth icon on the BEx analyzer design toolbar. You will automatically switch into design mode. Left-click the new button to open the SELECT COMMAND TYPE screen, as seen in Figure 6.22.

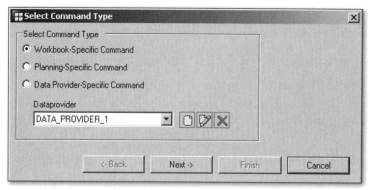

Figure 6.22 BEx Analyzer Button — Select Command Type

This is the start of the command wizard, a step-by-step process that will build a customized command for the button. In the first step of the wizard, you can choose from one of three different types of commands.

Workbook-Specific Commands

Choosing WORKBOOK-SPECIFIC COMMAND and clicking the NEXT button will display the different commands available that impact the workbook as a whole. These commands include bringing up the variable screen (with personalized variables either shown or hidden) and toggling drag-and-drop navigation for the workbook.

Notice that these commands do not impact any specific DataProvider, so the DataProvider assigned to the button does not matter. See Figure 6.23 for the second page of the command wizard showing workbook-specific commands. None of these commands require additional configuration, so clicking the Finish button will display the Button Properties window, which we will discuss later.

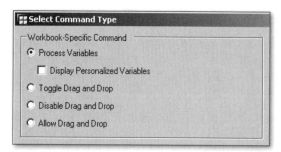

Figure 6.23 BEx Analyzer Button — Workbook-Specific Commands

Planning-Specific Commands

The PLANNING-SPECIFIC COMMAND section deals with commands that only apply to input-ready queries created for BI Integrated Planning. These commands are shown in Figure 6.24.

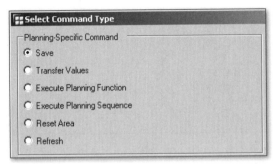

Figure 6.24 BEx Analyzer Button — Planning-specific Commands

The SAVE command will save any changes made to input-ready fields to the relevant InfoCube if the check is successful. TRANSFER VALUES will save changes to the planning buffer.

The next two commands, EXECUTE PLANNING FUNCTION and EXECUTE PLANNING SEQUENCE, both have follow-up screens, available by clicking the Next button at the bottom of the window. These follow-up screens allow you to choose a planning function of planning sequence to execute when the button is clicked.

The RESET AREA command will clear all planning data entered into input-ready fields that have not yet been saved. Finally, the REFRESH command will refresh the workbook and load current data for all DataProviders. The Refresh command is also useful for workbooks not related to planning.

Data Provider-Specific Commands

The final series of commands is specific to a single DataProvider, so one must be chosen in Figure 6.22 before the next step of the command wizard can be displayed. The DATA PROVIDER-SPECIFIC COMMAND section is shown in Figure 6.25.

The first two commands, EDIT and DISPLAY, are specific to input-ready queries created for BI Integrated Planning. The EDIT command will switch an input-ready DataProvider to change mode, while the Display command will switch the DataProvider to display mode.

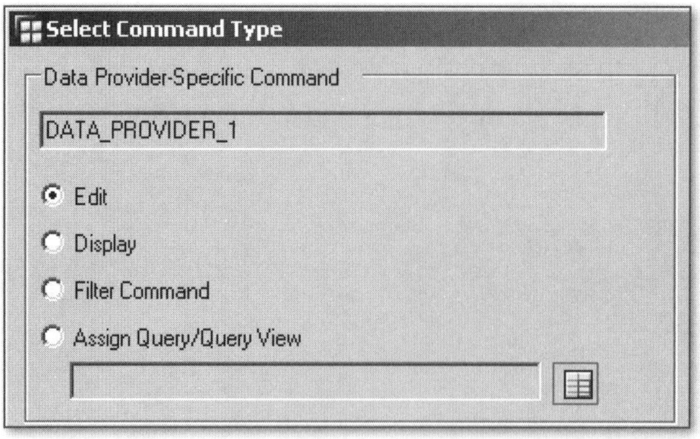

Figure 6.25 BEx Analyzer Button — Data Provider-Specific Commands

The FILTER COMMAND is one of the most commonly used commands available in the command wizard — it allows a button to remove an existing filter or set a specific filter value for a characteristic. We will see later in the chapter how useful the FILTER COMMAND can be when included in a *command sequence*, where a single button can perform a number of filter operations and other commands at once.

The last Data Provider-specific command available here is ASSIGN QUERY/QUERY VIEW. This command allows the user to change the query or query view assigned to the selected DataProvider with a single click.

User Experience Tip 6.2: Use Assign Query in Buttons with Caution

The ASSIGN QUERY/QUERY VIEW command is a very powerful one — not only does it change which query is displayed, it also throws out the current navigation state of the DataProvider. If the user has spent time customizing the navigation state by changing filters and adding or removing drilldowns, all those changes will be irrevocably lost if the user does not save before executing the ASSIGN QUERY/QUERY VIEW command.

Later in the chapter we will look at how to add a confirmation box by modifying the button's underlying Visual Basic code.

6.4.2 Configuring and Fine-Tuning Commands

Now that we've explored the different categories of commands available via the command wizard, let's continue to the properties box of the button design item. To do this, we must first step through the command wizard to the end. Our sample button will automatically filter on Company Code 0001, so let's set up the button accordingly.

Left-click the new button you created earlier in this section to bring up the Select Command Type screen (Figure 6.22) if it's not already showing. Select the Dat-aProvider-Specific Command option and choose the relevant DataProvider — in this case, DP_ACTUALPLAN. Click the Next button to continue to the next step in the wizard.

You should now see the Data Provider-Specific Command screen shown in Figure 6.25. Choose the Filter Command option. Because the Filter Command requires additional configuration before it can be implemented in a button, you'll need to click the Next button to move on to the next step, as seen in Figure 6.26.

Now select the Company Code characteristic, and the Set Filter option. The Set Filter field allows you to manually type in a value or select a value from the value help at the right side of the field. Type 0001 in the Set Filter field, or select a company code more relevant to your system using the value help. Click the Finish button (not shown in Figure 6.26) when you're done.

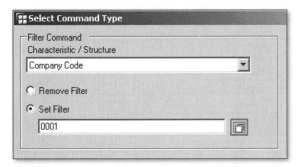

Figure 6.26 BEx Analyzer Command Wizard — Filter

Once you click the Finish button, the Properties of Button window will appear, as seen in Figure 6.27. The automatically generated name of the button is shown on the top left, followed by the cell range — in this case, the button only occupies cell E2, but the button can be expanded in a fashion similar to other design items.

The Button Text field controls the text displayed on the button in the worksheet, ideally a brief description of what the button does. We'll come back to the next field, Command Range, later in this section. The Shape field allows you to choose a different graphic to use for the button instead of SAP's default gray rectangle.

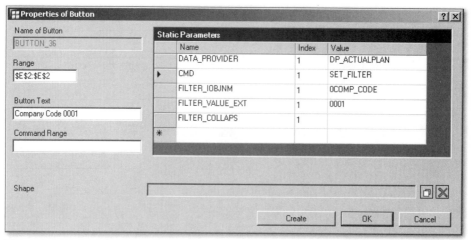

Figure 6.27 BEx Analyzer Button Properties

Stepping through the command wizard automatically populates the STATIC PARAM-ETERS section of the PROPERTIES OF BUTTON window with the commands selected in the wizard. The parameters in our simple filter command, which filters the Company Code characteristic on a single value 0001, are explained in Table 6.1. A more complete list of commands can be found later in the book — these commands are derived from the SAP BW 3.x Web Design API.

You can modify the parameters and parameter values manually by editing the fields in the STATIC PARAMETERS section. You can also add new parameters by editing the last line under STATIC PARAMETERS; a new blank line will appear after you edit the last line.

You may have noticed that each parameter has an index, in addition to a name and parameter value. Because commands typically require multiple parameters, the index value is a way of grouping parameters together so they all apply to the same command. We only have a single command in this button, so all of the parameters have an index of 1, but we will see later in the chapter how we can implement multiple commands in a single button by using different index values.

Instead of manually entering parameters in the STATIC PARAMETERS section, you can also dynamically populate parameter names, index values, and parameter values using the COMMAND RANGE field. If you enter a range of cells three columns wide, the parameters will be populated based on the values of these cells. Parameter names will be taken from the first column of the cell range, index values from the second column, and parameter values from the third.

DATA_PROVIDER	The name of the DataProvider this command will be affecting. Only required for DataProvider-specific commands.
CMD	The name of the command, in this case SET_FILTER.
FILTER_IOBJNM	The technical name of the characteristic that will be filtered on. In this case, the technical name of the Company Code characteristic is 0COMP_CODE.
FILTER_VALUE_EXT	The value that will be included in the filter. EXT refers to external display — for example, July 16th, 2009, would be 07.16.2009 in external display format (versus 20090716 in SAP's internal format).
FILTER_COLLAPS	If this parameter is marked with an X, the characteristic specified in FILTER_IOBJNM will be removed from any active drilldown. If the parameter is blank (as it is here), the characteristic will not be removed. This parameter is optional, and if it is not included the default value is X, indicating that the characteristic will be removed from active drilldowns.

Table 6.1 Filter Command: Basic Parameters

The COMMAND RANGE cells can also be contained within an analysis grid, so parameter information for a button can be provided by a BW query. If both the STATIC PARAMETERS section and the COMMAND RANGE field are already populated, the full list of commands executed by the button is determined by taking the STATIC PARAMETERS section and appending all of the parameters within the command range.

Finally, next to the OK and CANCEL buttons at the bottom of the dialog box, you will see a CREATE button. This button will reopen the command wizard again, allowing you to add additional commands to the button. We will explore this functionality in the next section.

6.4.3 Buttons with Multiple Commands

If you click the OK button in the PROPERTIES OF BUTTON window, the parameters will be saved and you will be back in design mode. Switching to analysis mode will draw the button, and clicking on it will execute the specified filter command.

Creating a button to filter on a single value for a single characteristic is interesting, but it really isn't a big time-saver. Let's add an additional command to this button, so in addition to filtering on company code 0001, the button will also filter on fiscal periods 1, 2, and 3, to show only data from the first quarter of the fiscal year.

Procedure 6.3: Adding Additional Commands to an Existing Button

1. Make sure you are in design mode, and left-click the existing button.

2. Confirm that the existing Static Parameters are correct for the button's first command.

3. Click the Create button at the bottom of the Button Properties window to launch the command wizard.

4. Because we will be implementing a second filter command, choose the DP_ACTUALPLAN DataProvider.

5. Select Data Provider-Specific Command and click the Next button.

6. Select Filter Command and click Next.

7. To filter on only data from the first fiscal quarter, we will need to set up a filter on Posting Periods 1, 2, and 3. Select Posting Period from the Characteristic/Structure dropdown.

8. Select the Set Filter option and click on the value help.

9. Note that the value help only allows us to select one posting period at a time, so we can't select all three posting periods through the command wizard. For now, select posting period 1 and click OK.

10. Click the Finish button to return to the worksheet, then left-click the button again to reopen the Button Properties window.

Note that there is now a new set of parameters with an index value of 2 — this is the second command the button will execute. However, the second command will only filter on posting period 1. To correct this, we will need to change parameters manually to set up a range of values.

1. Select the new FILTER_VALUE_EXT line (make sure it has an index value of 2), and change FILTER_VALUE_EXT to FILTER_VALUE_LOW_EXT. This will set posting period 1 as the lower bound of the filter range.

2. Scroll down to the bottom of the Static Parameters section until you see a blank line, click the Name field in this line and type "FILTER_VALUE_HIGH_EXT."

3. In the same line, enter the number "2" in the second column (indicating this parameter is part of the second command) and the number "3" in the third column to specify posting period 3 as the upper bound of the filter range.

4. Change the Button Text on the left side of the dialog box to reflect the button's new functionality — something like Q1, Company 0001 would work.

5. Confirm that the PROPERTIES OF BUTTON window looks like Figure 6.28, then click the OK button to return to BEx analyzer design mode.

If you switch back to analysis mode and click the new button, it will automatically filter on Company Code 0001 and Posting Periods 1 through 3.

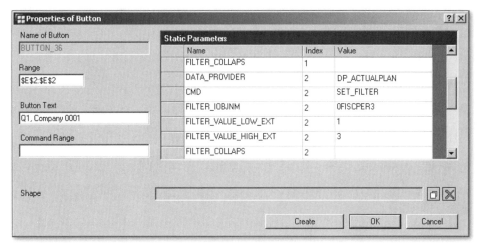

Figure 6.28 BEx Analyzer Button with Multiple Commands

6.4.4 Manually Adding Commands to Buttons

In the previous section, we created a single button that executed two filter commands on two different characteristics. Let's build on that and add different types of commands to the same button. By the end of this section, this button will not only execute two filters on company code and posting period — it will also drill down by Cost Element and deactivate the Cost Element display hierarchy.

There is a minor roadblock in adding these two commands: if you look through Section 6.4.1, The Command Wizard, you will not see commands to add a drill-down or change the hierarchy properties of a characteristic. The command wizard only lists a small subset of the available commands — documentation for these commands, which are derived from the BW Web API, can be found later in the book.

Fortunately, it is not required to use the command wizard to add new commands, and if you know the correct parameters you can add them yourself in the Static

Parameters section of the Properties of Button window. Let's take a look at the documentation for the commands that deal with adding drilldowns and changing the status of a characteristic's display hierarchy in Tables 6.2 and 6.3.

DATA_PROVIDER	The name of the DataProvider this command will be affecting. Only required for DataProvider-specific commands.
CMD	The name of the command, in this case EXPAND.
IOBJNM	The technical name of the characteristic that will be drilled down. In this case, the technical name of the Cost Element characteristic is 0COSTELMNT.
AXIS (optional)	Controls whether the characteristic is drilled down in the columns (value = 'X'), in the rows (value = 'Y'), or removed from drilldowns (blank value). If the parameter is not specified, characteristics are automatically added to the rows and structures are added to the columns.
PARENT_IOBJNM (optional)	If this parameter is specified, the new drilldown will be added just after the characteristic is identified. Otherwise, the new drilldown will be added to the end of the rows or columns.

Table 6.2 Drilldown Command Parameters

DATA_PROVIDER	The name of the DataProvider this command will be affecting. Only required for DataProvider-specific commands.
CMD	The name of the command, in this case SET_HIERARCHY_STATE.
IOBJNM	The technical name of the characteristic with the display hierarchy. In this case, the technical name of the Cost Element characteristic is 0COSTELMNT.
ACTIVE or TOGGLE_STATE	Either one of these two parameters may be used with this command. With the ACTIVE parameter, a value of X will activate the display hierarchy, and a blank value will deactivate it. With the TOGGLE_STATE parameter, a value of X will activate the display hierarchy if it is inactive, and deactivate it if currently active. TOGGLE_STATE with a blank value will have no effect.

Table 6.3 Activate/Deactivate Display Hierarchy Command Parameters

In this case, we will leave out the optional parameters for the drilldown command, because we are OK with the Cost Element characteristic drilldown being added to the end of the rows. For the second command, because we want to make sure the hierarchy is deactivated, we will use the ACTIVE parameter with a blank value.

To enter these parameters, switch to design mode and left-click on the button. Click the last row in the Static Parameters section and start entering the parameter names, index values, and parameter values. Because this button already has two commands, the index value for the drilldown command would be 3, and the index value for the hierarchy deactivation command would be 4.

The final result is shown in Figure 6.29. Don't forget to change the BUTTON TEXT to indicate that the button will now also drill down by the Cost Element characteristic.

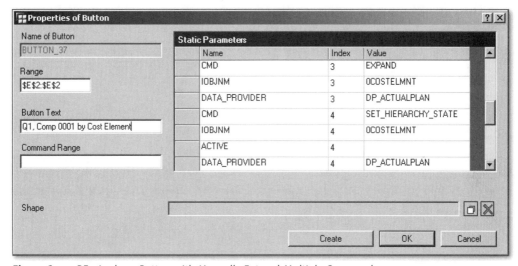

Figure 6.29 BEx Analyzer Button with Manually Entered Multiple Commands

If you switch out of design mode into analysis mode and click the button, the filters for the two characteristics will be set up as before, Cost Element will be drilled down in the rows, and the Cost Element hierarchy will be deactivated. This could be a significant time saver for users if they regularly execute this sequence of commands, especially as the workbook will only need to refresh once instead of four times.

6.5   Dropdowns, Checkboxes, and Radio Buttons

The next design items we will explore all involve filtering on characteristic values or elements of a structure: dropdown boxes, checkbox groups, and radio button groups. While all three of these design items perform similar functions, only one of them may be appropriate depending on business requirements.

In this section, we will look at these three types of design items, and then discuss when to use each one.

6.5.1   Dropdown Boxes

As with the other design items, the procedure for adding a new dropdown box is simple. Switch to design mode in BEx analyzer, select the cell where the dropdown box will be placed, and click the sixth button in the design toolbar to insert the dropdown box. Left-clicking once on the new dropdown box in design mode will open the PROPERTIES OF DROPDOWN BOX screen, as seen in Figure 6.30.

General Tab

The options on the GENERAL tab to select a DataProvider assignment and a cell range are the same as those on other design items that have been discussed earlier in the chapter. With a dropdown box, it is recommended to have a cell range consisting of only one cell. While it is possible to make the dropdown box larger, it will not provide any benefit to the user, as the font size will remain the same and you would still be able to view only one item at a time.

Note that the DataProvider in the GENERAL tab will be used to build the items in the dropdown list. We will see later in this section how to assign which DataProviders will be affected by the dropdown box selection.

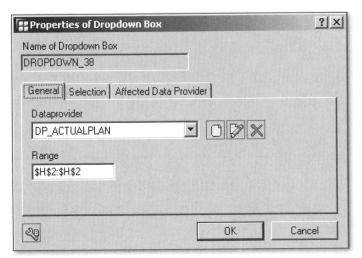

Figure 6.30 Dropdown Box Properties — General Tab

The SELECTION tab in the PROPERTIES OF DROPDOWN BOX window, as seen in Figure 6.31, controls how the dropdown box is populated. There are two potential uses for a dropdown box: it can be used to filter on a specific characteristic value or structure element, or it can be used to switch between query views.

Using Dropdowns to Filter

To use the dropdown box as a filtering tool, make sure the DIMENSIONS option is selected. You can choose the characteristic or structure to use — if you choose a characteristic, the dropdown box will be populated with the values of that characteristic, and if you choose a structure, the dropdown box will list the elements of that structure (selections and formulas).

The READ MODE option specifies how the system retrieves the list of characteristic values. Each READ MODE option is described in Table 6.4.

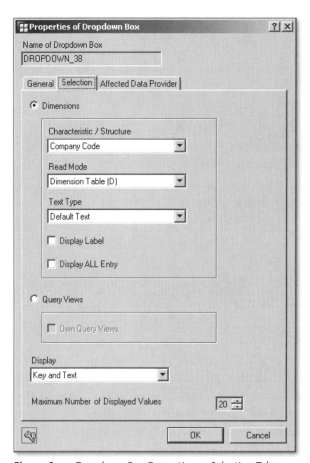

Figure 6.31 Dropdown Box Properties — Selection Tab

Master Data Table (M)	Returns all values that exist in the characteristic's master data table. Returns the most records, but many values may not be applicable, as they may not exist as data in the InfoProvider. Fastest performance.
Dimension Table (D)	Returns characteristic values from the dimension table. Slower performance than the Master Data Table read mode, but more relevant results are returned.
Posted Values (Q)	Returns only data that will be displayed in the query based on existing filter values. This is the slowest read mode, but all values returned will be usable.

Table 6.4 BW Read Modes

The next option, TEXT TYPE, controls whether short text, medium text, or long text is displayed in the dropdown box. The default value is "default text," which will automatically use the longest text available.

The DISPLAY LABEL checkbox will show the name of the characteristic or structure to the left of the dropdown box if checked.

If you want to provide a way for the user to remove a filter value using a drop-down menu, make sure to check the DISPLAY ALL ENTRY checkbox. When checked, a new ALL value will be added to the dropdown box. If a user selects this value, all existing filter values on the characteristic will be removed.

The DISPLAY item at the bottom of the window controls whether the dropdown box displays the key value of each characteristic value, the text value, or both.

Using Dropdowns to Change Query Views

Dropdown boxes can also be used as a shortcut to opening different query views. If you select the QUERY VIEWS option in the SELECTION tab, the dropdown box will be populated with a list of all query views that have been created on the query in the selected DataProvider.

The OWN QUERY VIEWS checkbox is grayed out unless the QUERY VIEWS option is selected. If this box is unchecked, all query views created on the query in the selected DataProvider will be listed in the dropdown box, regardless of who created the query view. If checked, only those query views created by the current user will be shown.

When a user selects a query view from a dropdown box, the current navigational state is replaced by the query view, so it is advisable to warn users to save their work before switching views.

The last item in the SELECTION tab is MAXIMUM NUMBER OF DISPLAYED VALUES. Although it looks like this item is grayed out, you can change the maximum number by clicking the up or down arrows next to the field.

Affected Data Providers

Earlier in this section, we saw that you can assign a DataProvider to a dropdown box in the GENERAL tab — this DataProvider will be used to build the list of values in the dropdown box.

However, you can also control which DataProviders are affected by the dropdown box. By default, the dropdown box will only affect the DataProvider selected in the GENERAL tab, and this will be indicated by a checkbox next to that DataProvider in the AFFECTED DATA PROVIDER tab. Any DataProvider marked with a checkbox in this tab will be affected by the dropdown box selection.

For example, Figure 6.32 shows a screenshot of the AFFECTED DATA PROVIDER tab. Because our sample workbook has two analysis grids with two different DataProviders (and two different queries), there are two entries in the AFFECTED DATA PROVIDER tab.

Let's say both these entries were checked, and we've created a dropdown box that will display Cost Center characteristic values. As long as the same Cost Center characteristic exists in the queries connected to both DataProviders, selecting a cost center from this dropdown box will result in both queries being filtered on that cost center.

The identical characteristic must be in both queries — if one query had 0costcenter as a free characteristic and the other query had 0costcenter as an attribute of 0employee, only one query would be affected. The affected query would be the one connected to the DataProvider in the GENERAL tab.

Similarly, if the dropdown box displayed values from a characteristic such as Personnel Area that did not exist in one of the queries connected to a checked DataProvider, selecting a Personnel Area from the dropdown box would have no effect on that DataProvider.

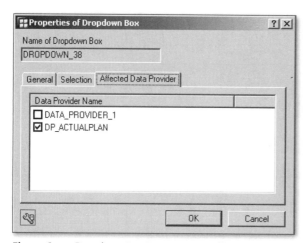

Figure 6.32   Dropdown Box Properties — Affected Data Provider Tab

As mentioned previously, a dropdown box can also be used to display query views instead of filtering on characteristic values. Let's say a dropdown box displaying query views has multiple DataProviders selected in the AFFECTED DATA PROVIDERS tab. If a user selects a query view, the characteristic filter values contained in that query view will be applied to all selected DataProviders, but again only if the characteristics are identical. Because the rest of the view's navigational state is specific to the query it was created on, any other DataProviders that do not share the same query will not have any further navigational state changes.

6.5.2 Checkboxes and Radio Buttons

The next two design items that can be used for filtering have very similar properties, so we will discuss them together. The buttons for adding new checkbox groups and radio button groups are the seventh and the eighth buttons on the design toolbar, respectively.

When you add a checkbox or radio button group to the worksheet, you will need to left-click it in design mode to bring up the PROPERTIES OF CHECKBOX GROUP screen. The GENERAL tab is shown in Figure 6.33.

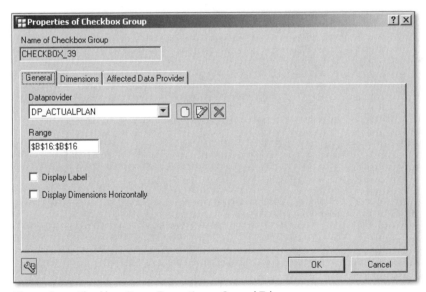

Figure 6.33 Checkbox Group Properties — General Tab

The same DATAPROVIDER assignment and RANGE options are present in these two design items. As with the dropdown box, the DataProvider assignment in this tab will be used to populate the list of values in the checkbox or radio button group.

You may notice that there are no clipping or AutoFit options for these design items — if you manually specify the size in the RANGE field to be smaller than the list of values, the range will automatically expand so all values can be displayed.

The DISPLAY LABEL checkbox will show the name of the characteristic or structure at the top of the checkbox or radio button group. Values in both of these design items are shown vertically by default; you can show values horizontally instead by checking the DISPLAY DIMENSIONS HORIZONTALLY checkbox.

The radio button group design item has an additional checkbox called Display ALL Entry. Much like the dropdown box, this option adds a new ALL value that has the effect of removing the filter value from the characteristic. This is not necessary with a checkbox design item, because users can simply check all of the values in the checkbox to effectively remove the filter. Unchecking all checkboxes has the same effect.

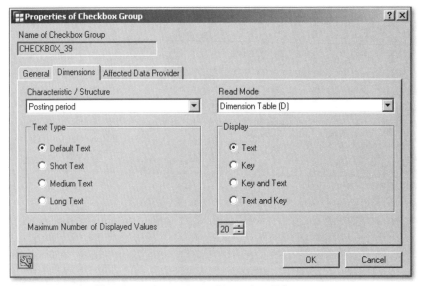

Figure 6.34 Checkbox Group Properties — Dimensions Tab

The DIMENSIONS tab in the checkbox and radio button design items includes options similar to the Selection tab in dropdown boxes (see Figure 6.34). You can choose the characteristic values or structure elements to be populated in the checkbox or radio button group using the CHARACTERISTIC/STRUCTURE setting, and you can also change the read mode (see the previous section for more information). The next two options, TEXT TYPE and DISPLAY, control the appearance of the characteristic values, and you can set the MAXIMUM NUMBER OF DISPLAYED VALUES at the bottom of the dialog box.

The last tab, AFFECTED DATA PROVIDER, works the same way as the corresponding tab in the dropdown menus (see Figure 6.35). Check the previous section for more information about this tab.

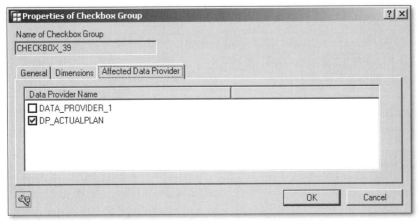

Figure 6.35 Checkbox Group Properties — Affected Data Providers

6.5.3 Choosing Which Filtering Control to Use

Dropdown boxes, checkbox groups, and radio button groups can all be used to present the user with an easy way to set up a filter value based on a list of characteristic values. Choosing which one to use will depend on the business requirement.

When screen real estate is at a premium, you will probably want to consider using a dropdown box. A dropdown box only takes up one cell (two cells if you display the label naming the characteristic) to display any number of characteristic values. Even if you do have plenty of room on a worksheet, you may also want to stick with a dropdown box if you have a large number of characteristic values, because more than 20 or so values in a checkbox group or radio button group can be awkward.

If you are presenting a list of query views to the user, you only have one choice, because the dropdown box is the only design item that supports a list of query views.

A screenshot of a dropdown box set up to show values for the POSTING PERIOD characteristic is shown in Figure 6.36. Note that the Display Label and the Display ALL Entry options have been enabled.

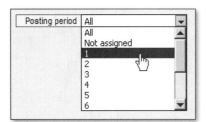

Figure 6.36　BEx Analyzer Dropdown Box

A significant limitation with the dropdown box design item is that you can only select and filter on one value at a time. If you want to provide an easy way for users to select multiple filter items directly on the worksheet, the checkbox group would be a good candidate.

The checkbox group allows users to check as many values as they wish, but unlike the other design items the user must click the SUBMIT button for the changes to take effect. After the SUBMIT button is clicked, the checkbox group continues to provide clear visual feedback for which values are currently filtered.

If there are a large number of characteristic values to choose from and business requirements dictate that multiple selections may be required, you are probably better off sticking with the Navigation Pane design item, outlined in Section 6.3, Navigation Panes.

Finally, the radio button group can be useful when you expect the user to be switching among a small number of filter values. As with the dropdown box, only one value can be selected at a time.

From a usability perspective, radio button groups are preferable to dropdown boxes (assuming a relatively small number of choices) because radio button groups display all possible choices without having to click a menu. On the other hand, if the characteristic values are sequential or users have prior knowledge of what the characteristic values are, a dropdown box would still work well, as displaying all possible values in these cases would be less important.

For example, in our POSTING PERIOD example a dropdown box would be appropriate from a usability standpoint, because users would already know that the POSTING PERIOD dropdown will contain sequential values corresponding to months of the year. However, as mentioned previously, using a radio button group would work well for users who are frequently switching between single value filters on the POSTING PERIOD characteristic.

Examples of the checkbox group and radio button group design items are shown in Figure 6.37. The Display Label option is disabled in the checkbox group and enabled in the radio button group.

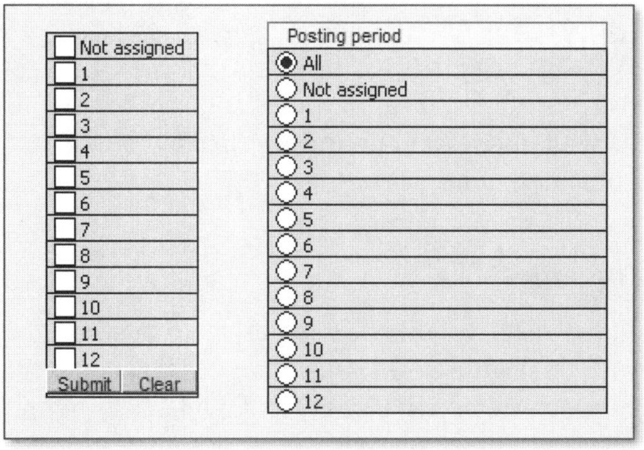

Figure 6.37   BEx Analyzer Checkbox Group and Radio Button Group

6.6   List of Conditions/Exceptions

The next two design items on the toolbar display a list of all of the conditions and exceptions defined in a specific query, respectively. Conditions are essentially filters based on transactional data (key figures and amounts) instead of master data (characteristic values), and they are defined in the query designer. Exceptions are similar to conditions in that they act based on transactional data, but instead of hiding the data, an exception will highlight data in a certain color based on specified thresholds. Both conditions and exceptions will be covered in detail later in the book.

The List of Conditions and List of Exceptions design items must be assigned to a DataProvider — the list will be populated based on the conditions or exceptions created in the query connected to that DataProvider. The description of each condition or exception will appear in the list, along with the status (Active or Inactive). Each condition or exception will also display an icon that allows the user to activate or deactivate it. When a condition or exception for a specific DataProvider is activated or deactivated, the analysis grid associated with that DataProvider is automatically refreshed.

We will revisit these design items later in the book, when we discuss how to set up conditions and exceptions in query designer, and how they are managed in both BEx Web analyzer and BEx analyzer.

6.7 Text Elements and System Messages

The final two design items exist for informational purposes and can be used to display text elements associated with queries and messages generated by the BW system. Let's take a look at the Text design item first.

6.7.1 Text Item General Properties

When you add a Text item to a BEx analyzer workbook and bring up the GENERAL tab in the PROPERTIES FOR TEXT screen (Figure 6.38), you will notice that you must assign a DataProvider. The query associated with this DataProvider will be the source of the text elements displayed in the design item.

As with other design items, you can specify a cell range, but the size of the Text item will automatically expand to fit all available data. However, column width will not be adjusted unless you check the AUTOFIT box.

The DISPLAY CAPTION option will display the name of each text element next to its value. It is recommended to enable this option unless you plan on manually entering descriptions next to the design item.

Finally, the DISPLAY FORMATS checkbox controls the appearance of the Text item. When disabled, the list of text elements will be standard text without a background, so any Excel-based formatting on the underlying cells will show through. If this box is checked, the BEx analyzer format will be applied, overriding any cell formatting in Excel. Check Section 6.3.1, General Properties, for more information and an illustration of how the design item's appearance changes.

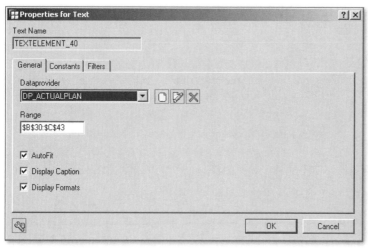

Figure 6.38 Text Item Properties — General Tab

6.7.2 Constant Text Elements

At this point, you may be wondering what exactly a text element is — text elements are essentially metadata that provide information about a query, such as who created the query and which InfoProvider it uses. Figure 6.39 shows the CONSTANTS tab, which allows you to select which text elements are displayed in the Text item by checking one or more text elements. You can select all text elements or deselect them all with the buttons at the bottom of the dialog box.

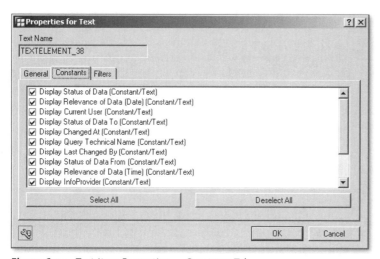

Figure 6.39 Text Item Properties — Constants Tab

A description of the text elements available in the CONSTANTS tab can be found in Table 6.5.

Status of Data	The date and time the last data request was posted to the InfoProvider associated with the query. If the query is built on a MultiProvider, the InfoProvider with the latest current data request is used.
Relevance of Data (Date)	The date component of the Status of Data text element.
Relevance of Data (Time)	The time component of the Status of Data text element.
Status of Data From, Status of Data To	For queries based on MultiProviders, these two text elements display the date and time of the last data request posted to the InfoProviders with the least recent data request and the most recent data request, respectively.
Query Technical Name, Query Description	The technical name and description of the query associated with the selected DataProvider.
InfoProvider	The technical name of the InfoProvider the query is based on.
Last Changed By, Changed On	The username of the user who last modified the query in Query Designer, and the date and time it was last modified.
Created By	The username of the user who first created the query.
Current User	Username of the user currently running the workbook.
Last Refreshed	The date and time the workbook was last refreshed.
Key Date	If time-dependent master data is used in the query, the key date determines which master data is displayed. This text element displays the key date if it has been assigned in the query definition or via a variable. If no key date has been assigned, the current system date is shown.

Table 6.5 Constant Text Elements in BEx Analyzer

6.7.3 Displaying Global Filters

Earlier in the book, in Chapter 3, Section 3.2, Restricting Data at the Query Level, we explored how to create filters at the query level in the Query Designer. The two types of hard-coded query-level filters were Characteristic Restrictions, which cannot be changed at query runtime, and Default Values, which can be modified after the query has been run just like any other filter. While Default Values can be displayed as a filter in the navigation pane, we have not seen a way to display Characteristic Restrictions — until now.

The FILTERS tab of the PROPERTIES FOR TEXT screen displays all characteristics with hard-coded values specified in the Characteristic Restrictions section of the query definition. Characteristics with only hard-coded Default Values or variable Characteristic Restrictions are not included in this list, because the former is viewable in a navigation pane, and the latter can be modified via the variable screen.

If a query has hard-coded Characteristic Restrictions that the user should be made aware of, it is common to set up a Text item to display those characteristics in the FILTERS tab (keeping all text elements in the CONSTANTS tab unchecked). This Text item can be placed adjacent to a Navigation Pane or List of Filters item for a relatively seamless display of all restrictions on the query.

Figure 6.40 shows the FILTERS tab with CONTROLLING AREA and CURRENCY TYPE listed. The query definition for the query associated with this DataProvider is displayed in Figure 6.41, where you can see the hard-coded values for the two characteristics.

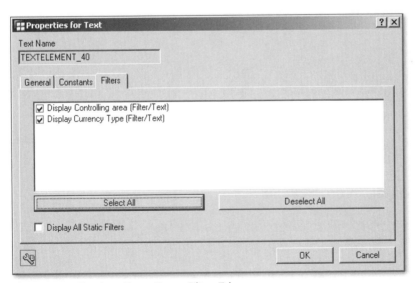

Figure 6.40 Text Item Properties — Filters Tab

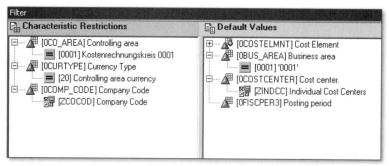

Figure 6.41 Query Design with Hard-Coded Characteristic Restrictions

6.7.4 Displaying System Messages

The Messages design item allows for the display of messages generated by BEx analyzer or by the BW backend system. The properties of this design item are relatively straightforward, and you can see the options on the GENERAL tab in Figure 6.42.

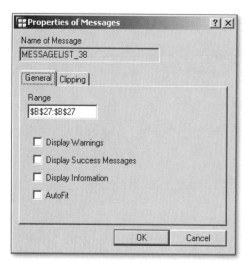

Figure 6.42 Messages Item Properties — General Tab

The Messages item is not associated with any specific DataProvider, so any message generated by either BEx analyzer or the BW system will be displayed. The RANGE field works the same way as with other design items to specify the size and location of the list on the worksheet.

The first three checkboxes allow you to control which types of messages are displayed. Warnings indicate a problem that may or may not prevent a BEx analyzer function from executing. An example of a Success Message is a notification that a workbook was successfully saved. Finally, an Information message is typically generated by the BW system — for example, the system could generate an informational message informing users of upcoming outages.

The last checkbox enables the AUTOFIT feature, which will expand column widths to fit the entire length of the message. You will want to be careful using this feature in the Messages item — some messages can be quite long, which would result in AUTOFIT increasing column width by a large amount to compensate.

Figure 6.43 shows the CLIPPING tab of the Message item. By default, the Message item will automatically expand to show all messages, but you can change this behavior to simply cut off messages beyond the cell range specified in the GENERAL tab, with or without a scroll bar.

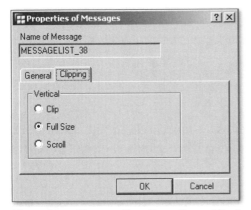

Figure 6.43 Messages Item Properties — Clipping Tab

6.8   Workbook Settings

The last item on the design toolbar opens the Workbook Settings screen, which includes a number of options specific to the current BEx analyzer workbook. This differs from the Global Settings screen on the analysis toolbar (see Chapter 5, Section 5.5.5, Global Settings), which focuses on options that apply to the BEx analyzer application as a whole.

6.8.1   General Workbook Properties

The first tab in the WORKBOOK SETTINGS screen contains a number of general properties, as seen in Figure 6.44. The first option in this tab, REFRESH WORKBOOK ON OPEN, controls whether or not the workbook is automatically refreshed when it is opened by the user. Enabling this option ensures that data in the workbook will be as up to date as possible, but it also adds to the time it takes to open the workbook.

If the REFRESH WORKBOOK ON OPEN option is disabled, users would need to click the Refresh button on the analysis toolbar to see updated data. In this case, it may be helpful to display the Last Refreshed text element in the workbook using the Text item (see Section 6.7.2, Constant Text Elements) so users are aware of when the workbook was refreshed.

The ALLOW DRAG AND DROP checkbox, enabled by default, can be unchecked to disable all drag-and-drop navigation in analysis grids and navigation panes in the current workbook. See Chapter 5, Section 5.3.1, Drag-and-Drop Navigation, for more information about drag and drop navigation in BEx analyzer. This option can also be changed with a button, as explained in Section 6.4, Buttons and Commands.

The next two fields determine what BEx analyzer displays in a cell if the cell contains a nonexisting value or a nonunique value.

Once you start adding multiple design items and worksheets, the file size of a BEx analyzer workbook can increase dramatically. SAP has provided built-in compression functionality, which can be enabled by checking the USE COMPRESSION WHEN SAVING WORKBOOK checkbox.

If this checkbox is grayed out (as it is in Figure 6.44), you may not have the correct software installed to support workbook compression. To fix this issue, you can download Microsoft J#, which can be found by doing an Internet search for "Microsoft Visual J# Version 2.0 Redistributable Package."

If you are running BI Frontend Support Package 1001 or later, Microsoft J# should already be installed (see Online Service System (OSS) Notes 1101143 and 1373214 for more information). It is also important to note that client PCs without Microsoft J# installed may get an error message when opening compressed workbooks.

The dropdown box in the middle of the GENERAL tab controls how values entered in input-ready fields are transferred to the server. This feature only applies to queries built for the BI Integrated Planning component. The default option is to have plan values automatically transfer to the server when you navigate away from an input-ready cell. You can change this setting to pop up a confirmation box before plan values are transferred automatically, or require users to manually select the Transfer Plan Values item from the context menu (or a button with the Transfer Values command, as seen in Section 6.4.1).

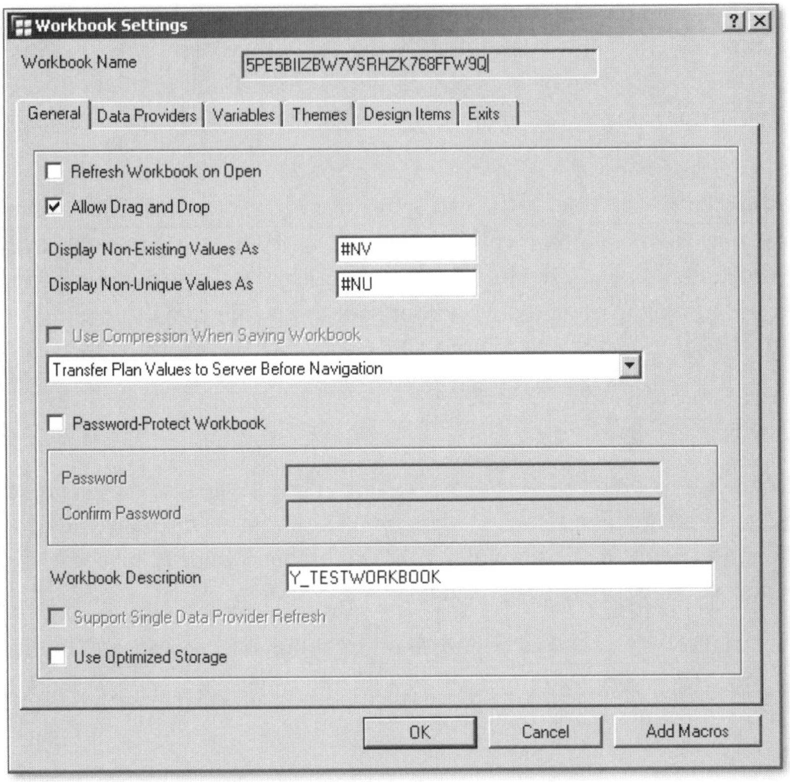

Figure 6.44 BEx Analyzer Workbook Settings — General Tab

BEx analyzer also provides password protection to workbooks that applies specifically to design mode changes. If you enable the PASSWORD-PROTECT WORKBOOK option and enter a password, you will be prompted for that password before you can add a new design item or make changes to existing items in design mode.

Unlike Excel's workbook protection feature, BEx analyzer workbook protection still allows users to navigate queries in analysis mode without entering a password. BEx analyzer workbook protection will prevent Excel formatting (such as changing cell colors and borders) while in design mode, so you'll need to switch to analysis mode to format cells using Excel native functionality.

The WORKBOOK DESCRIPTION field is useful when saving BEx analyzer workbooks to the server. The description entered in this field will be displayed when the BEx analyzer Open Workbook menu item is selected.

When the SUPPORT SINGLE DATA PROVIDER REFRESH box is checked, a new item is added to the analysis grid context menu allowing users to refresh only the DataProvider associated with the analysis grid rather than all DataProviders in the workbook. This feature only works correctly with BI Frontend Support Package 1001 or later.

The last checkbox in this tab, USE OPTIMIZED STORAGE, should be checked if you are having performance issues opening workbooks with Excel 2007. This option exists for a BI add-on Patch for GUI 7.10 patch level 800 or higher. Clients below patch level 800 will still be able to open the workbook, but they will not be able to make any changes in design mode. See OSS Note 1260213 for more information.

6.8.2   List of Data Providers

The DATA PROVIDERS tab is simply a list of all DataProviders in the workbook. From this screen, you can create new DataProviders by using the first button at the bottom of the window, delete a DataProvider using the second button, or open the Properties window for a specific DataProvider.

Section 6.2.1, DataProviders, has more information about setting up DataProviders. A screenshot of the DATA PROVIDERS tab in a BEx analyzer workbook with two DataProviders is shown in Figure 6.45.

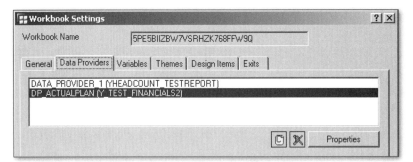

Figure 6.45   BEx Analyzer Workbook Settings — DataProviders Tab

6.8.3 Settings for Variables

The next Workbook Settings tab deals with variables – a screenshot of the VARIABLES tab is shown in Figure 6.46.

If the first checkbox, PROCESS VARIABLES ON REFRESH, is enabled, any variable selections made in the BEx analyzer workbook will be saved with the workbook and will be populated the next time the workbook is opened. If this setting is disabled, the default values for variables (based on the query definition) will be populated when the saved workbook is reopened.

In Section 6.2.4, we mentioned that one of the options in WORKBOOK SETTINGS can change the look of the variable screen for a BEx analyzer workbook with multiple DataProviders. By default, the DISPLAY DUPLICATE VARIABLES ONLY ONCE option is enabled, resulting in a variable screen like the one in Figure 6.12 — variables that are used by more than one DataProvider are separated into a Common Variables section.

If this option is disabled, the variable screen would have no Common Variables section, as all common variables would appear under their DataProviders. You may want to disable this setting if users would need to set different values for the same variable used in multiple DataProviders within a workbook.

When you save a variant in the BEx analyzer variable screen, it is either saved to the query associated with the relevant DataProvider, or it is saved to the workbook, assuming the workbook has been saved on the BW server. When there is only a single DataProvider, variants are saved to the query. When multiple DataProviders are present, the variant is saved to the workbook.

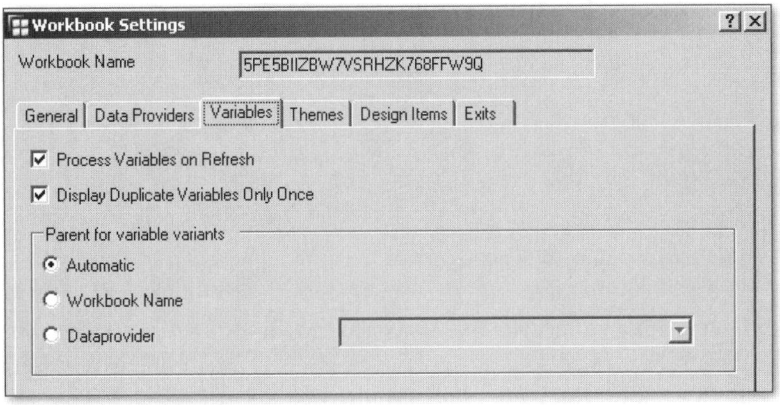

Figure 6.46 BEx Analyzer Workbook Settings — Variables Tab

This is the behavior associated with the Automatic selection for the Parent for variable variants option. If you'd always like to save variants to the workbook, even when there is a single DataProvider, select the WORKBOOK NAME option. To always save variable variants to a specific DataProvider, select the DATAPROVIDER option and choose a DataProvider from the list on the right. Note that with the last option, all variable values may not be saved to the variant if multiple DataProviders are present, because only the DataProvider specified here will have a saved variant.

6.8.4 BEx Analyzer Themes

Microsoft Excel includes a native Cell Styles feature, which can apply a number of different formatting options to cells automatically, including colors, borders, and font styles. In BEx analyzer, Themes are stored on the BW server and essentially consist of a collection of predefined style definitions. The THEMES tab, seen in Figure 6.47, lets you switch between existing themes or create your own.

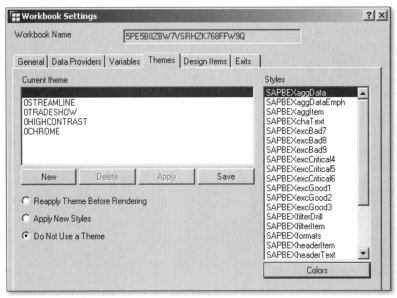

Figure 6.47 BEx Analyzer Workbook Settings — Themes Tab

The list of themes available from your BW server is shown in the CURRENT THEME list. The theme currently applied to your workbook is selected, and if no theme is applied (meaning the default theme is in effect), the first blank line is selected.

Clicking the New button will create a new theme using the current cell styles. Figure 6.48 shows the Cell Styles dropdown under the Home tab in Excel. All styles controlled by a BEx analyzer theme start with SAPBEX. Existing themes can be deleted using the Delete button.

The Apply button *does not* apply the selected theme to the workbook — instead, it applies all current cell style definitions *to the selected theme*, overwriting any existing cell styles in that theme.

The list on the right side of the Themes tab contains a list of BEx analyzer cell styles. You can either change the styles in this list, or change them in Excel by right-clicking the style in the Cell Styles dropdown seen in Figure 6.48 and selecting Modify. Once you finish making changes to cell styles, you can use the New button to create a new theme with the current styles or apply the current styles to an existing theme with the Apply button.

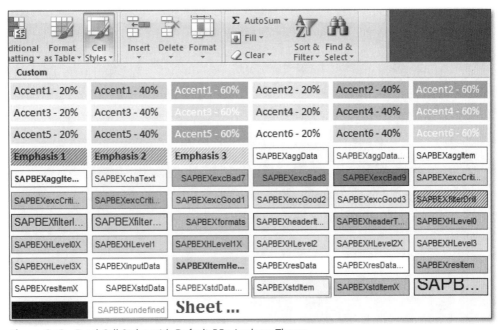

Figure 6.48   Excel Cell Styles with Default BEx Analyzer Theme

You can save these theme changes to the BW server by clicking the SAVE button. To modify and save themes on the server, your account will need the S_RS_TOOLS authorization object with the value THEMES in the COMMAND field.

If you want to apply an existing theme to the current workbook, select the theme and click either REAPPLY THEME BEFORE RENDERING or APPLY NEW STYLES, then click OK. The first option will automatically load all styles in the theme an apply them to the workbook, while the second option will only load new styles that have been added to the theme, leaving existing styles in the workbook unchanged. Remember not to click the APPLY button under the theme, as its function is to apply existing workbook styles to a theme, not the other way around.

Figures 6.49 and 6.50 show examples of two different themes applied to an analysis grid: the default theme and the chrome theme, respectively. In this case, the differences are relatively subtle, but themes can include any number of changes to cell styles.

Table		Headcount	
	Fiscal year	J4/2008	
Cost center.	Employee\Posting period	1	2
12345	1181		
	1726		
	3004		
	3549		
	4174		
	5396	1.000	1.000
	5397	1.000	1.000
	5413	1.000	1.000

Figure 6.49 Analysis Grid with Default Theme

Table		Headcount	
	Fiscal year	2008	
Cost center.	Employee\Posting period	1	2
12345	1181		
	1726		
	3004		
	3549		
	4174		
	5396	1.000	1.000
	5397	1.000	1.000
	5413	1.000	1.000

Figure 6.50 Analysis Grid with Chrome Theme

6.8.5 List of Design Items

Similarly to the VARIABLES tab discussed earlier in this section, the WORKBOOK SET-TINGS screen also contains a tab that lists all Design Items contained in the workbook. While you cannot create design items from this tab, you can delete them and modify their properties. A screenshot of a sample DESIGN ITEMS tab in a worksheet with a number of existing design items is shown in Figure 6.51.

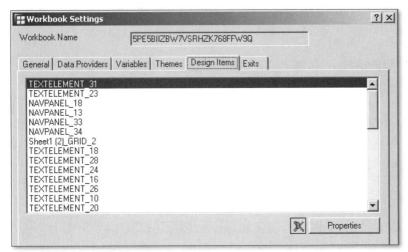

Figure 6.51 BEx Analyzer Workbook Settings — Design Items Tab

6.8.6 Exits Tab and Visual basic for Applications (VBA) Integration

The EXITS tab is the last tab in the WORKBOOK SETTINGS box, and it controls whether or not an Excel macro is run when the workbook is refreshed. In the screenshot shown in Figure 6.52, the workbook is configured to run the CallBack macro each time the workbook is refreshed.

The CallBack macro is written in VBA. To make changes to the macro, you need to enable the Developer tab first. In Excel 2007, this is done by clicking the Office button at the top left of the Excel window and selecting Excel Options. In the POPULAR section, check the SHOW DEVELOPER TAB IN THE RIBBON box, as seen in Figure 6.53.

Figure 6.52 BEx Analyzer Workbook Settings — Design Items Tab

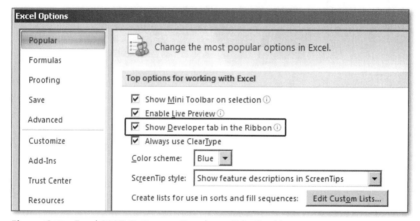

Figure 6.53 Excel 2007 Options — Developer Tab Checkbox

In Excel 2010, you can bring up the Excel Options screen by clicking the File button, then Options on the left side. Click Customize Ribbon on the left, and check the Developer checkbox in the list on the right side.

While in the Excel options box, you may want to confirm that the security settings for VBA macros are set up correctly. Click TRUST CENTER on the left side, then click the Trust Center Settings button on the right side of the window. In the Macro Settings section, make sure the Trust access to the VBA project object model box is checked. If you don't have trusted locations set up, you will also need to select the Enable all macros option in Macro Settings, but be sure to check with your information security department before changing this setting.

Once you have made these changes, you should see the DEVELOPER tab in your Excel interface. Switch to the DEVELOPER tab and click the VIEW CODE button in the middle of the tab, as seen in Figure 6.54. This will open the VBA development environment, shown in Figure 6.55.

On the left side of the VBA development environment, you will see the BEx analyzer Excel add-in (XLA) along with any open BEx analyzer workbooks. The Call-Back routine can be found by expanding the VBAPROJECT entry for the relevant workbook, expanding MODULES, and selecting DEFAULTWORKBOOK. From here, you can modify the VBA code to suit your business requirements — and any code added to the CallBack routine will be executed automatically when the workbook is refreshed, based on the setting in the Exits tab.

Figure 6.54 Excel 2007 Developer Tab

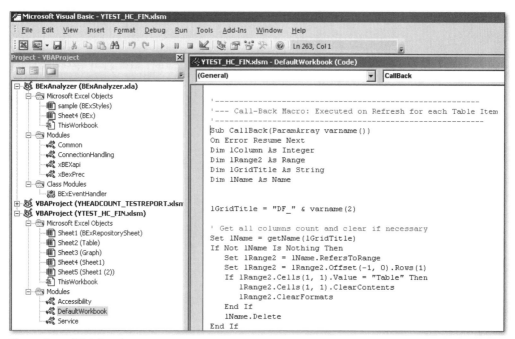

Figure 6.55 VBA Development Environment

Note that Button items also have a VBA routine associated with them. The VBA routines do not perform the commands specified in the buttons; they are essentially a shell that tells the BEx analyzer API to execute the commands defined in the Button design item.

You can view the VBA code associated with a button by selecting the button in design mode, switching to the Developer tab, and clicking the View Code button — this will jump directly to the button's VBA code. If you are already in the VBA development environment, you can select the worksheet containing the button from the list on the left side.

In Section 6.4.1 and Section 6.5.1, Dropdown Boxes, we introduced the Button and the Dropdown Box, both of which could be used to switch query views. We also suggested that prompting the user to confirm these actions might help prevent inadvertently overwriting the existing navigational state.

Figure 6.56 shows the VBA code for two buttons on a worksheet. The first button (BUTTON_37) does not load a new query view, so its code is unchanged. However, because the second button (BUTTON_36) switches to a new query view, the BUTTON_36_Click routine has been modified by adding a confirmation box asking the user if they really want to load the new query view.

If the user clicks Yes, the BEx analyzer function is called and the button is executed. If the user clicks No, nothing will happen and the current navigational state will be unchanged. For the purposes of the screenshot the confirmation message is relatively short, but ideally the message would include a sentence stating that opening a new query view will overwrite existing query navigation.

Figure 6.56 VBA Code for BEx Analyzer Buttons

6.9   Summary: Workbook Design

In this chapter, we introduced BEx analyzer's design mode, a toolset that allows powerusers and developers to customize workbooks with a number of interactive and informational design items. Most of these design items are assigned to DataProviders, a concept that provides an additional layer of abstraction between the workbook and queries or query views.

The core design items for most workbooks are Analysis Grids and Navigation Panes, which display data from the BW system and provide the user with a number of options to perform analysis via query navigation. In Section 6.2.4, we saw how multiple analysis grids can be added to a workbook to provide integrated analysis for a number of different functional areas.

One of the most powerful design tools, the Button item, was explored in Section 6.4. While there are a number of built-in button commands offered in the command wizard, the button's real power lies in stringing multiple commands together and adding custom commands from the BW Web API.

BEx analyzer provides a number of other tools to help users set up filters via dropdown boxes, checkboxes, and radio buttons. Informational displays can also be added to workbooks to display query metadata or system messages.

Finally, we explored the Workbook Settings available, including the ability to customize the look and feel of a workbook with themes (Section 6.8.4, BEx analyzer Themes). We also took a brief look at how Excel macros written in VBA are integrated into BEx analyzer, and we saw an example of how to customize BEx analyzer buttons using VBA code.

The tools outlined in this chapter will provide a foundation for building BEx analyzer workbooks for users with the right level of functionality for their business requirements. In the next chapter, we will start building web-based analytics using the Web's equivalent of BEx analyzer design mode: Web application designer (WAD).

*SAP's Web application designer (WAD) toolset is the cornerstone for deliv-
ering web-based Business Warehouse (BW) reporting customized to your
business requirements.*

7   Customizing Web-Based Analytics with Web Application Designer

We will now switch gears from the Business Explorer (BEx) analyzer Excel reporting interface to web-based BW reporting. You may recall that Chapter 4, Running
Queries on the Web: Business Explorer Web analyzer, highlighted BEx Web analyzer, the default runtime environment for BW web reports. This default environment was actually a *web application* created by a web template called 0ANALY-
SIS_PATTERN, a standard framework delivered by SAP to provide a basic set of
business intelligence (BI) functionality.

A simplified overview of the different components of a BI web application is
shown in Figure 7.1. You'll notice that this diagram looks similar to Figure 6.3,
which examined what makes up a BEx analyzer workbook. This is no accident, as
both web templates and BEx analyzer workbooks use the same concept of Data-
Providers and design items.

The big difference here is that instead of placing design items in an Excel worksheet, we are putting web items in a web template, which is essentially an XHTML
document. When the web template is executed, it runs as a web application in the
client's web browser as an HTML document with embedded JavaScript. The web
application typically runs on the SAP Portal platform.

Because the web application itself is generated dynamically, it can't be modified
directly. Instead, we will be modifying the underlying web template using SAP's
WAD tool.

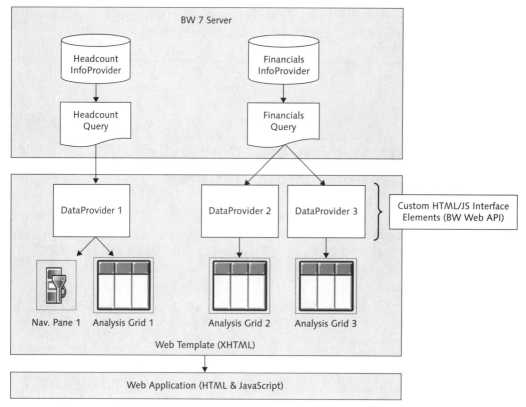

Figure 7.1 BW Web Application Overview

7.1 Introducing Web Application Designer

In the last two chapters, we saw the two different sides of the BEx analyzer toolset: analysis mode and design mode, which were both incorporated into Microsoft Excel. Looking at the web equivalents of these two modes, we find that the Web's analysis mode is the web application run in a browser, and design mode is covered by a completely separate desktop application called WAD.

WAD is included with the BI frontend software installation, and it is located in the BEx folder under Programs in the Start menu.

When you open WAD you will be presented with the interface shown in Figure 7.2. There are several options for creating a new web template: you can build a template using the pattern wizard, modify an existing web template, or create an entirely new blank template from scratch.

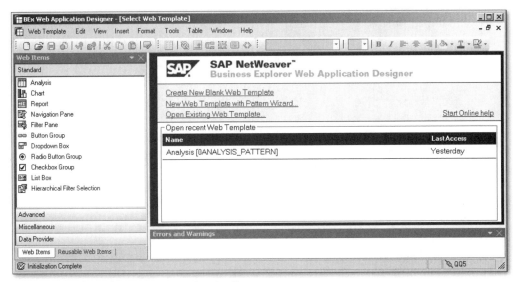

Figure 7.2 Web Application Designer Starting Screen

Under these options, you will see a list of existing web templates that have been opened recently in WAD. You can reopen any of these templates by clicking on them.

7.2 Using the Pattern Wizard

Building a new web template using the pattern wizard is the easiest method, but it's also the most restrictive. *BI Patterns* are ready-made web applications delivered by SAP that can be customized to a certain extent with the pattern wizard.

7.2.1 Types of BI Patterns

There are three types of patterns available in BW 7, each of which is targeted to a specific audience. The Information Consumer Pattern (ICP) is tailored for casual users and includes limited navigational functionality to keep the web application simple. Small Web Template patterns are even more restrictive and offer data presentation without any extraneous interface elements. Users who require more intensive analytical tools are better served with the Analysis Pattern, which is also known as BEx Web analyzer.

To illustrate the differences between these patterns, see Figures 7.3 and 7.4, which show the same query run in an ICP and BEx Web analyzer, respectively. Another example showing a Small Web Template web application is shown at the end of Section 7.2.3, Small Web Template Patterns.

Test Demo Headcount Report							Last Data Update: 08/23/2010 21:21:38

| Information | Send | Print Version | | | | | | Filter |

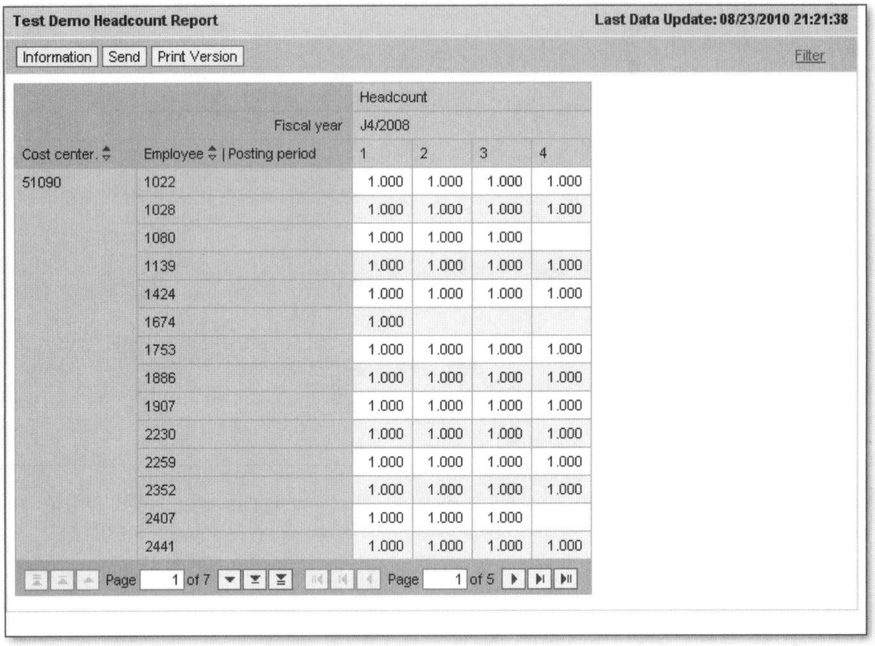

		Headcount			
	Fiscal year	J4/2008			
Cost center. ⇕	Employee ⇕ | Posting period	1	2	3	4
51090	1022	1.000	1.000	1.000	1.000
	1028	1.000	1.000	1.000	1.000
	1080	1.000	1.000	1.000	
	1139	1.000	1.000	1.000	1.000
	1424	1.000	1.000	1.000	1.000
	1674	1.000			
	1753	1.000	1.000	1.000	1.000
	1886	1.000	1.000	1.000	1.000
	1907	1.000	1.000	1.000	1.000
	2230	1.000	1.000	1.000	1.000
	2259	1.000	1.000	1.000	1.000
	2352	1.000	1.000	1.000	1.000
	2407	1.000	1.000	1.000	
	2441	1.000	1.000	1.000	1.000

Page 1 of 7 | Page 1 of 5

Figure 7.3 Query in ICP Web Template

Of the three different types of patterns, only the Information Consumer and Small Web Template patterns can be used to create new web templates using the pattern wizard. To create a new web template using the Analysis pattern, you'll need to open an existing web template, such as 0ANALYSIS_PATTERN, and save it as a new template.

We will start by looking at the different types of patterns available with the pattern wizard. From the starting screen in WAD (Figure 7.2), click NEW WEB TEMPLATE WITH PATTERN WIZARD. In the window that appears, click the All Patterns and Web Templates tab. The screen shown in Figure 7.5 will appear.

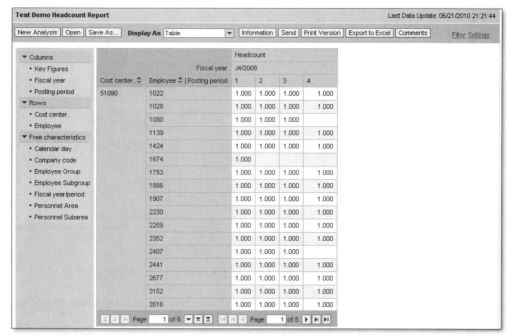

Figure 7.4 Query in BEx Web Analyzer (Analysis Pattern) Web Template

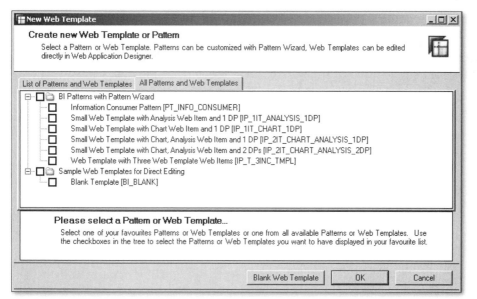

Figure 7.5 New Web Template with Pattern Wizard Screen

You'll notice six different patterns under the BI PATTERNS WITH PATTERN WIZARD heading, and one BLANK TEMPLATE entry under SAMPLE WEB TEMPLATES FOR DIRECT EDITING. Selecting the BLANK TEMPLATE entry and click OK (or just click the BLANK WEB TEMPLATE button at the bottom) to open up a new blank web template for editing; we will cover this template creation method later in the chapter.

All six of these patterns in the first section can be used to create simple web templates for casual users who do not need the full functionality of BEx Web analyzer. The first pattern, INFORMATION CONSUMER PATTERN, is the only one that allows you to create a web template with a toolbar using preconfigured items — we will see later that the other SMALL WEB TEMPLATE patterns generate templates with no visible navigation options.

7.2.2 Information Consumer Pattern

We will start by selecting the INFORMATION CONSUMER PATTERN — click once on the name of the pattern itself to select it. Clicking the checkbox next to the pattern will not select it, as the checkbox controls whether or not the item is displayed on the first tab, LIST OF PATTERNS AND WEB TEMPLATES. You can think of the first tab as a "favorites" tab that can provide easy access to commonly used items; this feature is used throughout WAD.

Toolbar Setup

After you select the Information Consumer Pattern, click OK to launch the pattern wizard. The first step of the wizard (seen in Figure 7.6) involves configuring the toolbar that will be displayed in the web template.

On this screen, you can choose to hide the toolbar completely, display a single-row toolbar, or display a double-row toolbar. You can also selectively hide or show groups of buttons as indicated by Figure 7.6. For example, unchecking the VISIBLE checkbox under the SEND and PRINT VERSION buttons in the ONE-ROW TOOLBAR section will hide both buttons, but you cannot show one of these buttons while keeping the other hidden using the pattern wizard.

You will notice that more functionality is available if you select the double-row toolbar, specifically the EXPORT TO EXCEL and PERSONALIZE buttons. Most of the other buttons should be familiar to you from the explanation of toolbar buttons in chapter 4 except for the PERSONALIZE button, which corresponds to the Personalize Web Application feature outlined in Chapter 4, Section 4.7.6, Save View/Personalize Web App.

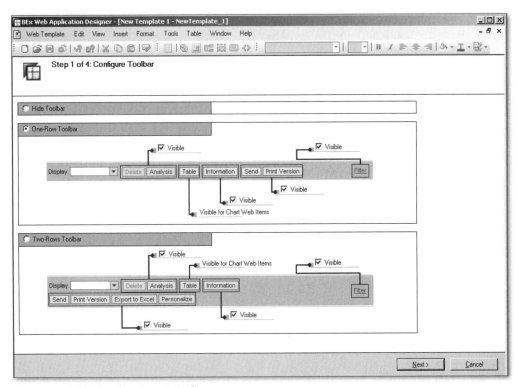

Figure 7.6 ICP Wizard — Step 1: Toolbars

Another new button is ANALYSIS, which opens up a new window showing the current query in an analysis pattern web application. This allows the user to create a new view using full BI functionality and save that view so it appears in the DISPLAY menu. The DELETE button will delete the current saved view.

Let's stick with the default selection of the ONE-ROW TOOLBAR with all items visible for now. Click the NEXT button to move on to the next step in the wizard, seen in Figure 7.7.

Display Dropdown Box

In the second step of the pattern wizard, we can configure the DISPLAY dropdown box, which lets users quickly jump between different queries and views. You can enter any number of DataProviders into the list, and each entry will correspond with an item in the DISPLAY dropdown box. When you click the empty cell under DataProvider, you will see a Value Help icon on the right side that can be used to select a DataProvider.

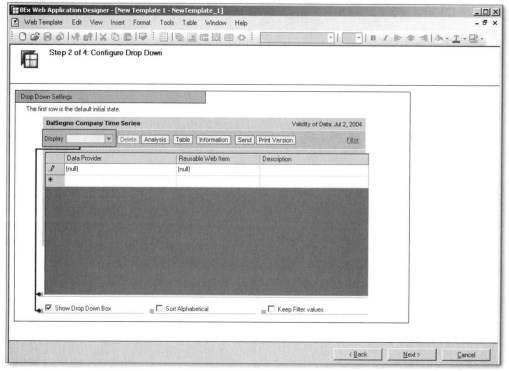

Figure 7.7 ICP Wizard — Step 2: Display Dropdown

The DataProviders here are equivalent to DataProviders in BEx analyzer. As discussed in Chapter 6, Section 6.2.1, DataProviders, a DataProvider can be connected to a query, query view, InfoProvider, or InfoObject.

You can also select a REUSABLE WEB ITEM for each DataProvider to tell the template how to present the data in the DataProvider. We haven't made any reusable web items yet, but luckily SAP includes a number of such items with your BW 7 installation.

Figure 7.8 shows the same dropdown configuration screen with two items filled out. Both entries use the same DataProvider (based on the query Y_TEST_FINANCIALS2), but the first uses the analysis web item 0PATTERN_TABLE_STANDARD, and the second uses the bar chart web item 0PATTERN_BARS_STANDARD. Based on the DESCRIPTION column, the DISPLAY dropdown in this web template will have two entries: FINANCIALS TABLE and FINANCIALS BAR CHART.

Even though this example includes two different presentations of the same DataProvider, depending on your business requirements you can have any number of different DataProviders as entries in the dropdown menu.

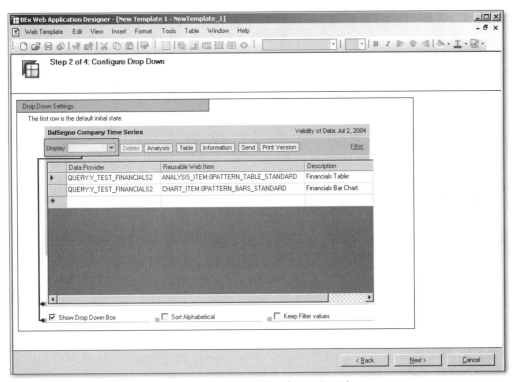

Figure 7.8 Display Dropdown Configuration Populated with DataProviders

Three checkboxes at the bottom of the screen offer additional configuration options. The first two checkboxes control whether or not the Display dropdown is displayed in the web template and the sorting of the entries: either as listed in the wizard screen or alphabetically.

When checked, the KEEP FILTER VALUES checkbox will automatically apply the currently selected filters to the new DataProvider when an item in the DISPLAY menu is chosen. If Keep FILTER VALUES is unchecked, the currently applied filters will be removed and the filters for the new DataProvider will be based on the query or view definition.

Choosing Visible Filters

Clicking the NEXT button will move us along to the filter configuration step of the wizard. In this screen, you can enter a number of characteristics or structures to be displayed when the user clicks the FILTER link at the top right of the template. For more information about the FILTER link, see Chapter 4, Section 4.3, Setting Filter Values.

If you selected a DataProvider in step 2 of the wizard, you can use the value help next to each empty cell under CHARACTERISTIC to choose the technical name of a characteristic or structure. You can also type the technical name of the characteristic or structure directly into an empty cell.

Figure 7.9 shows a screenshot of step 3 of the wizard with three characteristics already filled out. In this web template, when the user clicks the FILTER link, they will only be able to set up filters on the cost element, business area, and cost center characteristics, even if the query definition contains other free characteristics.

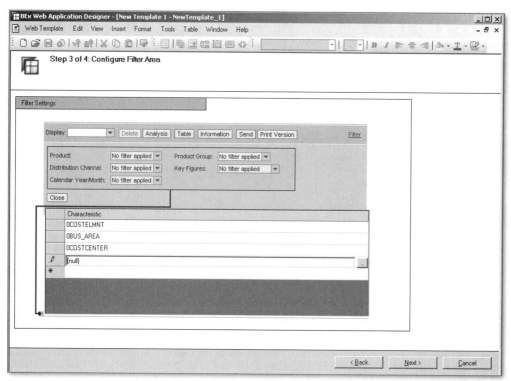

Figure 7.9 ICP Wizard — Step 3: Configure Filters

If you leave the list of characteristics blank, all characteristics and structures in the query definition (free characteristics, rows, and columns) will be displayed in the filter section.

Additional Settings

The final step of the pattern wizard for the ICP includes several miscellaneous options, as seen in Figure 7.10.

In ICP web applications, the variable screen is hidden by default unless there are required variables with no default values (see Chapter 3, Section 3.3, Variables, for more information on the variable screen). However, if the VARIABLE SCREEN VISIBLE box is checked, the variable screen will always be displayed first. Note that ICP web applications do not allow users to navigate back to the variable screen after it has been initially displayed, so use caution when including queries with variables.

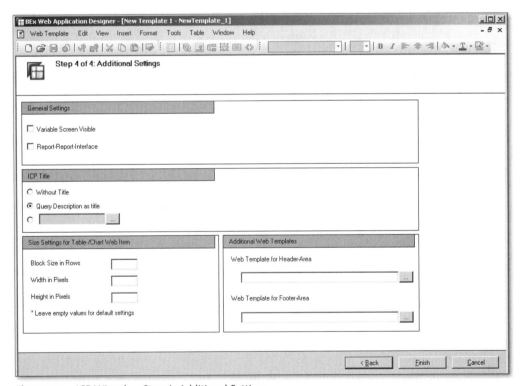

Figure 7.10 ICP Wizard — Step 4: Additional Settings

If a query utilizes the Report-to-Report Interface (RRI) as configured in Transaction RSBBS to jump to other queries or transactions, you'll want to make sure the REPORT-REPORT INTERFACE box is checked. Otherwise, this functionality will not appear in the context menu of the web application.

By default, the title of the ICP web application is the description of the query connected to the DataProvider. By changing the options in the ICP TITLE section, you can choose not to display a title or to display a custom title.

The next section allows you to change the properties of the main web item displayed (either the table or the chart). The BLOCK SIZE IN ROWS option controls how many rows of data are displayed in the table at one time, and the width and height of the table (and chart) can also be specified manually.

Finally, you can incorporate other existing web templates to serve as the header or footer of your ICP web application. This is often used to apply consistent branding or functionality across all of your company's BI web applications.

Once you are finished making changes, click the FINISH button at the bottom right to exit the wizard and save your web template. You can run the ICP web application by pulling down the Web Template menu in the main WAD screen and selecting Execute in Browser.

We will revisit the rest of the WAD interface later in the chapter. For now, let's close the current web template by clicking the innermost X button in the top right corner and start creating a web application using a different BI pattern.

7.2.3 Small Web Template Patterns

The ICP includes fewer interface elements than BEx Web analyzer, but there may be situations where you want to present data in tabular ("analysis") or graphical ("chart") form without any buttons or navigational functionality.

The Small Web Template BI patterns can meet this requirement. There are a number of different patterns of this type available, depending on the type of data presentation (analysis, chart, or both) and the number of DataProviders. For this example, we will generate a web application that shows both an analysis table and a chart for a single DataProvider, similar to the ICP example in the previous section.

On the main WAD screen, click the New Web Template with Pattern Wizard link, then the ALL PATTERNS AND WEB TEMPLATES tab. The window shown in Figure 7.11

will appear. Click the selected line (SMALL WEB TEMPLATE WITH CHART, ANALYSIS WEB ITEM AND 1 DP) and click OK to launch the wizard for this particular BI pattern, the first step of which is shown in Figure 7.12.

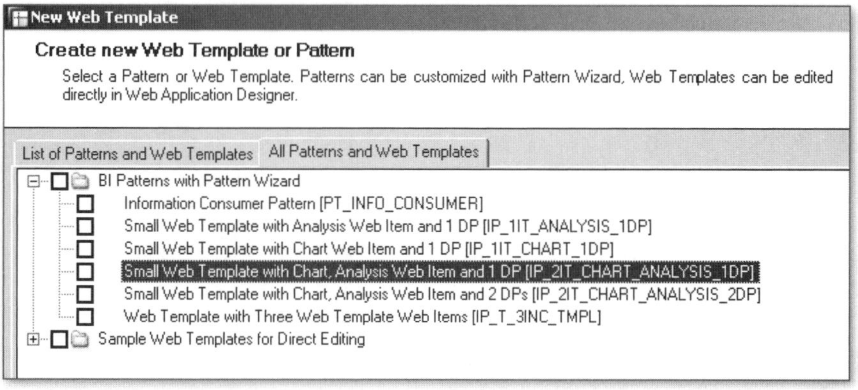

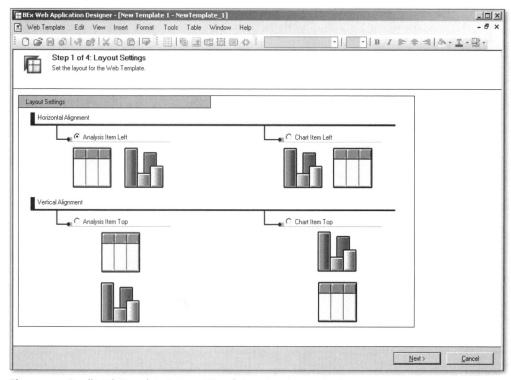

Figure 7.11 Start of Small Web Template Pattern Wizard

Figure 7.12 Small Web Template Pattern Wizard: Step 1 — Layout Settings

195

Layout Settings

Unlike the ICP web application, which has the user toggle between the display of a table and a chart, this web application will show both at the same time. The first step of the wizard determines how the two items will be displayed in the application — they can be arranged horizontally or vertically, with either the table or the chart displayed first.

Web Template Properties

Clicking the NEXT button will lead to step 2 of the wizard, shown in Figure 7.13, where you can modify the title and properties of the template. The title settings here are a little different from the ICP title settings: here you can specify no title, a custom title independent of language, or a language-dependent title.

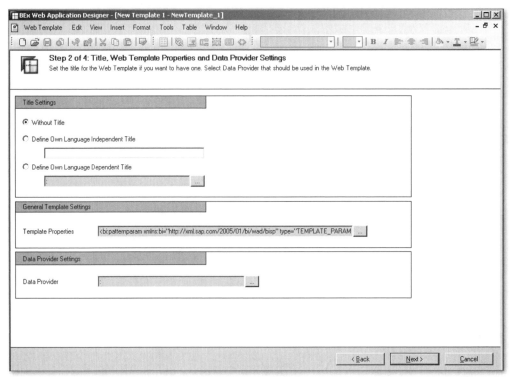

Figure 7.13 Small Web Template Pattern Wizard: Step 2 — Template Settings

The next item allows you to customize a number of different properties of the web template itself; we will explore web template properties later in the chapter. For now, the default template properties will work.

To select the query, view, InfoProvider, or InfoObject to use as a DataProvider, you can click the Value Help button next to the DATA PROVIDER field. Because this BI pattern is for a single DataProvider, there is only one field here, so the same DataProvider will be used for both the chart and the table. However, if you choose the SMALL WEB TEMPLATE WITH CHART, ANALYSIS WEB ITEM AND 2 DPs pattern, you can select one DataProvider for the chart and a different one for the table.

Analysis Item Settings

The next step of the wizard involves setting up the analysis item (table) that will be displayed in the query, as seen in Figure 7.14. While the ICP required the use of reusable web items (see the Display Dropdown Box heading in the previous section), with the Small Web Template pattern we can create a new web item for both the analysis and the chart.

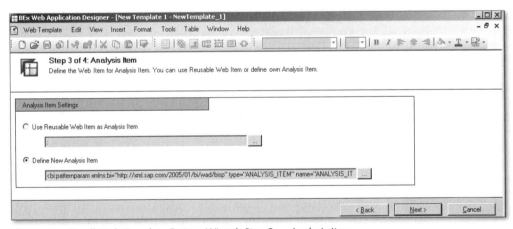

Figure 7.14 Small Web Template Pattern Wizard: Step 3 — Analysis Item

If you would like to use a previously created reusable web item for the analysis, you can select the first option and use the value help to find the item. Otherwise, make sure the DEFINE NEW ANALYSIS ITEM option is selected.

You can change the properties of the new analysis item by clicking the value help next to the field. The EDIT WEB ITEM screen in Figure 7.15 will appear, displaying a wide variety of parameters that can be used to customize the analysis item. For now, let's leave the settings as they are — we will revisit these parameters later in the chapter.

If you are still in the EDIT WEB ITEM window, click OK to return to the wizard, then click Next to move on to the last step.

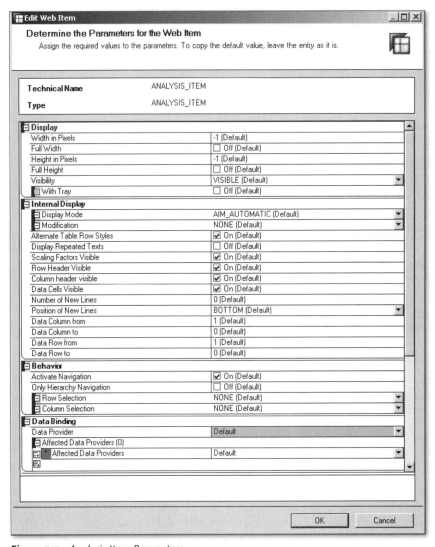

Figure 7.15 Analysis Item Parameters

Chart Item Settings

Step 4 in the wizard is similar to step 3, except we are now setting up the chart item that will be shown next to the analysis item in the web application. See Figure 7.16 for a screenshot.

As with the previous step, you can select a reusable web item or define a new one. The CHART ITEM parameters available by clicking the value help next to the DEFINE NEW CHART ITEM field are similar to the Analysis item parameters.

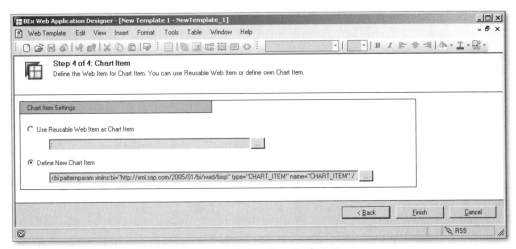

Figure 7.16 Small Web Template Pattern Wizard: Step 3 — Analysis Item

Click the FINISH button to exit the wizard and save the web template. You can now run the web template by pulling down the Web Template menu in the main WAD screen and selecting Execute in Browser.

The end result will look something like Figure 7.17. Note that queries that show a lot of data will not have a clean-looking chart unless you set up filters to restrict the amount of data shown. For this reason, it might make sense to use a different DataProvider for charts, with a query that already has these restrictions, especially because navigation functionality in a Small Web Template web application is extremely limited.

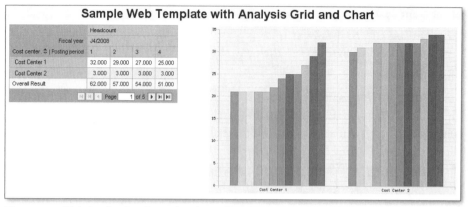

Figure 7.17 Web Application Created with Small Web Template BI Pattern

7.2.4   Pattern Wizard Summary

While the different BI patterns available in the pattern wizard have limited customizability, they are an easy way to start building simplified templates for users who may not have a need for flexible analytics. Let's take a moment to briefly summarize the different BI patterns available in Table 7.1:

Pattern Name	Wizard-Editable	Navigational Features
Information Consumer	Yes (reusable web items only)	Display query views, set filters, export, switch to analysis pattern, no context menu available
Small Web Template	Yes (can generate new web items)	None visible, navigation only available via context menu
Analysis (BEx Web Analyzer)	No (must copy existing template)	All (see chapter 4 for details)

Table 7.1 Available BI Patterns

Before this section, we did not bring up the context menu's availability in web applications generated by different BI patterns. BEx Web analyzer (the analysis pattern) obviously provides full access to the context menu. Surprisingly, the Small Web Template pattern, which has no other navigational options, also allows the user to navigate using the context menu. The Information Consumer pattern does not include a context menu — however, if the Analysis button is available, the user can switch to analysis mode and gain access to the features of the analysis pattern, including the context menu.

In practice, if the pattern wizard does not meet your needs, you may want to consider spending some time getting familiar with the features of the analysis pattern template so you can deploy a customized version of this template to your users. When customized, this web template will be able to provide functionality targeted to your specific business requirements that may not be available with the pattern wizards.

Later in this chapter, we will look at how WAD can customize the analysis pattern template to suit your needs. For now, though, we will jump in and start creating a new web template from scratch.

7.3 Creating a Basic Web Template

In the previous section, we mentioned customizing the existing analysis pattern template as a means to create feature-rich web templates for your users. So you may be wondering why we are now creating a blank web template from scratch instead of starting with the existing analysis pattern — the reason for this should be apparent in Figure 7.18.

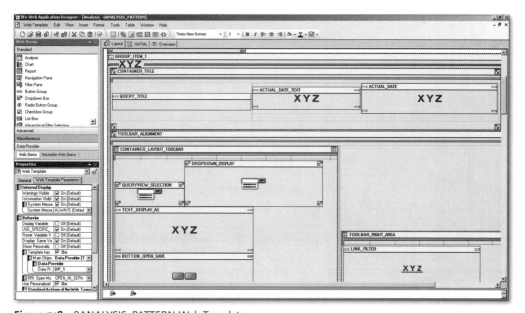

Figure 7.18 0ANALYSIS_PATTERN Web Template

The screenshot in Figure 7.18 represents about one-fifth of the layout of the default analysis pattern. Unlike BW 3.x web templates, which were relatively straightforward, BW 7 web templates typically contain several levels of nested web items of various types. As a result, diving into the analysis pattern web template without an understanding of how each web item works presents a significant challenge.

Don't worry if Figure 7.18 looks a little (or very) complicated — by the end of this chapter, you should have a better idea of how the analysis pattern web template was built. In fact, the last section of this chapter is an overview of the functionality contained in this web template.

For now, we will create a new web template from scratch by clicking the Create New Blank Web Template link on the starting screen of WAD. The resulting window will look like Figure 7.19.

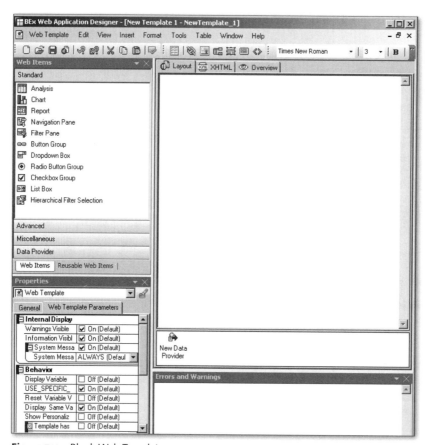

Figure 7.19 Blank Web Template

There are six main areas of the WAD interface: the menu bar, the toolbar, the WEB ITEMS area, the PROPERTIES area, the main workspace (with the Layout, XHTML, and Overview tabs), and the ERRORS AND WARNINGS section. Instead of going over all of the features offered by these different areas now, we will discover the functionality organically as we build the template.

7.3.1 Adding Web Items

Let's start by creating a very basic template with two web items: an analysis grid to display data and a navigation pane to help users modify the navigational state of the query.

Adding a Navigation Pane and Analysis Grid

In the WEB ITEMS section, make sure the Standard web items are displayed (click on the Standard heading if it's not already selected) and drag a NAVIGATION PANE out to the main workspace under the Layout tab. Next, drag the ANALYSIS ITEM to the main workspace to create a new analysis grid. The result should look like Figure 7.20.

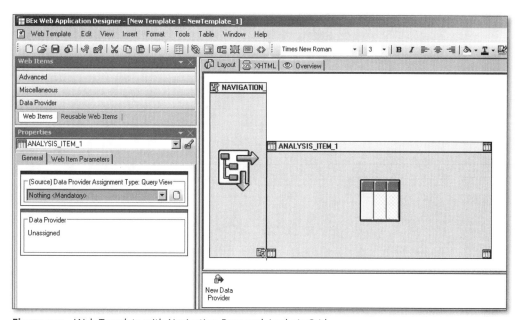

Figure 7.20 Web Template with Navigation Pane and Analysis Grid

If you click the navigation pane or the analysis item in the main workspace, the properties for that web item are displayed in the PROPERTIES section on the bottom left of the WAD interface. You'll notice that the properties for both of these web items show the data provider assignment (the first option in the Properties General tab) highlighted in orange: this means that there is a problem with that setting that needs to be resolved.

In this case, the problem is pretty obvious: we have not yet assigned a DataProvider to either one of these web items. To assign a DataProvider, we first have to create one, so click on the Create icon next to the DATA PROVIDER field in the PROPERTIES pane. You can also double-click the NEW DATA PROVIDER icon at the bottom of the main workspace.

Creating and Assigning DataProviders

Both methods will open the NEW DATA PROVIDER window, seen in Figure 7.21. The default DataProvider name will be DP_1, but it is a good practice to change the name to something a little more relevant. In this example, we will be connecting the DataProvider to a headcount query, hence the DataProvider name DP_HEADCOUNT.

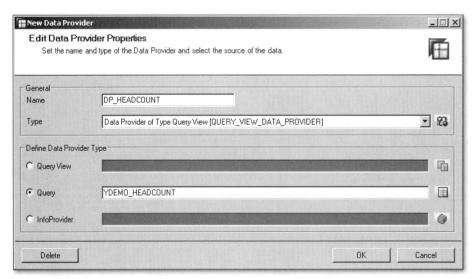

Figure 7.21 New DataProvider Window

For now we will leave the TYPE field alone — the default value is to create a Query View DataProvider, which is the most versatile type of DataProvider, as it can connect to a query view, query, or InfoProvider. The other type is a Filter DataProvider, which is typically used to populate web items such as dropdown boxes and radio button groups. Filter DataProviders can be connected to reusable saved filters, queries, and InfoProviders.

Note that if you select the Filter DataProvider type, the window will change to "advanced mode," which is the only mode available for this DataProvider type. Click the Green and Red icon next to the Type dropdown to toggle advanced mode for Query View DataProviders.

In this case, we will be connecting a specific query to the DataProvider, so that query will be run each time the template is run. However, later in the chapter we will see that it is OK to leave the DEFINE DATAPROVIDER TYPE section blank, as queries can also be assigned via URL parameters.

Click OK once you've assigned a query to return to the main WAD window. Select each web item and make sure the new DataProvider is assigned to both in the PROPERTIES section. The result should look similar to Figure 7.22, with no more orange warning in the PROPERTIES section. The name of the DataProvider (and the attached query) will also appear in the title bar of each web item.

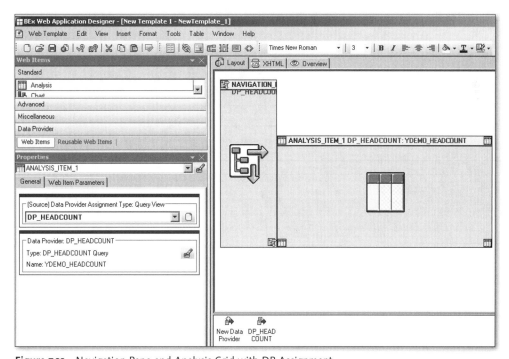

Figure 7.22 Navigation Pane and Analysis Grid with DP Assignment

Test Driving the Web Application

So far, so good: we've created a basic web template that provides users with a navigation pane to help them drill down on new characteristics and an analysis grid. Save the web template by clicking the Save button on the toolbar or selecting the Save option from the Web Template menu, and run the web template by clicking Execute in the toolbar or from the Web Template menu.

The results, seen in Figure 7.23, may not be what you anticipated — while the web template layout in WAD displayed the analysis grid next to the navigation pane, the analysis grid in the web application itself is below the navigation pane.

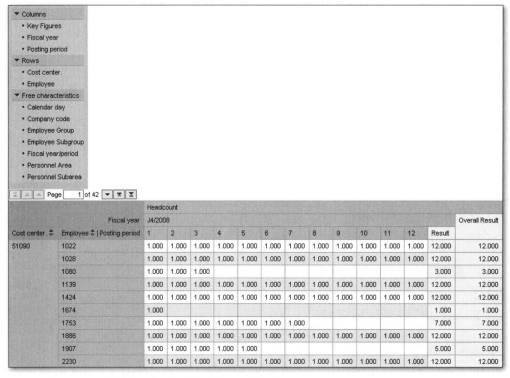

Figure 7.23 Web Application Test Drive — Take One

The reason for this discrepancy lies in how the BEx runtime engine builds the HTML web application from the XHTML web template. If you go back to the web template and click the XHTML tab in the main workspace, you will see a screen similar to the one shown in Figure 7.24. The third tab, OVERVIEW, displays a simple list of web items, a more compact view than the LAYOUT tab.

The XHTML code (enclosed by two boxes for emphasis) corresponds to the navigation pane and the analysis grid, respectively. When the web template is executed, this XHTML code generates an HTML page that the web browser can read, including actual characteristics and key figure data from the DataProvider. The HTML generation process does not allow web items placed directly on the template itself to appear next to each other in the web application, as there is a line break between each web item.

In BW 3.x web templates, this problem could be solved by manually creating HTML tables to arrange each web template in a specific order. The HTML table solution still works in BW 7, but WAD now has a new tool to handle web item arrangement: the Container Layout. We will explore the Container Layout tool in the next section.

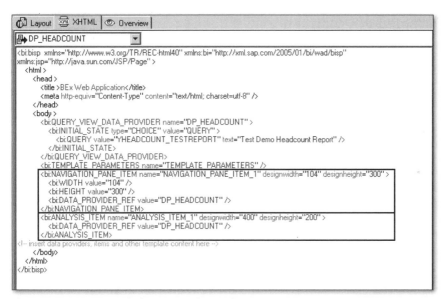

Figure 7.24 XHTML Code for Basic Web Template

7.3.2 Arranging Web Items

To customize the layout of the web items in our web application, we will need to place both the navigation pane and the analysis grid within the Container Layout web item. The properties of the Container Layout will control where each web item appears.

Creating a Container Layout

Let's switch back to the LAYOUT tab of the main WAD workspace. From the WEB ITEMS section in the top left, click the ADVANCED heading, and drag a CONTAINER LAYOUT out to the white space just to the left of the navigation pane.

The new container layout will probably take up the whole main workspace. If you scroll down, you will see the navigation pane and analysis grid below the container layout. Drag the navigation pane inside the container layout, and scroll back up to confirm that the web item is now within the container layout. Do the same with the analysis grid web item. The main workspace should now look like Figure 7.25, with both the navigation pane and the analysis grid within the container layout.

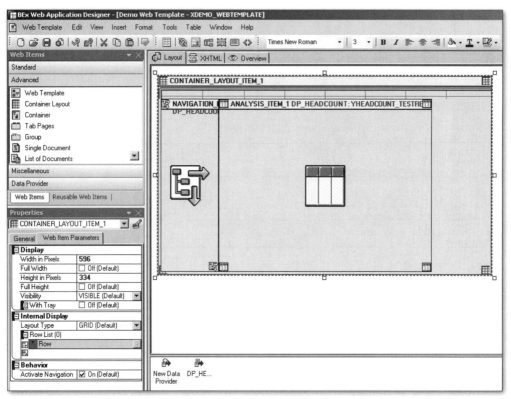

Figure 7.25 Navigation Pane and Analysis Grid inside Container Layout

Assigning Items within the Layout

Now that the web items are within the container layout, we will assign where each web item will display. Because the container layout is essentially a table, we can assign each web item to a specific row and column. In this case, there are only two web items, both of which will be displayed in the same row, so the container layout will end up consisting of one row and two columns.

Click the container layout in the main workspace, and select the WEB ITEM PARAMETERS tab in the PROPERTIES section. We are interested in the INTERNAL DISPLAY section for now, because it controls the location of web items within the layout.

The LAYOUT TYPE option allows you to change the alignment of the cells within the layout: you can choose between the default option of a fixed grid, floating rows, or floating columns. The differences between these options are illustrated in Figure 7.26.

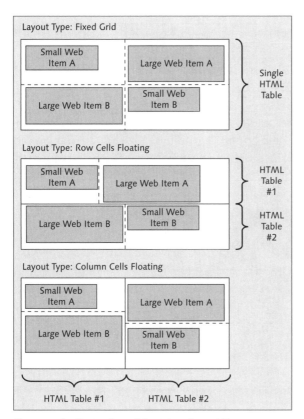

Figure 7.26 Illustration of Container Layout Types

In the Fixed Grid layout, the entire layout acts as a single HTML table, so row widths and column heights are determined by the largest item in that row or column. In the floating rows or floating columns layout, each row or column is its own separate table, with the column width or row height calculated independently.

Because we only have a single row in this container layout, we will leave the layout type at the default fixed grid setting.

Next is the Row List, where each row in a container layout has its own entry. Click the Value Help button next to the only row in the list to see that row's column list, as seen in Figure 7.27.

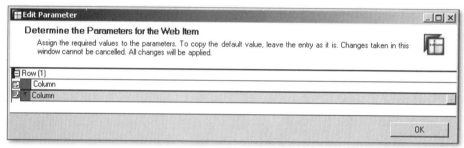

Figure 7.27 Column List for Container Layout Row

We will define two columns here, one to hold the navigation pane and one for the analysis grid. Click the Value Help button next to the only column item on the screen to open the screen that lets us assign a web item to that column, shown in Figure 7.28.

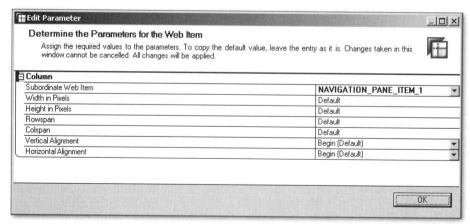

Figure 7.28 Individual Column Assignment

To assign a web item, pull down the SUBORDINATE WEB ITEM dropdown box and select the Navigation Pane (NAVIGATION_PANE_ITEM_1). The other properties can be left at their default values for now, so click the OK button to return to the column list. There should be a new empty column item at the bottom of the list — click the value help next to this empty column, select the analysis grid (ANALYSIS_ITEM_1), and click OK. Click OK one more time to return to the main WAD window.

If you look at the Internal Display properties of the container layout now, you should see two rows, one of which is designated by an asterisk. Clicking the value help of the first row will confirm that the columns in that row are assigned to the two web items.

User Experience Tip 7.1: Missing Subordinate Web Items in Dropdown Menu

If you create a container layout, move web items within the layout, and immediately open the container layout properties to assign the web items to columns, you may not see them in the Subordinate Web Item dropdown menu. To correct this issue, you can exit out of the Edit Parameter dialog boxes, click another tab in the main workspace (either XHTML or Overview), and switch back to the Layout tab. You can now reopen the container layout parameters and assign subordinate web items.

Basic Analysis Item Properties

While we're here, let's take a look at some of the properties of the analysis grid. Looking back at Figure 7.23, you will notice that the analysis grid has a scrollbar at the top to scroll through data rows — there is another scroll bar at the bottom of the analysis grid, not shown in the screenshot.

Let's get rid of that top scrollbar. Click the existing analysis web item in the main workspace, and make sure the WEB ITEM PARAMETERS tab is displayed in the Properties pane. Scroll down until you see the PAGING section, and uncheck the PAGING AREA ON TOP OF TABLE VISIBLE checkbox.

By default, analysis grids will display 25 columns and 100 rows at a time. For the purposes of this example, let's say we want to only display 6 columns and 15 rows at a time. To make these changes, click the NUMBER OF DATA COLUMNS and NUMBER OF DATA ROWS fields, and enter 6 and 15, respectively.

The end result should look like Figure 7.29. Note that the settings we have changed are all in bold — this reflects that they have been modified from their default setting. The Data Provider is also in bold, because the default setting for Data Provider is empty and we manually assigned one.

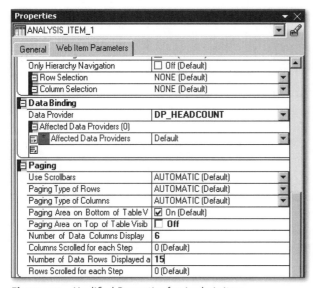

Figure 7.29 Modified Properties for Analysis Item

Another Test Drive

Now that we've set up the container layout, assigned the web items to their own columns, and made a few changes to the analysis item properties, it's time to take a look at the web application again.

Click the Save button in the toolbar, then click the Execute button. The results should look something like Figure 7.30. The navigation pane and analysis grid are side-by-side, the number of rows and columns displayed in the analysis grid are limited, and there is no more scrollbar on the top of the grid.

Our humble web template is starting to take shape — it looks similar to the default analysis pattern seen in Figure 7.4. The only thing missing is the header and the toolbar. We will get to the header later, for now let's explore how to add a toolbar to the web template.

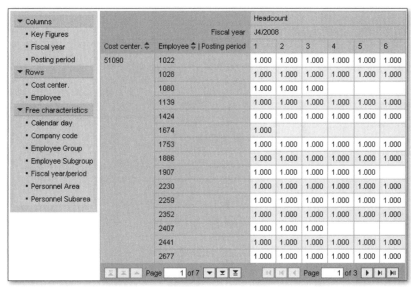

Figure 7.30 Web Application Test Drive — Take Two

7.4 Adding Toolbars and Headers

There are a number of different web items involved in creating and placing toolbars and headers. The toolbar itself consists of one or more Button Group web items. These button groups are placed within a Container Layout web item, which is in turn included in a Container web item.

The header of a web application will typically include a number of text elements, such as the query description and the last rollup time. Again, these text elements are placed within a Container Layout to ensure they are arranged correctly, then within a Container. It sounds a little convoluted, but the reasoning for using each of these web items will become clear by the end of this section.

We will start out by creating the toolbar, and then we will look at incorporating the toolbar into a full header.

7.4.1 Button Groups and Commands

Switch back to the main WAD window. Look for the BUTTON GROUP web item under the Standard heading at the top left of the screen (you may have to scroll down), and drag the button group to the whitespace above the container layout. The result will look like Figure 7.31.

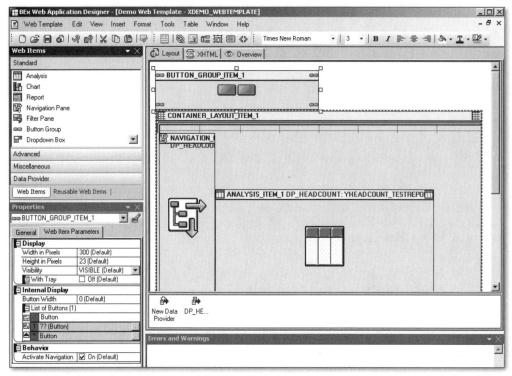

Figure 7.31 Button Group above Container Layout

Click the new button group web item once, and make sure the WEB ITEM PARAMETERS tab is selected in the PROPERTIES pane. Now look for the LIST OF BUTTONS item in the INTERNAL DISPLAY section. In this list you will see an item called ?? (BUTTON), click the value help button to the right of this field to define the first button.

Adding a Back Button

The screenshot in Figure 7.32 shows the default parameters for the first button in the button group. Back in Chapter 4, Section 4.7.1, Back, we mentioned that the Back feature, which takes the user back one navigation step, is one of the most useful functions in BW. In that same section we said we would show how to add a Back button to the toolbar — and now you will get your chance.

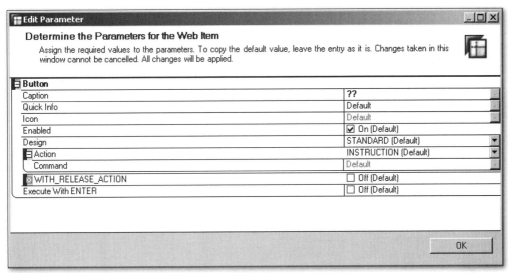

Figure 7.32 Parameters for Individual Button in Button Group

Click in the CAPTION field and type "Back" to give our button a description. The next field, QUICK INFO, controls what is displayed in the tooltip, so you can type a longer description here such as "Go back one navigation step."

WAD allows icons to be added to buttons, but for now we will just stick to text. We want to make sure the button is enabled, and we'll keep the standard design for now.

The ACTION parameter allows you to choose between specifying a command via the command wizard (similar to what we saw in BEx analyzer, Chapter 6, Section 6.4.1, The Command Wizard) or by selecting a preexisting script. We will be using the command wizard to specify the Back command, so make sure Command via Command Wizard is selected and click the Value Help button next to the COMMAND field.

The command wizard will open. As with the pattern wizard from Section 7.2.2, Information Consumer Pattern, the command wizard starts with a tab showing your "favorite" commands. Click the All Commands tab and expand Commands for Web Templates, the resulting screen is shown in Figure 7.33.

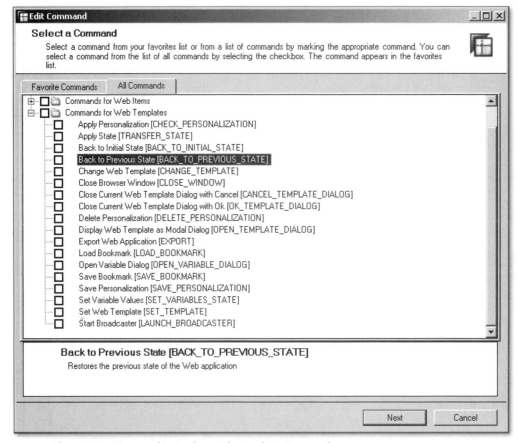

Figure 7.33 Command Wizard — Web Template Commands

This screen lists all of the commands pertaining to web templates in the BW Web Application Programming Interface (API). There are many other commands available for modifying web items, planning applications, and DataProviders — all are accessible by expanding the relevant folder. You'll notice that there is a much larger variety of commands available here versus the BEx analyzer command wizard (see Chapter 6, Section 6.4.1).

In this case, we will choose the BACK TO PREVIOUS STATE command. Select it once by clicking on the name of the command itself — recall how the checkbox controls which commands are on the "favorite" tab and not which are selected — and click the NEXT button. In most cases, there will be a follow-up screen, but as this command always applies to the entire web template, you can just click OK on the next screen.

If you look through the list of commands available in the command wizard, you may notice that there are three different Back commands in three different categories. Each Back command applies to a different component of the web application; they are listed below from most comprehensive to most specific.

BACK_TO_PREVIOUS_STATE (the command we selected in this example) will undo any navigational change made across the entire web application, regardless of which DataProvider or web item was changed.

BACK_TO_PREVIOUS_DP_STATE, under Commands for Data Providers and Basic Data Provider Commands, will roll back the last change made that affected one or more specific DataProviders, which must be selected in the command wizard.

Finally, BACK_TO_PREVIOUS_ITEM_STATE, under Commands for Web Items, will only undo the changes made to one or more web items specified in the command wizard.

After you exit the command wizard, you will return to the EDIT PARAMETER screen, which will look like Figure 7.34.

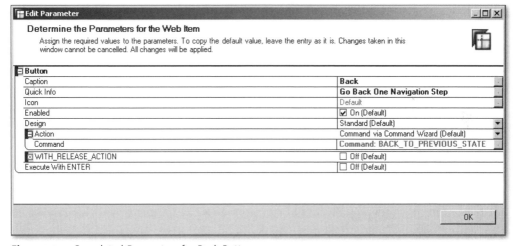

Figure 7.34 Completed Parameters for Back Button

There are two additional settings in this screen that we haven't discussed yet. When the WITH_RELEASE_ACTION option is checked, the button will stay pressed when it is clicked once. Clicking the button again in this state will return the button to its original status and execute the second command you assign under the WITH_RELEASE_ACTION option. We will see how this feature can be used later in the chapter.

The final setting, EXECUTE WITH ENTER, will automatically execute the button's command if Enter is pressed within the web template. If you use this feature, it is recommended to only enable the setting on one button in the web template.

Let's click OK to close out of the EDIT PARAMETER window and return to the main WAD workspace. The Back button is now complete, but we will proceed to add a few more buttons to round out our example toolbar.

Adding Load and Save Buttons

Before we add new buttons, let's take a look at the properties of the button group. Make sure the button group is selected, and look in the bottom left of the WAD window. The properties should look similar to Figure 7.35, indicating the BACK button is complete.

Figure 7.35 Properties of Button Group with Back Button

For future reference, you can add rows in the PROPERTIES pane by clicking the small Green icon just under LIST OF BUTTONS. To remove an existing row, click on it once to select it, and click the small Red icon — but don't remove the Back button row unless you want to recreate it.

We will now follow the same procedure we used with the Back button to create two additional buttons to allow users to load and save queries or web applications. Click the Value Help button next to the BUTTON row under the BACK BUTTON row in Figure 7.35.

The resulting window will look the same as Figure 7.32. Type a description such as "Load" or "Open" into the Caption field, and a longer description into the Quick Info field. Click the Value Help button next to the Command row to bring up the command wizard.

Click the ALL COMMANDS tab, expand COMMANDS FOR DATA PROVIDERS, and look under the OPEN/SAVE FUNCTIONS folder (seen in Figure 7.36). Select CALL OPEN DIALOG [LOAD] and click the NEXT button.

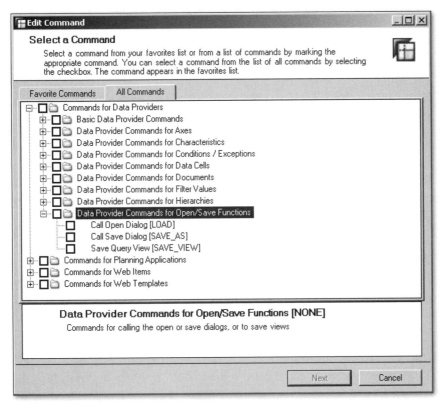

Figure 7.36 Command Wizard for Open/Save Functions

Unlike the Back button in the previous section, the Load command has a few additional configuration steps in the command wizard. The first additional step is to select a DataProvider, as seen in Figure 7.37.

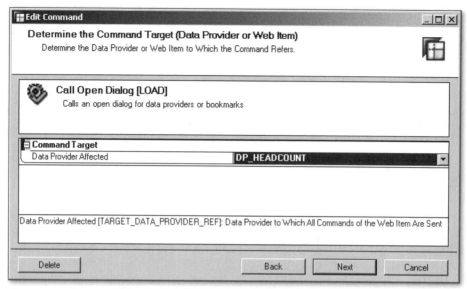

Figure 7.37 Command Wizard – DataProvider Assignment for Load Function

Both the Load and Save functions can either affect the whole web template or a specific DataProvider, depending on which option the user selects in the Load or Save dialog box. We briefly discussed this functionality in Chapter 4, Section 4.5, Opening and Saving Queries at Runtime, but we'll cover the Load and Save boxes in more detail in a bit.

For now, select a DataProvider. The query connected to the DataProvider specified in the Load command will be replaced by the query or query view selected by the user. Click the Next button to move on to the next step in the wizard, seen in Figure 7.38.

In this step, the first option allows you to choose whether or not to display single entries as dropdown menus. The second setting controls which options are available in the Open dialog box — the open function can load a new query, query view, or InfoProvider from the BW system into the selected DataProvider within the current web application, or it can load an entirely new web application from Favorites, My Portfolio, or BEx Portfolio in the portal system (as discussed in Chapter 4, Section 4.5).

The default choice, DISPLAY ALL OPTIONS, will show a dropdown menu in the Open dialog box to choose between looking at queries, query views, and InfoProviders from the BW system or saved web applications from the portal system. Selecting

Display Only Template Persistency Options will only show saved web applications from the portal system in the Open dialog box, while choosing Display Only Data Provider Persistency Options will only let the user see saved views, queries, and InfoProviders from the BW system.

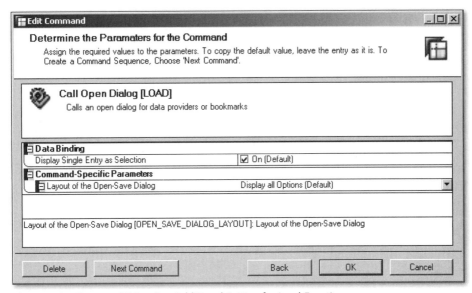

Figure 7.38 Command Wizard — Additional Setting for Load Function

Keep both of these options at their default settings and click OK to return to the Button Parameters screen. Click OK one more time to return to the main WAD screen.

To add a Save button to the toolbar, follow the same instructions as mentioned previously, but instead of selecting the CALL OPEN DIALOG [LOAD] command in Figure 7.36, choose the CALL SAVE DIALOG [SAVE] command. The configuration screens for the Save command are identical to the screens for the Load command.

Adding a Variable Screen Button

Next, we'll add a button that calls up the variable screen. This one should be relatively straightforward: in the Properties tab of the main WAD screen, click the value help button next to the blank Button row.

In the Caption field, enter "Variable Screen." You can also enter a suitable short description in the Quick Info screen if you want a tooltip to be available.

Click the Value Help button next to the Command field. Under the All Commands tab, expand Commands for Web Templates, click Open Variable Dialog, and click the Next button. No additional configuration is required for this particular function, so in the next screen click OK, then OK again.

The Toolbar So Far

Let's take a look at the toolbar we've built by saving and executing the web template. Our web application should look something like Figure 7.39.

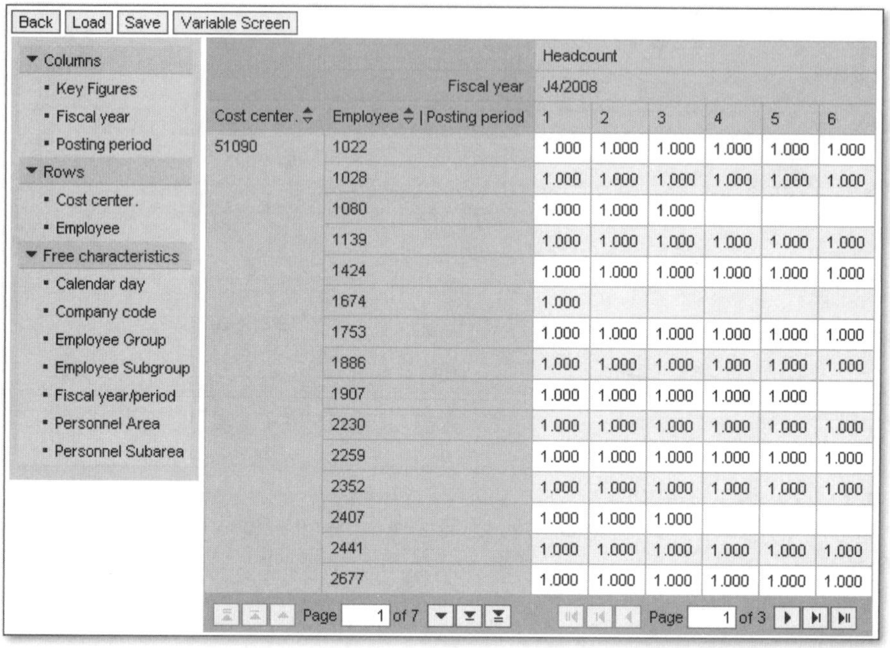

| Back | Load | Save | Variable Screen |

	Headcount					
▼ Columns						
• Key Figures	Fiscal year	J4/2008				
• Fiscal year	Cost center. ⇕	Employee ⇕ | Posting period	1	2	3	4	5	6
• Posting period	51090	1022	1.000	1.000	1.000	1.000	1.000	1.000
▼ Rows		1028	1.000	1.000	1.000	1.000	1.000	1.000
• Cost center.		1080	1.000	1.000	1.000			
• Employee		1139	1.000	1.000	1.000	1.000	1.000	1.000
▼ Free characteristics		1424	1.000	1.000	1.000	1.000	1.000	1.000
• Calendar day		1674	1.000					
• Company code		1753	1.000	1.000	1.000	1.000	1.000	1.000
• Employee Group		1886	1.000	1.000	1.000	1.000	1.000	1.000
• Employee Subgroup		1907	1.000	1.000	1.000	1.000	1.000	
• Fiscal year/period		2230	1.000	1.000	1.000	1.000	1.000	1.000
• Personnel Area		2259	1.000	1.000	1.000	1.000	1.000	1.000
• Personnel Subarea		2352	1.000	1.000	1.000	1.000	1.000	1.000
		2407	1.000	1.000	1.000			
		2441	1.000	1.000	1.000	1.000	1.000	1.000
		2677	1.000	1.000	1.000	1.000	1.000	1.000

Page 1 of 7   Page 1 of 3

Figure 7.39 Web Application with Simple Toolbar

We are getting closer to the look of the analysis pattern web application. The next step is to incorporate the toolbar into a full header that includes information about the query.

7.4.2 Creating and Populating a Header

To create a header, we will need the assistance of a few new web items. The ultimate goal of this section is to create a group web item with two different areas: one displaying text elements relating to the query and the other containing the toolbar we created in the previous section. Figure 7.40 shows a high-level overview of the eventual structure of our web template.

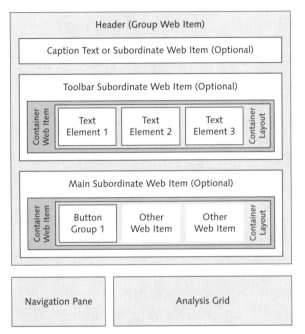

Figure 7.40 Overview of Web Template Structure with Header

As we will see later, the group web item has three different sections, two of which are optional. Each section can display content from only one web item, called a subordinate web item. In Figure 7.40, the main subordinate web item is the container holding the button group, and the subordinate web item assigned to the toolbar option is the container holding text elements. In this example, the option to show the caption section is disabled, so there is no web item or text associated with that section.

Note that the toolbar subordinate web item does not actually have to contain a toolbar, it is just the name of the parameter that controls the display of the section just above the main section.

It is possible to assign an individual text element or a button group web item directly to a group as a subordinate web item, but in doing so you lose the ability to show additional content in that section. However, if you put a web item within a container item and assign the container as the subordinate web item, you are free to add additional web items to the container if you want them to appear in the relevant section of the Group.

Putting Web Items in Containers

In Section 7.3.2, Arranging Web Items, we saw how web items can be placed inside other items — in that case, the Container Layout item was used to arrange the navigation pane and analysis item in a specific manner within a grid.

Another web item, simply called Container, can also hold other web items. Unlike the Container Layout, a Container does not allow you to specify the arrangement of its constituent web items its main purpose is to serve as an additional layer of abstraction between individual web items and their assignment in other interface elements such as groups or tab pages.

Container Layouts also provide the same abstraction, but their primary purpose is to set the position of each web item. That's why you will often see a container layout within a container — this setup also allows for additional web items to be added to the container that may not need to be included in the container layout's grid.

Because we are building a header with two rows (to match the analysis pattern header seen earlier), the first step is putting all of the web items for each row into two containers. We haven't built the web items for the header yet, so let's focus on the toolbar we created in the previous section.

In the main WAD interface, click the ADVANCED header in the WEB ITEMS pane. Drag a Container into the main workspace in the whitespace next to the button group created earlier. Next, drag the button group web item inside the container. (Feel free to change the size of the container web item if necessary.) The resulting workspace should look like Figure 7.41.

Because we only have a single button group in the toolbar right now, a container layout is not necessary. We will revisit this later when we add more web items to the toolbar.

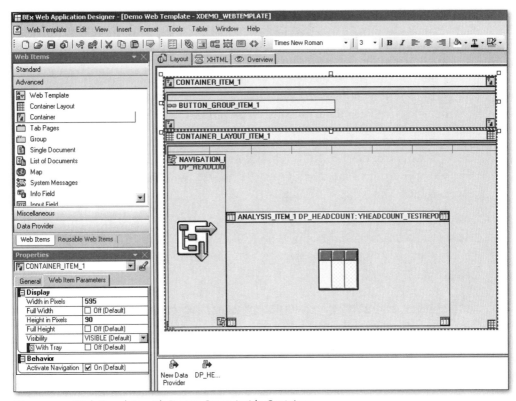

Figure 7.41 Web Template with Button Group inside Container

Adding a Text Element

Now let's start building our header. In the analysis pattern, the header shows the name of the current query and the date data was last updated in the InfoProvider. These are both examples of text elements, which are metadata about a query that provides useful information to the user. We want the first part of our header to show the name of the query being displayed, and for that we will need the text web item.

The text web item functions similarly to the Text design item in BEx analyzer, which was covered in Chapter 6, Section 6.7, Text Elements and System Messages. It can be found under the MISCELLANEOUS heading of the WEB ITEMS pane.

Don't add the text web item quite yet — remember that we need to create a container for the header, so we can include it in the group web item. Switch back to the ADVANCED heading of the WEB ITEMS pane and drag another container to the whitespace just above the existing container.

Before we continue, let's rename our containers so we don't confuse them later. Click the first container you created to hold the button group. Look in the PROPERTIES pane just above the GENERAL and WEB ITEM PARAMETERS tabs; you should see a dropdown box with the name of the container (CONTAINER_ITEM_1).

Click the icon to the right of the dropdown box to change the name of the web item to something like CONTAINER_TOOLBAR. Now do the same with the new empty container you just created. Because this container will be holding the header, you can call it CONTAINER_HEADER.

Now that the new container is ready, we can create the text web item. Click the MISCELLANEOUS heading in the WEB ITEMS pane and drag a text item from the WEB ITEMS pane directly into the new container. The screen should now look like Figure 7.42.

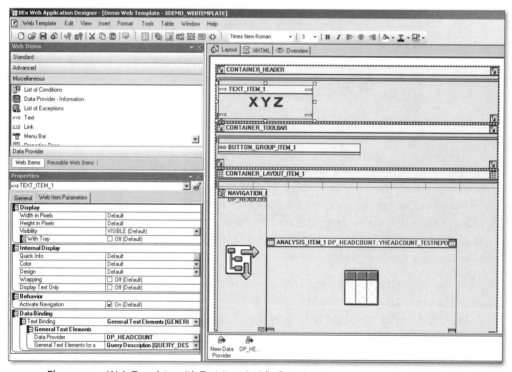

Figure 7.42 Web Template with Text Item inside Container

Configuring the text element is relatively straightforward. Click the Text item and make sure the Web Item Parameters tab is displayed in the Properties pane. We are primarily concerned with the Data Binding properties.

Text items can be used one of three ways: to display a custom text string, to indicate the name (description) of a characteristic, or to show a text element. Because we will be using this text item to show the description of the current query, select General Text Elements in the Text Binding dropdown menu.

The next step is to choose which DataProvider should be used to acquire the query metadata — because there is only one DataProvider in this web template, DP_HEADCOUNT, this is an easy choice.

We will now select which text element to display. For the most part, the list of text elements in Chapter 6, Section 6.7.2, Constant Text Elements, applies here as well, with a few additions such as the name of the web template. Choose Query Description from the dropdown menu, this will display the description of the query connected to DP_HEADCOUNT when the web application is executed.

If you look at the header of the analysis pattern web template in Figure 7.4, you'll notice that it also displays the date and time data was last rolled up in the InfoProvider. We can add that to our web template by creating another Text web item.

In the Miscellaneous heading of the Web Items pane, drag another Text item into the CONTAINER_HEADER container, next to the existing Text item. Click the new Text item and make sure the Web Item Parameters tab is selected in the Properties pane, as in Figure 7.43.

As with the last Text item, we will want to change the Text Binding to General Text Elements and select DP_HEADCOUNT as the Data Provider. Click the General Text Elements dropdown and select Last Data Update. The Last Data Update text element will display the date and time the InfoProvider for the query connected to DP_HEADCOUNT was last rolled up.

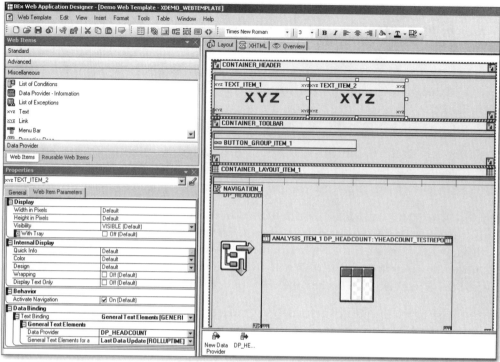

Figure 7.43 Web Template with Two Text Items inside Container

Checking Our Work

Let's take a moment to save the web template and execute it to see what the header looks like so far. We haven't added the group web item yet, so we still have some work to do, but it doesn't hurt to check your progress and make sure the web items you have added are configured correctly. Based on what we have built so far, the web application will look similar to Figure 7.44.

You may be wondering why the query description and the last update date are running together — this is because we added both text items to a container, but we did not include a container layout. If you recall from earlier in this section, the container does not specify the position of each text item, so it just displays each text item one after another without any spaces.

We can correct this issue by creating a container layout to hold the two text items, and we will do exactly that in the next section.

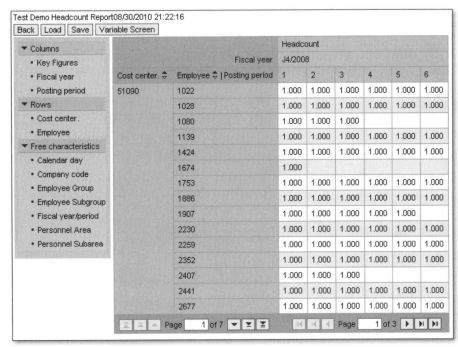

Figure 7.44 Web Application with Two Text Items Directly in Container

Aligning Multiple Text Elements

To display these two text elements correctly, we will need to put the two text items into a container layout. Under the ADVANCED heading of the WEB ITEMS pane, drag a CONTAINER LAYOUT to an empty space within the CONTAINER_HEADER container, next to the second text item. The CONTAINER LAYOUT will be displayed below the two text items.

Now drag each text item one by one into the new container layout. Next, click the container layout in the main workspace, and click the rename button at the top of the Properties pane to give the container layout a more descriptive name, such as CONTAINER_LAYOUT_HEADER. Now look under the DISPLAY section of the web item parameters and find the FULL WIDTH setting. Because we want the header to be shown across the entire width of the screen, make sure FULL WIDTH is set to On.

The results should look similar to Figure 7.45. Note that the container layout is larger than necessary by default, but unlike with the container, you should not manually adjust the size of the container layout web item, as this will modify its settings and may have an impact on how the text items are displayed.

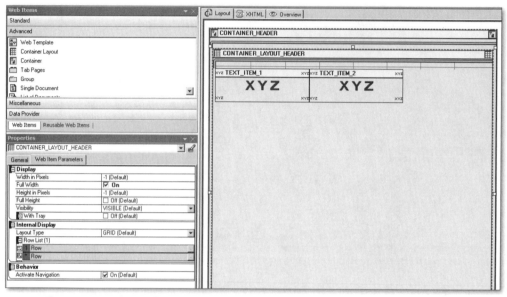

Figure 7.45 Web Template with Two Text Items inside Container Layout

As we saw in Section 7.3.2, it is not enough to drag web items within a container layout, each one must be assigned to a specific row and column before it can be displayed. Click the container layout, look under the INTERNAL DISPLAY section, and click the value help button next to the first row.

In the next dialog box (see Figure 7.46), click the Value Help button next to the first column and assign TEXT_ITEM_1 as the subordinate web item. If TEXT_ITEM_1 does not appear in the subordinate web item dropdown menu, click OK twice to return to the main WAD workspace, switch to the Overview tab, then switch back to the Layout tab and reopen the properties for the row and column.

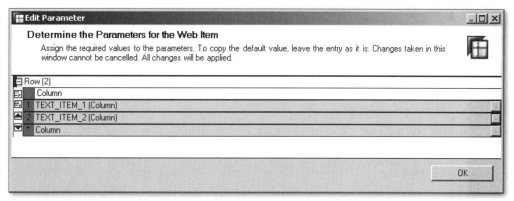

Figure 7.46 Edit Parameters for Container Layout First Row

Once you have assigned TEXT_ITEM_1 in the first column, click the Value Help button next to the second column and assign TEXT_ITEM_2 as the subordinate web item there, as in Figure 7.47. Because we want the second text element (last update date) to be aligned to the right side of the header, change the HORIZONTAL ALIGNMENT setting in the second column parameter screen to END.

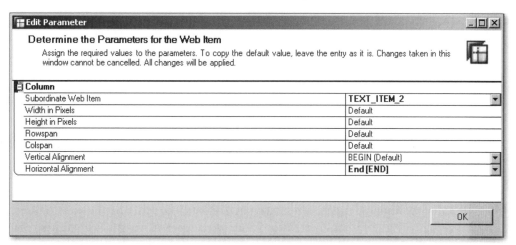

Figure 7.47 Edit Parameters for Container Layout First Row, Second Column

Click OK to return to the list of columns, and then OK again to return to the main workspace.

Now let's add a description so users will know the meaning of the date and time displayed in the web application. We will use yet another text item for this, so go back to the MISCELLANEOUS tab of the WEB ITEMS pane and drag another text item next to the first two. Make sure the new web item is within the container layout.

Click the third text item and look at the DATA BINDING settings in the WEB ITEM PARAMETERS tab of the PROPERTIES pane. Because we just want to display a simple text phrase in this web item, change the TEXT BINDING option to SIMPLE TEXT. In the TEXT field, type in the description you want to display, such as DATE LAST ROLLED UP: . Make sure to include the colon and space at the end of the description so there is some padding between the description and the date.

Figure 7.48 shows all three text items in the container layout, and the properties for the third text item.

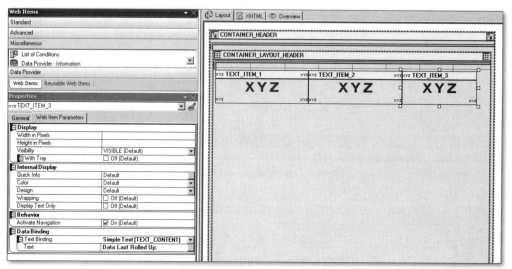

Figure 7.48 Web Template with Three Text Items inside Container Layout

We've added a third web item to the container layout, but the new text item will not display until we assign it in the layout. Click on the container layout, and then click the Value Help button next to the first Row item in the Internal Display section of the Properties pane.

Because we want the third text item to display before the second, we'll need to do some shuffling. Click on the third column, assign TEXT_ITEM_3 as the subordinate web item, and change HORIZONTAL ALIGNMENT to END as we did with the last column. The screen should look like Figure 7.49. Click OK to return to the list of columns once you've made these changes.

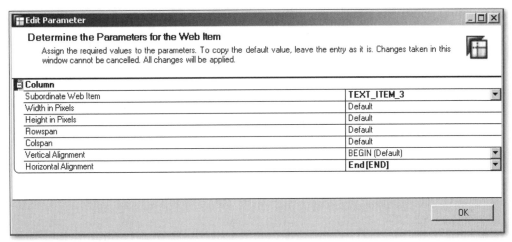

Figure 7.49 Parameters for Third Column of Header Layout

Now let's change the order of the web items. Look for the TEXT_ITEM_3 line, and click it once to select it. Once you've selected this line, click the small up arrow on the left side of the window. The list of columns should now look like Figure 7.50, and the third text item will be displayed before the second one.

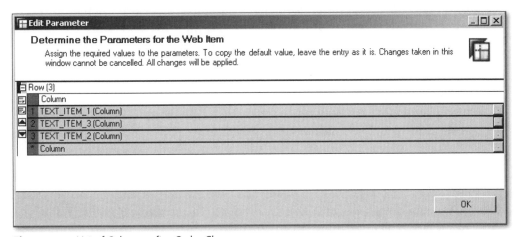

Figure 7.50 List of Columns after Order Change

> **User Experience Tip 7.3: Web Item Placement within Container Layouts in the Layout Tab**
>
> You may notice that the order of the web items within the container layout is unchanged in the main workspace, even after you moved the third text item before the second one in the Layout Parameter screen. This is because the display of web items within container layouts is only determined by the subordinate web item assignments to different columns and rows in the layout properties. The order web items appear on the Layout tab has no effect on their display order in the web application.
>
> On the other hand, because container web items do not have subordinate web item assignments, the display order of web items within the container is determined by the order they appear in the main workspace. The same is true for web items placed directly on the web template.

Let's click OK now and return to the main workspace. It's time to save and execute the web template. The header portion of the resulting web application is seen in Figure 7.51.

Figure 7.51 Header for Web Application with Three Text Items

As you can see, the header now takes up the full width of the web application. Other than a minor issue with the spacing between the second and third text item — which we will correct in the next section — the header is really starting to shape up.

7.4.3 Putting It All Together in a Group

In this section, we will see how the group web item can be used to pull together a header with a unified visual theme. As seen earlier in Figure 7.40, the group web item can display up to three subordinate web items in three separate lines.

In the previous section, we created container web items to hold the toolbar and the header. As a result, we can easily add both the toolbar and the header to the group item simply by assigning each container as a subordinate web item for the group.

Before we create the group item, though, let's tie up a loose end and correct the spacing issue we saw at the end of the previous section.

Spacing Adjustments in Container Layouts

The DATA LAST ROLLED UP label in Figure 7.51 is separated from the actual date and time by some whitespace — ideally we'd like to have the label and the date/time closer together.

The reason for the whitespace has to do with how the container layout web item is translated into HTML when the web application is rendered. It creates an HTML table with one cell for each of the columns specified in the container layout properties. Each cell has a default width, and if the content of the cell does not fill the complete cell, the remainder will be whitespace. If the content is wider than the default width, the cell will automatically expand as necessary.

Because we specified that the container layout should take up the whole width of the web application in the previous section (see Figure 7.45), and there are three columns assigned to subordinate web items (see Figure 7.50), each column takes up roughly one-third of the screen. The second and third columns were set to be aligned to the right horizontally, but the text in the second column is aligned against the end of the second cell, not the text in the third column.

One way to approach this issue would be to change the third column to be aligned left instead of right. However, this would leave whitespace on the right side of the date and time, and we'd like to have both the rollup label and the date/time aligned to the right side of the web application.

Instead, let's try reducing the width of the last column so there is no extra whitespace around the date and time. To do this, select the header container layout and click the value help next to the first Row field in the properties. Next, locate the third column (it should be assigned to subordinate web item TEXT_ITEM_2) and click the Value Help button.

In the resulting screen (Figure 7.52), locate the WIDTH IN PIXELS field. Because the width of the column will automatically expand beyond the specified width to hold the content of the web item, we can enter a value of 1 in this field, indicating a new width of 1 pixel. The end result of this adjustment is that the column will expand to exactly fit the contents of TEXT_ITEM_2, specifically the date and time.

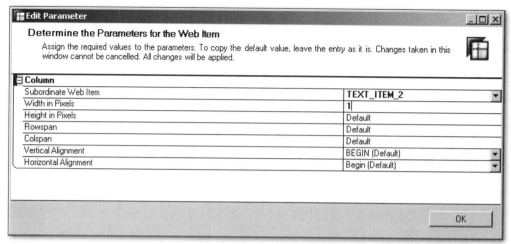

Figure 7.52 Parameters for Header Container Layout, Third Column

If we save and execute the web template, the header of the resulting web application should look like Figure 7.53.

Figure 7.53 Header of Web Application after Whitespace Adjustment

Consolidating Web Items in a Group

The final step of creating the complete header is placing all of the web items we've created within a group web item. We'll start by creating the group web item itself: in the main WAD workspace, look under the Advanced heading of the Web Items pane, and drag the group item to the whitespace just above the toolbar container.

Because all of the other components of the header are already enclosed within containers, all we have to do now is drag both the toolbar container and the header container into the group item we just created. Be sure to drag the container itself and not the container layout or any other individual web item. Also, take care not to drag one container inside another; both containers should be dropped on empty space within the group item.

The end result should look like Figure 7.54. Once you have confirmed that the containers are both inside the group item, click the group item itself and select the WEB ITEM PARAMETERS tab in the PROPERTIES pane.

We want to make sure the group item stretches across the entire width of the web application, so check the box next to the FULL WIDTH setting. We don't need to modify the WIDTH IN PIXELS setting, because FULL WIDTH overrides that entry.

Now let's check the Internal Display settings. As seen earlier, a group item can have up to three sections (listed in order of display from top to bottom): a caption, a toolbar, and a main section. The first item under INTERNAL DISPLAY, DESIGN, controls the look of the group item. We will leave that setting as it is for now.

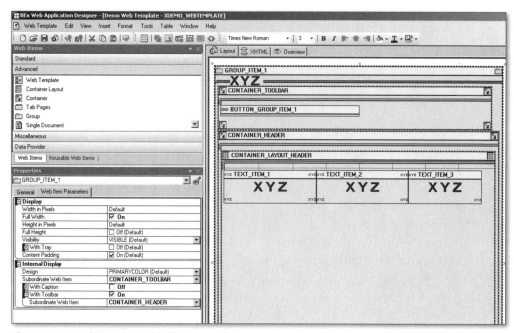

Figure 7.54 Web Template with Completed Group Item

The next field, SUBORDINATE WEB ITEM, determines which web item is displayed in the main section of the group item. Under the SUBORDINATE WEB ITEM setting are two checkboxes: WITH CAPTION and WITH TOOLBAR. By default, both of these boxes are unchecked, which results in a group item that only displays one web item. In this example, we will leave WITH CAPTION unchecked, but we will check the WITH TOOLBAR option. When you check WITH TOOLBAR, a new SUBORDINATE WEB ITEM field appears, and the web item assigned here will be displayed in the toolbar section.

Once you've checked WITH TOOLBAR, look back at the first SUBORDINATE WEB ITEM option. The web item specified here will be displayed in the main section at the bottom of the group item. Because we want the toolbar to be displayed as the second line, select CONTAINER_TOOLBAR from the dropdown list. If this web item does not appear in the list, try switching to the OVERVIEW tab in the main workspace, then back to the LAYOUT tab.

Now locate the second SUBORDINATE WEB ITEM option, under WITH TOOLBAR. This web item will be the top line of the group item, so select CONTAINER_HEADER from the dropdown list.

> **User Experience Tip 7.4: A Group Item's Toolbar Section Doesn't Have to Display a Toolbar**
>
> In this example, the container holding the toolbar button group ended up in the main section of the group item rather than in the toolbar section. There is nothing special about the WITH TOOLBAR option that makes it better suited to display toolbars versus other content; it just happens to be the name of the setting that controls the middle section of the group item.
>
> Similarly, the WITH CAPTION setting does not have to hold a caption, although there is a CAPTION TYPE setting that allows you to specify the display of straight text in this section instead of a web item.
>
> Here is an easy way to remember when to use which group item option:
>
> ▸ First Subordinate Web Item option = bottom section of group item (required)
> ▸ With Caption Subordinate Web Item option = top section (optional, can contain text instead of web item)
> ▸ With Toolbar Subordinate Web Item option = middle section (or top section if no caption exists)

Once you've completed these changes, the web template should look like Figure 7.54. Let's save and execute the web template, the resulting web application will look like Figure 7.55. Congratulations, you've now duplicated the basic functionality of the analysis pattern!

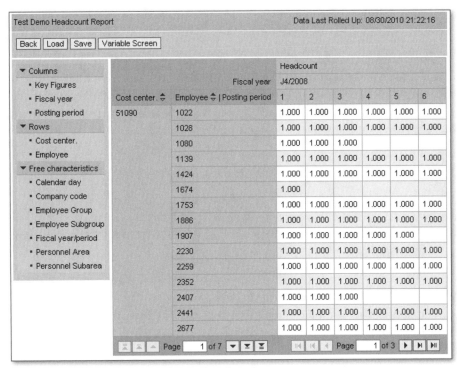

| Test Demo Headcount Report | | | | Data Last Rolled Up: 08/30/2010 21:22:16 | | | | | |

Back | Load | Save | Variable Screen

		Headcount						
▼ Columns		Fiscal year	J4/2008					
• Key Figures								
• Fiscal year	Cost center. ⬍	Employee ⬍ | Posting period	1	2	3	4	5	6
• Posting period	51090	1022	1.000	1.000	1.000	1.000	1.000	1.000
▼ Rows		1028	1.000	1.000	1.000	1.000	1.000	1.000
• Cost center.		1080	1.000	1.000	1.000			
• Employee		1139	1.000	1.000	1.000	1.000	1.000	1.000
▼ Free characteristics		1424	1.000	1.000	1.000	1.000	1.000	1.000
• Calendar day		1674	1.000					
• Company code		1753	1.000	1.000	1.000	1.000	1.000	1.000
• Employee Group		1886	1.000	1.000	1.000	1.000	1.000	1.000
• Employee Subgroup		1907	1.000	1.000	1.000	1.000	1.000	
• Fiscal year/period		2230	1.000	1.000	1.000	1.000	1.000	1.000
• Personnel Area		2259	1.000	1.000	1.000	1.000	1.000	1.000
• Personnel Subarea		2352	1.000	1.000	1.000	1.000	1.000	1.000
		2407	1.000	1.000	1.000			
		2441	1.000	1.000	1.000	1.000	1.000	1.000
		2677	1.000	1.000	1.000	1.000	1.000	1.000

Page 1 of 7 ▼ | Page 1 of 3 ▶

Figure 7.55 Web Application with Completed Header

7.5 Hiding and Showing Web Items

In the last few sections we've been recreating some of the basic functionality of the analysis pattern web template from scratch. So far, we've built a web application that shows an analysis grid, a navigation pane, and a heading that displays some query metadata along with a few commands on a toolbar.

One of the keys to creating useful web applications for analytics is the ability to dynamically change how data is displayed with minimal effort. One way to do this is by using the navigation pane and the context menu to change the navigational state of the displayed query, but that method only works to an extent.

Let's say you are facing a business requirement to build a web-based analytical report that allows the user to switch between seeing data in a tabular format, a graphical format, and both side by side. You could create three separate web templates and deliver all three to users via a role menu, but a better solution would be to use one web template, and create interface controls that can hide and show tables and graphs on command. Luckily, WAD includes a number of tools allowing us to do just that.

In this section, we will discuss how to create a button and a dropdown box that can hide and show different web items within the template. We will also look at the Tab Pages web item, which offers another way to change the display of items in the web application. However, before we create these new controls we should take a closer look at the settings that control web item visibility.

7.5.1 Visibility Settings for Web Items

Every web item in WAD has something in common: they all have a setting in their Properties pane that controls whether or not the item is displayed in the web application. The setting is labeled VISIBILITY, and it is found in the DISPLAY section of the WEB ITEM PARAMETERS tab in the Properties pane of any given web item.

You can manually change the Visibility setting from the default setting of "Visible" to "Hidden" if you do not want the web item to display in the web application. This setting can also be changed programmatically by using the SET_ITEM_PARAMETERS command, which can then be called via a button or a dropdown menu.

Looking back at the web template we've been building, we only have a navigation pane and an analysis grid in the main section of the template. For the purposes of the example at the beginning of this section (the business requirement to change the display tables and graphs), let's create a new Chart web item. Click the STANDARD heading in the WEB ITEMS pane in the top left of the main WAD screen, and drag the Chart item to an empty space inside CONTAINER_LAYOUT_ITEM_1, next to the existing analysis item. The screen should look like Figure 7.56.

We will keep the chart's properties at their default setting for now. Note that the VISIBILITY setting is at its default setting, VISIBLE. However, because we added the chart item within a container layout, it won't actually appear in the web application unless we assign it to a cell within the layout.

Click on the layout (CONTAINER_LAYOUT_ITEM_1) and click the Value Help button next to the first row. Click the third item in the resulting screen and assign CHART_ITEM_1 as the subordinate web item. (If it does not appear in the list, go back to the main workspace, click the OVERVIEW tab, and then switch back to the LAYOUT tab.) Figure 7.57 shows the resulting configuration for the container layout row.

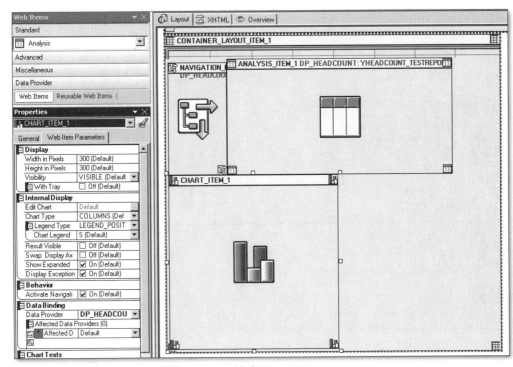

Figure 7.56 Web Template with Chart Item Added

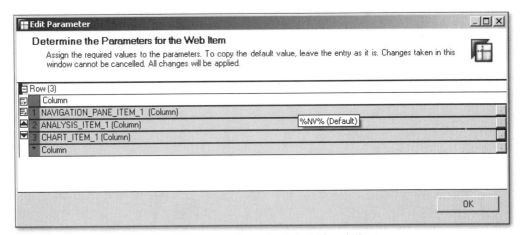

Figure 7.57 Container Layout with Navigation Pane, Analysis Grid, and Chart

Saving and executing the web template will result in a web application that looks something like Figure 7.58. Because the visibility setting of all of the web items are set to Visible by default, both the analysis grid and the graph are displayed when the web application is first run.

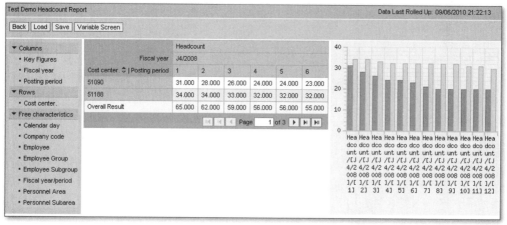

Figure 7.58 Web Application with Analysis Grid and Chart

7.5.2   Adding a Dropdown Box

Now that we've created a chart item, we can start looking at different ways to control the visibility of the table and the chart. In this case, we will have three different views: one with both the table and chart visible, one with only the table, and one that shows just the chart. We could add three buttons that would switch between the different views, but here it might make more sense to use a dropdown box.

Creating the Dropdown Box

The dropdown box web item has several uses: it can show a list of characteristic values, query views, or potential variable values. However, it can also be used to display a list of static options, each of which can run one or more commands — this is the configuration we will be using for our dropdown box. Each item in the dropdown box will run commands that change the visibility of the table and chart to produce the view described in the selected item.

Let's start by creating a new dropdown box. In the main WAD workspace, scroll to the top and locate the button group we created earlier for the toolbar. In the

WEB ITEMS pane, look under the STANDARD heading and drag DROPDOWN BOX to an empty space within CONTAINER_TOOLBAR, next to the existing button group (see Figure 7.59)

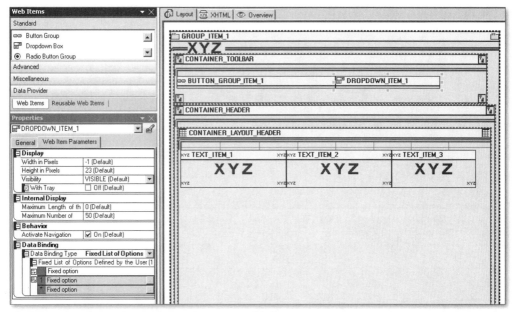

Figure 7.59 Web Template with Dropdown Item Added

Now click the new DROPDOWN_ITEM_1 we just created, and look in the Properties pane under the Web Item Parameters tab. In the Data Binding section, change Data Binding Type to Fixed List of Options. Click the Value Help button next to Fixed option to configure the first item in the dropdown.

Table Only Selection

We'll start with the table only view, where the analysis grid is shown and the chart is hidden. In the resulting configuration screen, type "Table Only" in the Description field and click the Value Help button next to Commands. This will start the same command wizard we saw in Section 7.4.1, Button Groups and Commands, but this time we will select SET WEB ITEM PARAMETERS, under COMMANDS FOR WEB ITEMS (see Figure 7.60).

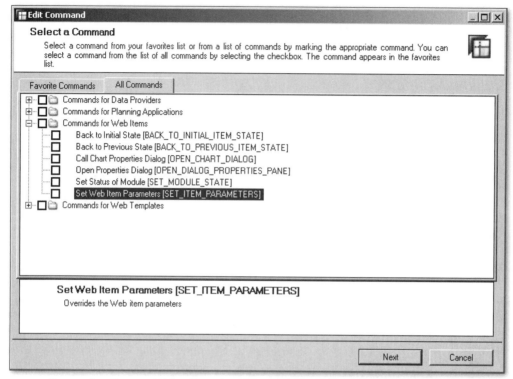

Figure 7.60 Command Wizard Step 1 — Commands for Web Items

Because we will be using this command several times in this section, you may wish to add it to the FAVORITE COMMANDS tab by clicking the checkbox next to the command. When you open the command wizard in the future, the SET WEB ITEM PARAMETERS command will be shown in the FAVORITE COMMANDS tab.

With the Set Web Item Parameters command selected, click the Next button to continue on to the next step in the wizard, seen in Figure 7.61. This step is where we select which web item will have its parameters modified.

Because we are configuring the Table Only option, you might think that we would only need to change the parameters of the chart web item, because the analysis grid is already visible by default. However, later in this section we will be creating a Chart Only option that hides the analysis grid, so if a user switches from Chart Only directly to Table Only we need to make sure the analysis grid is made visible again.

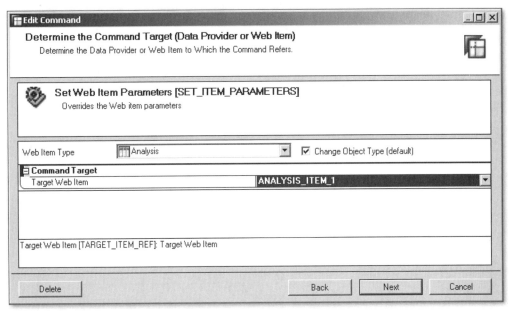

Figure 7.61 Set Web Item Parameters Step 2 — Select Target Web Item

In the Target Web Item field, select the analysis grid ANALYSIS_ITEM_1 and click the Next button to move on to the next step, seen in Figure 7.62. In this step of the wizard, we can see the properties of the analysis grid web item selected in the previous step. Any changes to parameters made here will overwrite existing parameter settings for this web item when the user selects Table Only from the dropdown menu.

The existing parameter settings are shown in nonbold text with (Default) next to the setting...it is important to note that if a setting does not appear in bold in this screen, *it will not be changed* by the command.

The Visibility parameter for the analysis grid is set to Visible (Default), so if we keep this setting unchanged the command will not work correctly. The trick is to change Visible (Default) to Visible (VISIBLE). It may seem like this change didn't really do anything, but you'll notice that the Visibility setting now appears in bold, which tells the command to go ahead and switch the parameter to Visible.

The other settings on this screen can be left alone, because the only thing we will be changing about the analysis grid is whether or not it is visible.

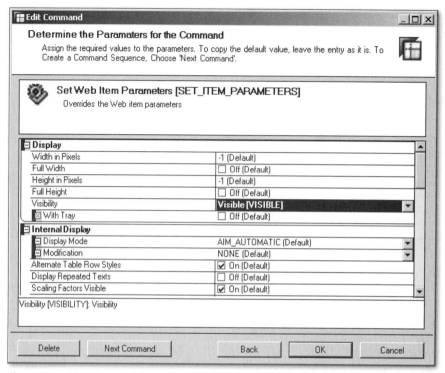

Figure 7.62 Set Web Item Parameters Step 3 — Change Parameters

Command Sequences

If you only wanted the Table Only dropdown item to make sure the analysis grid was visible without affecting any other web items, you would click OK at this point. However, we also want to hide the chart web item. We can make a single dropdown item (or button) perform multiple commands by stringing them together in a *command sequence*.

To create a command sequence by adding a second command to this dropdown item, click the NEXT COMMAND button. The COMMAND LIST EDITING screen, seen in Figure 7.63, will appear. This screen lists all of the commands that will be triggered by the dropdown item — so far, we only have one command, to make the analysis grid visible. To add a second command, click the INSERT button.

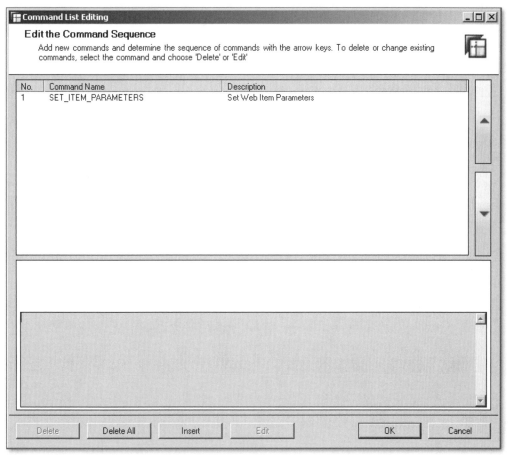

Figure 7.63 Command Sequence with One Command

Once you click the INSERT button, the command wizard will start again, as seen in Figure 7.64. This time, we will want to make sure the visibility of the chart item is set to "hidden." In the first screen of the command wizard, change the TARGET WEB ITEM setting to CHART_ITEM_1.

Click NEXT to go to the next screen (Figure 7.65) and change the VISIBILITY setting to HIDDEN [HIDDEN]. Again, note that the VISIBILITY setting is now in bold, which indicates that it will be modified by the command. Once you've changed the VISIBILITY setting, click OK to return to the command list screen (Figure 7.66).

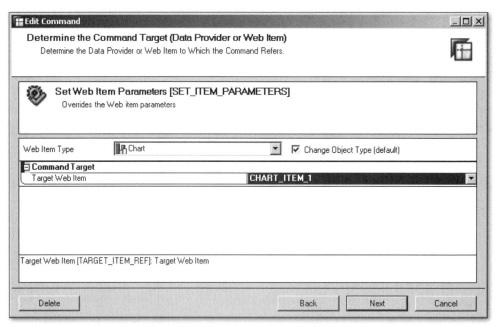

Figure 7.64 Command Wizard for Hiding Chart Item — Step 1

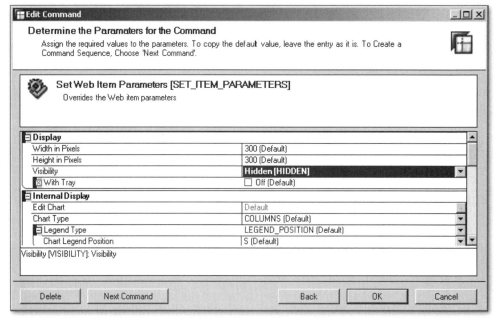

Figure 7.65 Command Wizard for Hiding Chart Item — Step 2

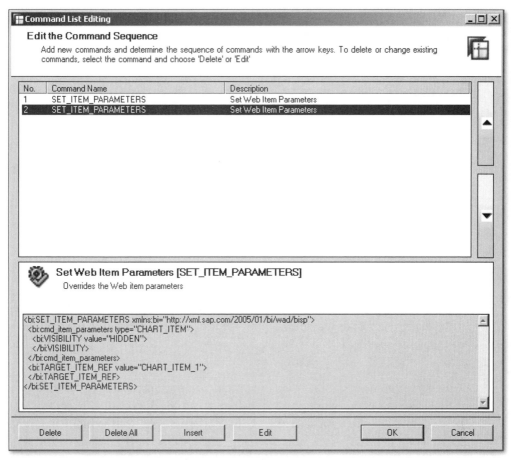

Figure 7.66 Command Sequence with Two Commands

Our dropdown item now has a two-command sequence, and both commands will be executed when the user selects the item in the dropdown menu. If you click on an existing command, you can see a preview of the XHTML code in the bottom pane. The buttons at the bottom of the command list allow you to delete a single command, delete all commands, insert a new command, or edit an existing command.

Clicking the OK button in the command list will return you to the parameter screen for the TABLE ONLY option, seen in Figure 7.67. The COMMAND parameter will now be populated with COMMANDS, indicating a command sequence. You can return to the command list screen by clicking the value help again, but for now let's click the OK button to return to the main WAD workspace.

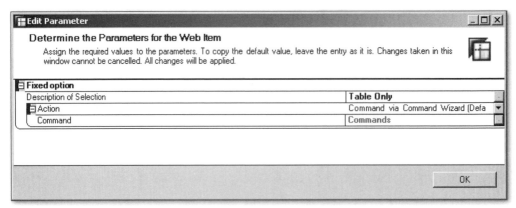

Figure 7.67 Parameter Screen for Table Only Dropdown Option

Adding More Dropdown Selections

Now that we've created the Table Only option for the dropdown menu, let's go back and create additional options for Chart Only and Table and Chart. Click the Value Help button next to the FIXED OPTION line under TABLE ONLY in the PROPERTIES pane of the dropdown item, and repeat the previous procedure for the CHART ONLY option, starting from the TABLE ONLY selection section. Repeat the procedure again for the TABLE AND CHART option.

The only differences for the other two dropdown options will be the Description of Selection parameter and which items are set to visible or hidden in the command wizard. For the CHART ONLY option, set the analysis item to hidden and the chart item to visible (make sure to change Visible (Default) to Visible [VISIBLE] and make sure that it turns bold). When you create the TABLE AND CHART option, change the settings on both web items to be visible.

Don't forget to add the second command to the CHART ONLY and TABLE AND CHART options by clicking the Next Command and Insert after finishing with the analysis grid setting changes.

Once you are done creating these two options, return to the main WAD workspace, click the dropdown item, and look at the list of options under the Data Binding section in the Properties pane. The first setting, Table Only, will be the displayed in the dropdown box by default. However, both the table and chart are visible by default (based on their parameter settings in the web template), so we want to make sure the default view of the web application matches what is shown initially in the dropdown box.

Luckily, it is easy to reorder existing options. Click on the number 3 next to the Table and Chart option in the Properties pane. Once it is selected, click the up arrow on the left twice. This will change the order of the options in the dropdown menu so TABLE AND CHART is displayed first, and when the web application is run, the dropdown menu will initially show the TABLE AND CHART option.

User Experience Tip 7.5: Matching Default Web Application View with Initial Dropdown Options

Why is it so important to match the default view of the web application with the option initially displayed in the dropdown box? The answer is apparent if you walk through the web application from the user's perspective. If the TABLE ONLY option was initially displayed in the dropdown box, but the web application showed both the table and the chart by default, the user would have to select the TABLE ONLY option by first switching to a different option, then back to TABLE ONLY.

On the other hand, if the default dropdown option is TABLE AND CHART, there is no usability issue — the user would never need to choose the TABLE AND CHART option when the web application is initially run, as that view would already be displayed. If another item is selected from the dropdown, the selected item becomes the new displayed option, so the option displayed on the dropdown box will always match the current view.

Container Layout Alignment

When we created this dropdown box, we did so directly in the container web item with the button group. As we saw in Section 7.3.1, Adding Web Items, this would result in the button group and dropdown box being shown on two different lines in the web application, because the container item does not handle alignment.

The solution is the same as the one in Section 7.3.2: we need to add a container layout within the container, and the container layout must be configured to display the two web items within the same row. Drag the container layout from the ADVANCED tab of the WEB ITEMS pane into the CONTAINER_TOOLBAR container, next to the existing button group and dropdown item. Drag both the button group and dropdown items inside the new container layout.

Let's rename the container layout so we can distinguish it from the other layout item we created before. Click the new container layout in the main WAD workspace, click the rename icon next to the web item name at the top of the Properties pane, and change the web item name to CONTAINER_LAYOUT_TOOLBAR. The result should look like the screen in Figure 7.68 — the screenshot in this figure is still showing the dropdown item properties after the TABLE AND CHART item was moved to the top.

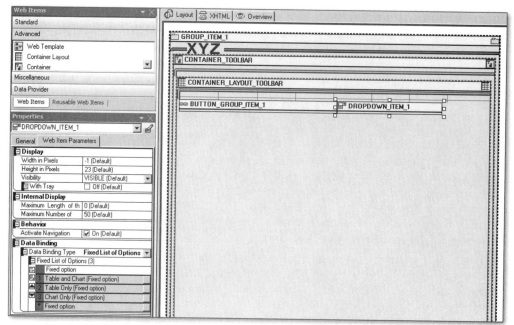

Figure 7.68 Web Template with Dropdown Item Populated with Three Options

Let's go back to the Properties pane of the new container layout, and click the Value Help button next to the first row to assign the button group and the dropdown item to cells within the layout. Just as we did before, click the Value Help button next to each column, assigning BUTTON_GROUP_ITEM_1 as the subordinate web item in the first column and DROPDOWN_ITEM_1 as the subordinate web item in the second column, as seen in Figure 7.69. Click OK to return to the main workspace.

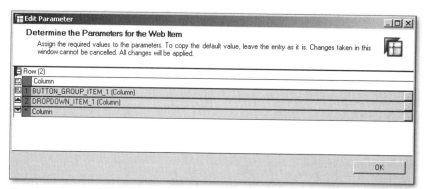

Figure 7.69 Columns of Toolbar Container Layout

We are now ready to save and execute the web template. The header from the resulting web application can be seen in Figure 7.70, and as you can see the toolbar and the dropdown menu are displayed side by side. The TABLE AND CHART dropdown option is displayed initially, but selecting Table Only or Chart Only from the dropdown menu will change the view accordingly.

Figure 7.70 Web Application Toolbar with Dropdown

You may notice that the default analysis pattern template included a Display As label before its dropdown menu. If you'd like to add a similar label, look back to Section 7.4.2, Creating and Populating a Header, and follow the instructions under Aligning Multiple Text Elements for adding a text item with the Simple Text option, this time between the button group and dropdown item. Don't forget to add the text item to the container layout.

7.5.3   Nesting Container Layouts

This implementation of hiding and showing web items works fine for relatively simple web applications, but when you start creating container layouts with multiple rows, you may run into visual spacing issues when changing web item visibility.

Figure 7.71 illustrates how this issue can appear. Let's say we have a web application with our existing three web items (navigation pane, analysis grid, and chart) along with three additional web items assigned to each column in the second row of the container layout.

The addition of three additional web items does not change our dropdown command, so if a user selected CHART ONLY, the analysis grid web item would be hidden. However, because WEB ITEM #5 would still be visible, there would be a large gap between the navigation pane and the chart.

One way to correct this issue is to create an additional container layout that contains both the analysis grid and the chart, and a third container layout that holds WEB ITEM #5 and WEB ITEM #6. These new container layouts would be assigned to the second column of the first and second row of the existing layout, respectively. (There would no longer be a third column in the existing layout.)

253

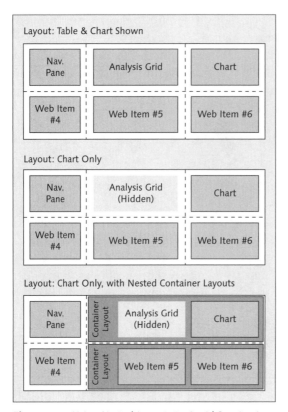

Figure 7.71 Using Nested Layouts to Avoid Spacing Issues

In this configuration, selecting the CHART ONLY option would not leave any whitespace in the web application, because the nested container layout holding the table and chart is a separate HTML table, and the chart would end up appearing next to the navigation pane.

The third container layout holding WEB ITEM #5 and #6 exists because the parent layout is now a 2 x 2 grid, and only one web item can be assigned to the second column of the second row in the layout. Therefore, both WEB ITEM # 5 and #6 are assigned to different columns in the third container layout, which is in turn assigned to the bottom right cell of the parent layout.

Going back to our web template, we will create the new container layout as an exercise, including both the analysis item and the chart item. Create the layout within the existing CONTAINER_LAYOUT_ITEM_1, next to the chart item, and drag the analysis and chart items inside the new layout, as seen in Figure 7.72.

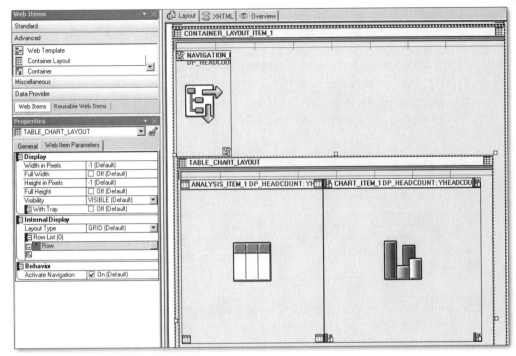

Figure 7.72 Nested Container Layouts

Now click the new container layout and rename it. To avoid confusion, you can call it something like TABLE_CHART_LAYOUT. Adjust the properties of the row so the two web items are assigned correctly, as in Figure 7.73. If the analysis and chart items don't appear as subordinate web items, don't forget to switch to the Overview tab then back to the Layout tab in the main workspace.

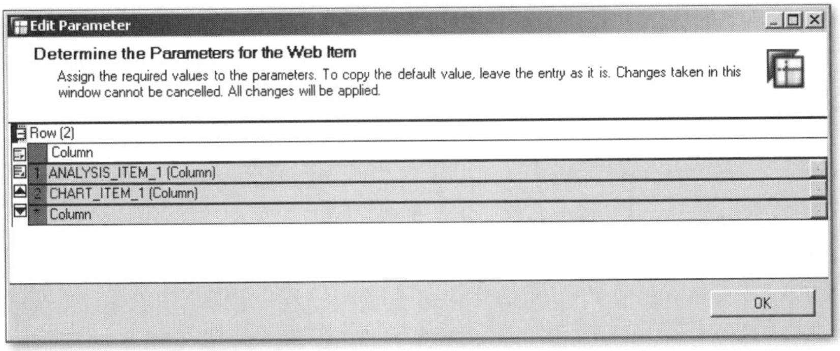

Figure 7.73 Assigning Analysis and Chart Items to Nested Layout

The next step is to assign the new layout we just created to the parent layout. Click the CONTAINER_LAYOUT_ITEM_1 layout and open the parameters for the first row. Modify the second column in the resulting screen to show TABLE_CHART_LAYOUT as a subordinate web item instead of the analysis item. Because TABLE_CHART_LAYOUT includes both the analysis item and the chart item, we can delete the third column item by clicking it once to select it and clicking the red icon on the left side of the screen (see figure 7.74).

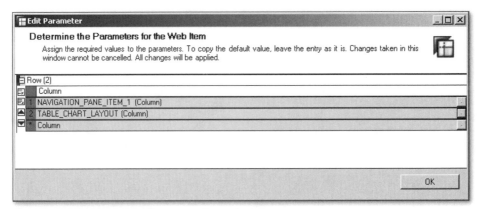

Figure 7.74 Assigning Nested Layout to Parent Layout

Click OK and save the web template. You can run the web application if you wish, but adding the nested container layout will have no impact on the look of the current web application. However, if you add new web items to the second row of the existing layout, there will be no whitespace issues when hiding the table or the chart.

Nesting container layouts is not the only solution to this issue. You may recall back in Section 7.3.2, under the heading Assigning Items within the Layout, we discussed the Layout Type option, illustrated in Figure 7.26. For the specific example in this section, changing the layout type of the existing container layout to Row Cells Floating would also eliminate whitespace without creating nested layouts, because the two rows in the existing layout would be rendered as independent HTML tables.

Using a different container layout for additional web items would also resolve this issue, but it would make it more difficult to line up web items across multiple rows.

Finally, it's also possible to dynamically change the Colspan parameter of individual columns within the container layout to make a single web item span multiple columns when other web items are hidden. However, this approach is more complex to implement and requires longer command sequences.

Creating nested container layouts offers greater flexibility to the application designer while maintaining a visual representation of the structure of the web template in the Layout tab. The tradeoff is that the Layout tab can become more cluttered, but now that you understand the role of each nested web item, you should be able to follow the subordinate web item assignments in any web template to better understand how it was built.

7.5.4 Using Buttons to Show Items

Buttons, introduced in Section 7.4, Adding Toolbars and Headers, can also be used to control the visibility of web items. Buttons are not as flexible as dropdown boxes, but they do work well for switching between two different views.

Two common implementations involve creating a button that toggles the visibility setting of a single web item (or multiple web items using a command sequence) between visible and hidden, or a button that displays a hidden web item, with another button on the item itself that hides it again.

We'll start by walking through the first type of implementation by creating a button that can change the visibility of the navigation pane. We will see an example of the second type of implementation later in the chapter.

The navigation pane is a very useful component of a BI web application, as it allows users to navigate a query by dragging and dropping characteristics. However, casual users may prefer sticking to predefined views instead of trying to navigate themselves.

For web applications aimed at these casual users, you may want to consider hiding the navigation pane by default. Let's make that change now: in the main WAD workspace, scroll down until you see the navigation pane item, and click on it once. In the PROPERTIES pane, change the VISIBILITY setting to HIDDEN, as seen in Figure 7.75.

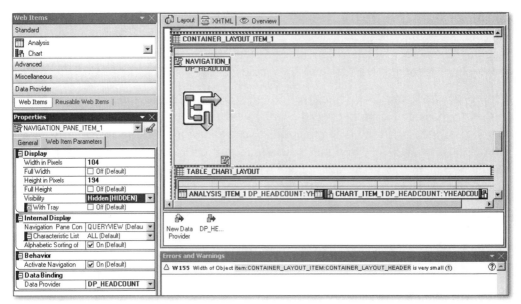

Figure 7.75 Hiding the Navigation Pane

Now we will create a button that will show the navigation pane when clicked, and hide it when clicked again. In the main WAD workspace, scroll up until you see BUTTON_GROUP_ITEM_1, also known as the toolbar we created in Section 7.4. Click the button group, and find the last row in the Internal Display section of the Web Item Parameters tab in the Properties pane. Click the Value Help button next to this row, and click the button next to the Command field in the resulting dialog box.

Because we will be changing the parameters of the navigation pane web item, select the Set Web Item Parameters command and click the Next button. In the following screen (see Figure 7.76) select NAVIGATION_PANE_ITEM_1 as the TARGET WEB ITEM, and click the NEXT button again.

As shown in Figure 7.77, the properties for the navigation pane will be displayed. Because we want this button to display the navigation pane, change the VISIBILITY setting to VISIBLE. Double-check that the VISIBILITY setting is the only item that is in bold (indicating that it will be changed by the button) and click OK.

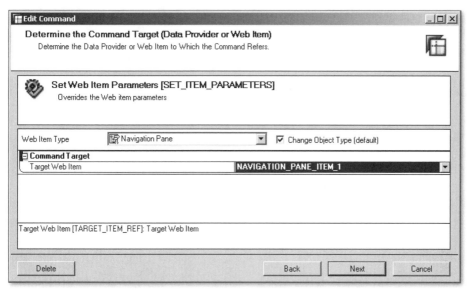

Figure 7.76 Setting the Navigation Pane as a Target Web Item

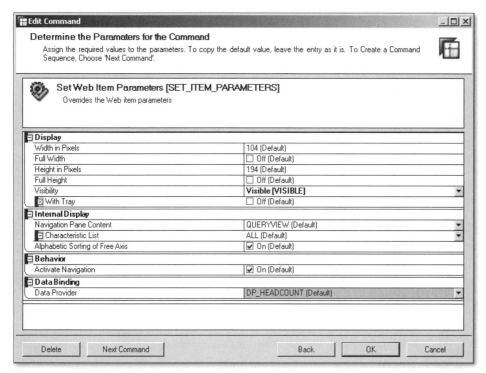

Figure 7.77 Navigation Pane Parameters to Be Changed

After clicking OK, you will return to the Edit Parameter screen for our new button. Let's type a caption for this button, something like "Show/Hide Drilldowns." If space on the toolbar is an issue, a simple label of "Drilldowns" would also work.

User Experience Tip 7.6: Rebranding SAP Interface Components for End Users

You may find it useful to rebrand certain user-facing elements of your SAP implementation to help clarify features for end users. For example, if users have the option of choosing between BEx analyzer, BEx Web analyzer (the analysis pattern), and an Information Consumer web application, you could refer to these tools using names such as BW Excel Reporting, Advanced Web Reporting, and Casual Web Reporting.

In the example in this section, instead of labeling the button "Show/Hide Navigation Pane," we are using "Show/Hide Drilldowns," which gives the user a better idea of the functionality offered by the button.

We are halfway there: the command we set up will display the navigation pane when the button is clicked. To add another action that will hide the navigation pane when the button is clicked again, we need to use the RELEASE ACTION setting.

In the EDIT PARAMETER screen for our new button, click the checkbox next to the WITH_RELEASE_ACTION setting, and confirm that it is set to ON. A new command parameter will appear below the setting — the command we enter here will be executed when the button is clicked a second time.

Click the Value Help button next to the new command parameter and follow the same instructions as mentioned previously for setting up a new command change for the web item parameters of the navigation pane. This time, change the Visibility setting to Visible [VISIBLE]. When you click OK, the EDIT PARAMETER screen should look like Figure 7.78.

Click OK one more time to return to the main WAD workspace. Save the web template and execute it to see the results, shown in Figure 7.79.

This screenshot shows our web application with the TABLE ONLY option selected from our dropdown. Note that the navigation pane is hidden by default, because we changed the web item parameters in the main web template.

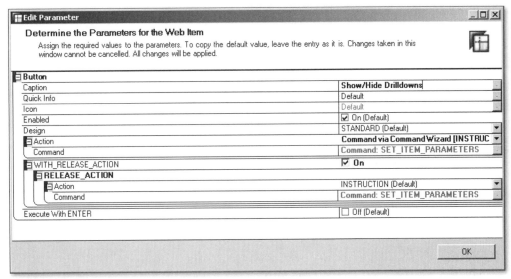

Figure 7.78 Properties for Show/Hide Drilldowns Button

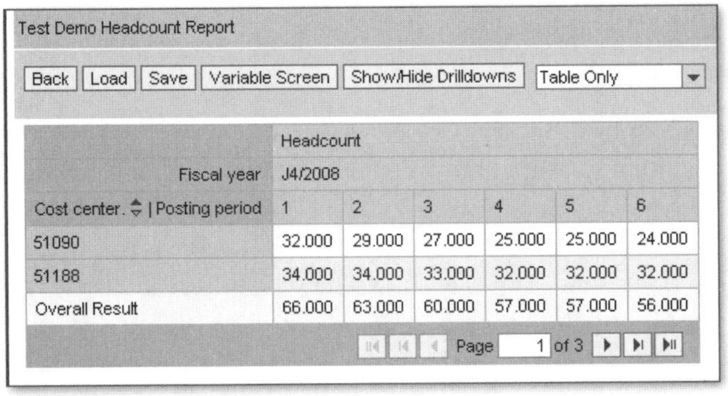

Figure 7.79 Web Application with Navigation Pane Hidden

If you click the SHOW/HIDE DRILLDOWNS button, the navigation pane appears. The look of the button also changes to indicate that it is now in the "pressed" status, seen in Figure 7.80. When you click the button again, the release action command will be executed, and the navigation pane will be hidden. The button will also return to its original look, seen in Figure 7.79.

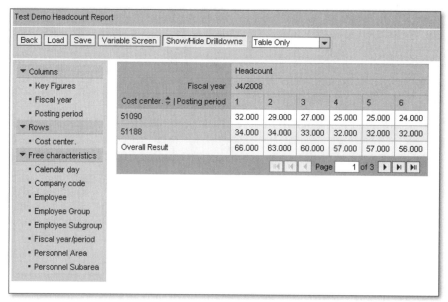

Figure 7.80   Web Application with Drilldowns Shown

7.5.5   Placing Items in Tab Pages

Another useful method to control the visibility of web items is to use Tab Pages items. A tab page item is similar to a single-row container layout in that it consists of a number of columns that can be assigned to one subordinate web item each. Unlike a container layout, which displays all of the columns at once, a tab page only displays one web item at a time. The user can select which item to display by clicking one of the tabs at the top of the tab page item.

The example in this section will introduce a number of different concepts: we will create a tab page item containing both a filter web item and a checkbox web item. The tab page item will be hidden by default, and a new button will be added to our toolbar to display the tab page item. A separate toolbar will also be created with buttons that are specific to the tab pages, including a button to hide the tab page item.

Creating the Tab Page Item

The first step is to create the tab page item itself. The tab page will be hidden by default, but when it is displayed we would like it to show between the toolbar and the navigation pane/analysis grid.

Because the tab page will have its own toolbar, we will be putting the tab page item itself inside a group item so we can easily assign a toolbar later. This group item will be placed inside a container layout so we can control web item placement.

Look in the LAYOUT tab of the main WAD workspace and scroll down until you see CONTAINER_LAYOUT_ITEM_1, the layout that contains the navigation pane, analysis grid, and chart item. Now look in the WEB ITEMS pane at the top left and click the ADVANCED header.

Drag a CONTAINER LAYOUT item to the whitespace just to the left of the existing container layout — this will create the new layout just above it. Click the new layout once and rename it to FILTER_LAYOUT. Now drag a group item from the WEB ITEMS pane into the new FILTER_LAYOUT item, and rename it to FILTER_GROUP. Finally, drag a TAB PAGES item into FILTER_GROUP.

Because we want this entire section to be hidden by default, click the FILTER_LAYOUT item, which is the highest-level web item we just created. Look in the PROPERTIES pane and change the VISIBILITY setting to HIDDEN.

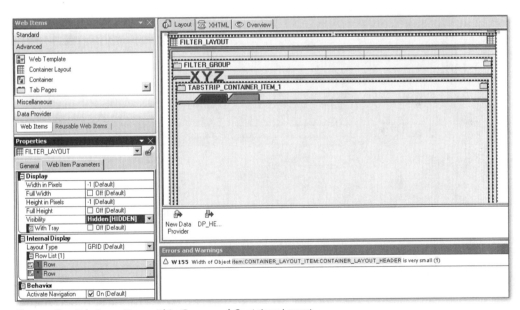

Figure 7.81 Tab Pages Item within Group and Container Layout

The result should look similar to Figure 7.81. While we're here, let's assign FILTER_GROUP as a subordinate web item to FILTER_LAYOUT by clicking the Value Help button next to the first row, then the first column, then making the assignment. This particular container layout will only hold one web item, but adding the layout makes it easier to add more items in the future.

We will assign the tab pages item to the group later, after we create the secondary toolbar.

Adding a Filter Pane and Checkbox Group

Now that the tab pages item has been created, let's add a few web items to it. Under the STANDARD heading of the WEB ITEMS pane, drag a Filter Pane and a Checkbox Group into the tab pages item (see Figure 7.82). As with the container layout, the order of the web items within the tab page item in WAD is not important, we will see later how to assign these web items to different tabs.

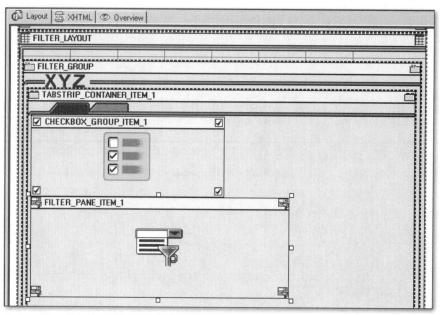

Figure 7.82   Checkbox Group and Filter Pane within Tab Pages

The checkbox group web item is similar to the checkbox item in BEx analyzer (discussed in Chapter 6, Section 6.5.2, Checkboxes and Radio Buttons), it can be used to list values from a selected characteristic or structure. The filter pane displays a number of different characteristics and structures, allowing the user to easily set filters for individual values or open the value selection screen.

Let's configure the checkbox group first: click on the checkbox group item and look in the Web Item Parameters tab of the Properties pane, under the Data Binding section. Click the Value Help button next to the Characteristic line to open the VALUEHELP SELECTOR screen shown in Figure 7.83.

In this example, we want this item to display checkboxes for each month of the year so the user can easily filter the report to display one or more months. The LISTED VALUE option at the top of this screen will display all characteristics and structures in the query associated with the DataProvider assigned to the web item. We will select the POSTING PERIOD characteristic after choosing the LISTED VALUE option — this will display all valid values for POSTING PERIOD as a series of checkboxes when we run the web application and show this web item.

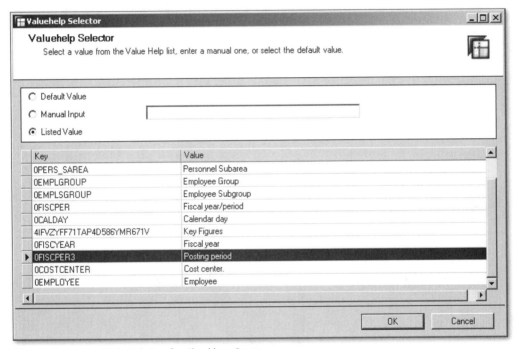

Figure 7.83 Value Help Selector for Checkbox Group

Once you've selected POSTING PERIOD, click OK to return to the main WAD workspace. Look in the checkbox group properties (Figure 7.84) and confirm that POSTING PERIOD shows up as the CHARACTERISTIC value.

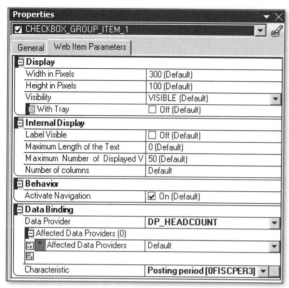

Figure 7.84 Checkbox Group Properties

The other web item we created, a filter pane, does not need to be configured at this time. By default, a filter pane web item will display a list of all characteristics and structures in the query associated with the selected DataProvider. We will see later how we can use a button to modify the filter pane properties and restrict which characteristics are displayed.

Assigning Items to Tabs

As we mentioned before, the tab pages web item is similar to the container layout in that subordinate web items must be assigned before they will display. Configuration of the tab pages item is simpler than the container layout in that there is only one row of web items, but in the tab pages each subordinate web item must be assigned a caption that will appear on the tab. If no caption is assigned, the tab will display "??".

Click the TABSTRIP_CONTAINER_ITEM_1 in the main WAD workspace and look at the Properties pane, shown in Figure 7.85.

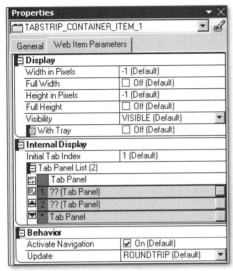

Figure 7.85 Tab Page Item Properties

Note that there are already two parameters in the TAB PANEL LIST: when you drag another web item into a tab pages item, WAD assumes that you want to display that web item on a tab, so it creates one for you.

In this example, we will be creating one tab called Filters to hold the filter pane item, and another tab called Months that will display the checkbox group item we configured in the previous section.

Start by clicking the Value Help button next to the first item in the tab panel list to bring up the EDIT PARAMETER screen for the first tab, shown in Figure 7.86. Type "Filters" in the CAPTION field, and select FILTER_PANE_ITEM_1 as the subordinate web item. (If the subordinate web items dropdown is not populated, use the trick of switching to the Overview tab and back to the Layout tab in the main WAD workspace.)

Click OK, then set up the second tab with a caption of "Months," and assign the subordinate web item CHECKBOX_GROUP_ITEM_1, as seen in Figure 7.87. Note that this web item has the capability to execute commands when a user clicks a specific tab (ACTIVATION ACTION) or navigates away from the tab (DEACTIVATION ACTION). We will not be using these features in this scenario, but keep this in mind as it may prove useful to meet your own business requirements.

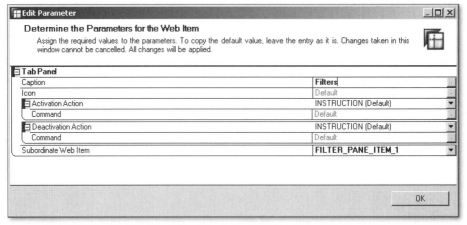

Figure 7.86 Parameters for Filters Tab

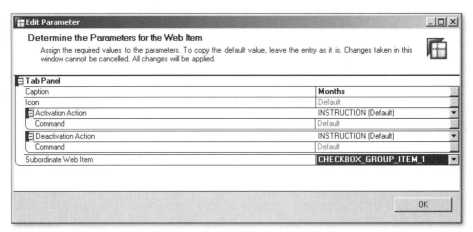

Figure 7.87 Parameters for Months Tab

Secondary Toolbars

Now that our tab pages item is set up and assigned to the appropriate subordinate web items, it's time to go back to the main WAD workspace and set up a secondary toolbar to provide functionality specific to content on the tab pages. Recall that we created the tab pages item within a group item for this purpose.

From the STANDARD heading of the WEB ITEMS pane, drag a button group to the FILTER_GROUP web item just above the tab pages item. It may help to drag the button group onto the XYZ illustration at the top of the group item. The end result should look like Figure 7.88.

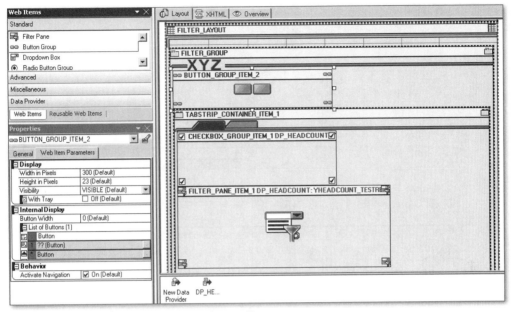

Figure 7.88 Button Group Item for Secondary Toolbar

This secondary toolbar will have just one button for now: Hide Filters. This button is necessary because we are creating a button in the main toolbar that will show the filter pane, but it will not be a toggle switch as we made in the previous section, and there will be no release action command that hides the filter pane again. Instead, this functionality will be incorporated into another toolbar, which will only be visible when the filter pane is shown.

Click the new button group item we just created, and click the Value Help button next to the first item in the list of buttons under the WEB ITEM PARAMETERS tab of the PROPERTIES pane. In the button parameters screen, type "Hide Filters" in the Caption field, click the Value Help button next to the Command field, select the Set Web Item Parameters command, and click the Next button to bring up the screen shown in Figure 7.89.

We need to be careful to hide the correct web item here — if we just hide the filter pane, the container layout, group, and tab pages item would still be shown. Instead, let's select the highest-level web item we've created in this section, the container layout. Select FILTER_LAYOUT as the target web item and click the NEXT button to show the web item parameters for the layout (Figure 7.90).

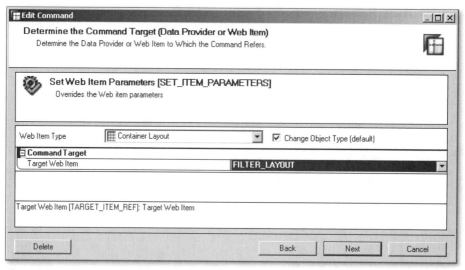

Figure 7.89 Web Item Assignment for Hide Filters Button

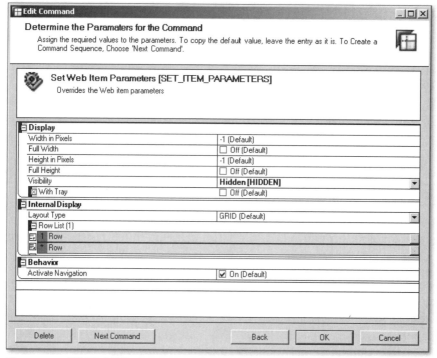

Figure 7.90 FILTER_LAYOUT Parameters for Hide Filters Button

The only change we will make to the container layout is the VISIBILITY parameter, which will be changed to HIDDEN [HIDDEN]. The container layout is already hidden by default, but this button is designed to hide the layout again after the user clicks the Show Filters button, which we will create next.

Click OK, and OK again to return to the main WAD workspace. Scroll up to the top of the layout section of the web template and locate the original toolbar we created, BUTTON_GROUP_ITEM_1. Click this button group, and then click the first available Button line in the List of Buttons under the Web Item Parameters tab of the Properties pane.

Follow the same procedure to create a button, this time typing "Show Filters" in the Caption field. After you select the Set Web Item Parameters command and choose FILTER_LAYOUT as the target web item, make sure to change the VISIBILITY setting to VISIBLE [VISIBLE], as seen in Figure 7.91.

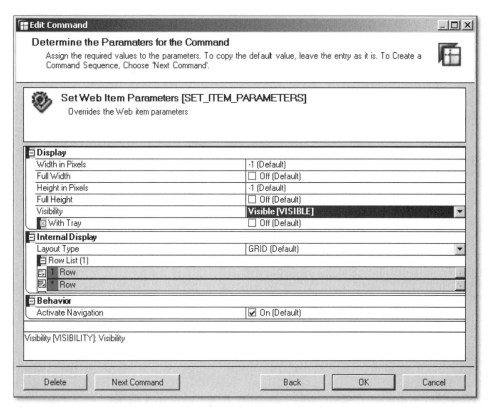

Figure 7.91 FILTER_LAYOUT Parameters for Show Filters Button

Click OK, and then OK again to return to the main WAD workspace.

Getting the Group Together

Now that all of the pieces have been created, it's time to take care of assignments to the group web item. Scroll back down to the middle of the web template and locate the FILTER_GROUP item. Click it once and look under the WAD, specifically the INTERNAL DISPLAY section.

As we did in Section 7.4.3, Putting It All Together in a Group, we will now assign a main subordinate web item and a web item for the toolbar. Recall that the toolbar section in the group is displayed above the main subordinate web item — in this case, we would like the Hide Filters button to appear on top of the tab pages item, so the toolbar we just created will actually be assigned to the toolbar section.

Make sure the WITH CAPTION setting is turned off and WITH TOOLBAR is on. Assign BUTTON_GROUP_ITEM_2 as the subordinate web item under WITH TOOLBAR. Because we want the tab pages item to appear in the main section of the group, make sure TABSTRIP_CONTAINER_ITEM_1 is selected in the first subordinate web item field (see Figure 7.92).

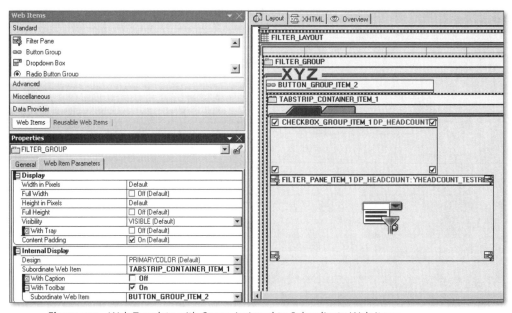

Figure 7.92 Web Template with Group Assigned to Subordinate Web Items

User Experience Tip 7.7: Keep Similar Interface Elements Together

It's usually a good idea to make sure similar interface elements are grouped in the same general area within your web application. For example, if we had displayed the Hide Filters button below the tab pages item in the group, the button would have been separated from the rest of the buttons in our original toolbar. Instead, the Hide Filters button appears directly below the original toolbar, leaving the rest of the web application an unbroken block of data-driven functionality (filtering characteristic values and displaying data in an analysis grid and chart).

Running the Web Application

Now that we have the filter pane and checkbox group assigned to the tab pages item, the tab pages and secondary toolbar assigned to the group, and the group assigned to the layout, we are ready to run the web application.

Save the web template and run the web application. Click the SHOW FILTERS button to display the tab pages item showing the filter pane, as seen in Figure 7.93.

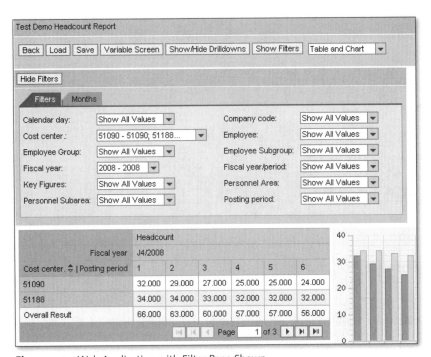

Figure 7.93 Web Application with Filter Pane Shown

If you click the Months tab, the tab pages item will display the checkbox group instead of the filter pane, as in Figure 7.94. The single-column format does not work that well to display months, but you can change this setting in the checkbox group web item parameters, specifically the Number of columns setting. Clicking the Hide Filters button will hide the entire group, including the secondary toolbar and the tab pages item.

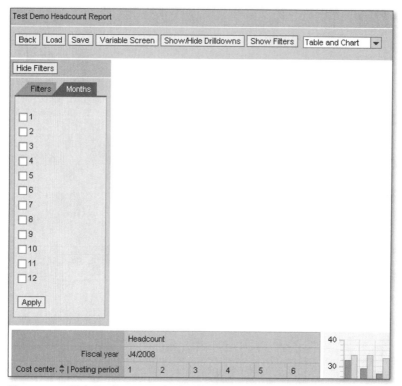

Figure 7.94 Web Application with Checkbox Group Shown

7.6 More Buttons and Commands

In the past few sections, we've recreated much of the functionality of the default analysis pattern web template delivered by SAP. We have a number of basic buttons within a header, and the capability to toggle the display of the navigation pane and the filter pane (the filter is controlled with a separate link in SAP's template, as opposed to the button we created in this scenario). We have also created an analysis grid and a chart item, and a dropdown menu that allows the user to change which is displayed.

Now let's go a little further and start adding additional functionality using the command wizard. This section contains a few examples that could improve the usability of your web applications by making relatively minor tweaks.

7.6.1 Making "Simple Views" of Web Items

The Set Web Item Parameters command we've been using throughout this chapter to create buttons is one of the most powerful commands available in WAD, as it can modify the settings for any number of existing web items in your application.

One such use for this command would be to allow users to switch between multiple "versions" of the same web item, by setting up a button to change the web item parameters.

When we created the filter pane item in the last section, we left the web item with its default parameters, which show all characteristics and structures in the relevant query attached to the DataProvider. This configuration would be appropriate for a user who might need to potentially filter on any one of these characteristics, but some users might only need to see a few of them.

To serve the latter user population, we can create a button that will simplify the filter pane by modifying its parameters and only including select characteristics. Because this button will only apply to the filter pane when it is shown, let's include it in the secondary toolbar we created inside the FILTER_GROUP item.

User Experience Tip 7.8: Use Secondary Toolbars Wisely

To maximize usability, the toolbar at the top of the web application should be reserved for functionality that applies to the entire web application, including hiding and showing various components.

With the group and button group web items, it is easy to add a secondary toolbar to any existing individual web item or container. If a specific button or dropdown implements functionality that applies only to a subset of your web application, you may be better off including those interface elements in a secondary toolbar connected with the relevant web item or container.

But don't go toolbar-crazy — if you are implementing functionality that will apply to a web item that is typically shown most of the time (such as the analysis grid), consider including the necessary buttons on the main toolbar to streamline the application.

In the main WAD interface, look in the Layout tab and scroll down until you see the BUTTON_GROUP_ITEM_2 web item we created within FILTER_GROUP. Click BUTTON_GROUP_ITEM_2 and look under the Web Item Parameters tab of the Properties pane. We already have a Hide Filters button in this toolbar, so let's add a second button that will change the filter pane to show only a few characteristics instead of all of them at once.

Click the value help button next to the blank row after the Hide Filters button. In this scenario, the new button will only show the Employee, Employee Group, and Employee Subgroup characteristics of our headcount report, so let's call the button "Empl/Group Filters Only." Set up the Set Web Item Parameters command as we've done before, and select the FILTER_PANE_ITEM_1 web item (Figure 7.95).

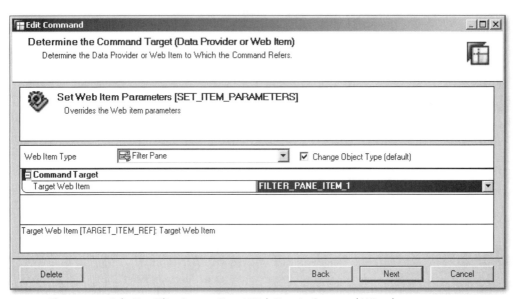

Figure 7.95 Selecting Filter Pane as Target Web Item in Command Wizard

When you click the NEXT button, you will have the opportunity to change the parameters of the Filter pane. Look under the DATA BINDING section and change the INITIAL CHARACTERISTIC SET parameter to LIST OF CHARACTERISTICS. This setting will allow you to select which characteristics are displayed in the Filter pane item, instead of all of the characteristics being displayed.

Once you have made this change, select the characteristics you want to display (in this case, Employee, Employee Group, and Employee Subgroup) in the characteristic parameters below the INITIAL CHARACTERISTIC SET setting. You may need to manually type in the technical names for each characteristic using the Value Help buttons next to each line. The result should look like Figure 7.96.

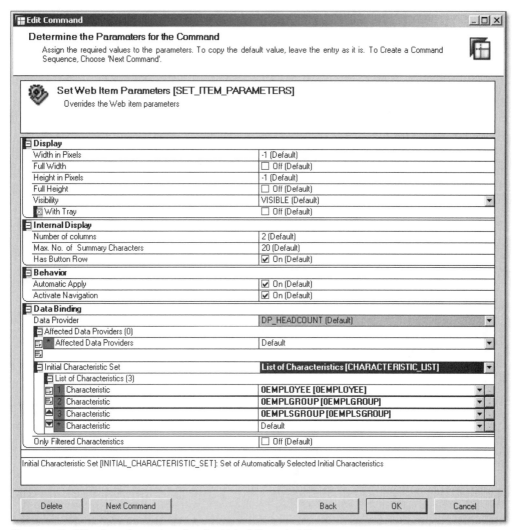

Figure 7.96 Filter Pane Parameters showing List of Characteristics

Click OK to complete the command wizard, and return to the main WAD workspace. Your users now have a way of simplifying the Filter pane to display only certain characteristics — but what if they want to switch back to the view showing all characteristics? You'll need another button for that!

Go back to the Button Group Properties pane and add another button called All Filters. Follow the same procedure as before, but when you get to the Properties screen of the Filter pane, choose ALL (ALL) for the INITIAL CHARACTERISTIC SET parameter. Make sure the parameter is in bold, indicating that the command will change that parameter when the user clicks the button. Figure 7.97 shows what the Filter Pane Parameter screen should look like in the command wizard for the All Filters button.

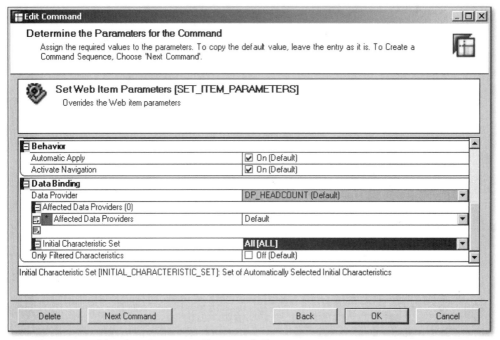

Figure 7.97 Filter Pane Parameters Showing All Characteristics

---

User Experience Tip 7.9: Plan for Common Use Patterns

As mentioned in an earlier chapter, a good way to iteratively design an application is to watch how people belonging to different user populations navigate through the existing version of an application or a prototype of a new design.

Applying that tip to this specific scenario involving the filter pane, you may find that in your own system most of your users prefer the simplified filter pane view, and the first thing they do after they show the filter pane is to click the button that hides extraneous characteristics.

There are a few different ways to handle this. One way would be to set up the initial view of the filter pane to start out with a simplified view — then you would only need one additional button on the secondary toolbar, to show all characteristics. Another potential solution would be to create multiple buttons on the main toolbar to show the filter pane: for example, an All Filters button would simply show the filter pane with all characteristics as per its initial setup, while a Simple Filters button would include a command sequence that shows the filter pane and applies the same parameter changes outlined earlier in this section. The second solution allows both types of users to show their preferred filter view with one click, at the cost of using additional space on the main toolbar.

7.6.2 Disabling Nonapplicable Buttons

Another important consideration for designing usable web applications is making sure users don't waste time clicking on buttons that do not have any function in the currently displayed interface.

In the example in the last section, we created a Show Filters button that displays the tab pages item containing the Filter pane (Figure 7.93 shows a screenshot). However, if the filter pane is already displayed, the user can still click on the Show Filters button, but nothing happens.

To avoid this situation and indicate to the user that the button is unavailable, we can modify the button group to uncheck the Enabled option of the relevant button. This will give the button a grayed-out look, and the user will not be able to click on it.

To make this change, we will need to modify the Show Filters button to not only display the filter pane, but also change its own parameters and uncheck the Enabled option. In the main WAD workspace, click the BUTTON_GROUP_ITEM_1 web item near the top of the Layout tab.

In the Properties pane, click the Value Help button next to the Show Filters button, then launch the command wizard. From here, we will insert a new command to create a command sequence. Click the Next button, and then Next Command. To insert a second command in the sequence, click the Insert button and select the Set Web Item Parameters command.

Now you will choose BUTTON_GROUP_ITEM_1 as the Target Web Item, because we want this button to modify its own parameters. Click the Next button to bring up the parameters for the button group, as seen in Figure 7.98.

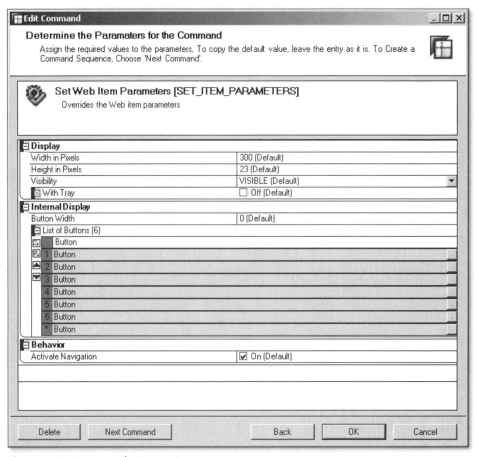

Figure 7.98 Parameters for Button Group

Unfortunately, in this screen the names of the buttons are not displayed. Looking back at the parameters of the button group in the properties pane of the main WAD workspace, Show Filters was the sixth button, so click the value help button next to button number six.

Figure 7.99 shows the parameters for the button itself. The only change we will make here is to uncheck the ENABLED setting, so it shows as OFF in bold. This will tell the command to disable the button. Click OK, and then OK again to go back to the command list. Next, you will click the OK button two more times to go back to WAD.

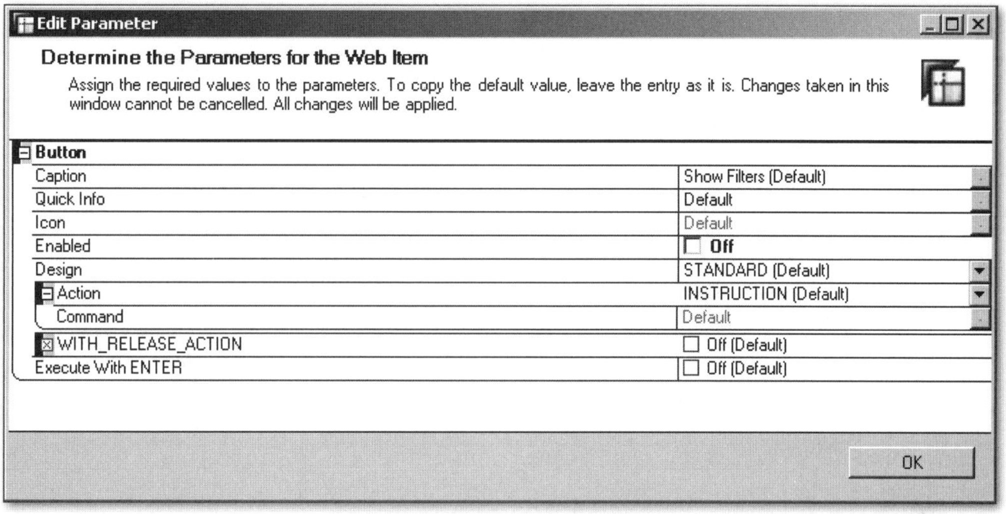

Figure 7.99 Parameters for Show Filters Button with Enabled Setting Off

The Show Filters button will now execute two commands: the first command will display the filter pane, and the second command will disable the Show Filters button. Sounds good so far, but what happens when the user clicks the Hide Filters button after they are done adjusting the filter settings? The Show Filters button will still be disabled, so the user will not be able to display the filter pane again.

To correct this issue, we will need to add another command to the Hide Filters button that changes the Show Filters button back to enabled status. Find the BUTTON_GROUP_ITEM_2 web item (our secondary toolbar) in the middle of the web template, and follow the same procedure as before. Modify the Hide Filters button and make sure to again select BUTTON_GROUP_ITEM_1 (the main toolbar) as the target web item. This time, when you get to the EDIT PARAMETER screen in Figure 7.99, click the ENABLED setting until it is set to On in bold.

Save and execute the web template. The resulting web application will look similar to Figure 7.100 — note that after the Show Filters button has been pressed, it is grayed out. In this screenshot, the EMPL/GROUP FILTERS ONLY button has been clicked, drastically simplifying the selections in the filter pane.

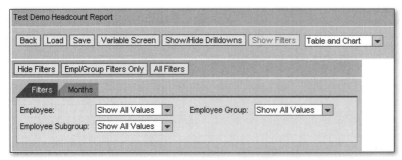

Figure 7.100 Web Application with Disabled Show Filters Button

7.6.3 Adding Icons to Buttons

Icons on buttons may seem superfluous if the text of the button already indicates its functionality. However, from a usability perspective, adding familiar icons to a web application can improve the efficiency with which users navigate the interface.

One of the most commonly used interface elements in software today is the Web browser's Back button. Most web browsers don't even display the word "Back," instead opting for a left-facing arrow. We will keep the word "Back" in the web application we've built, but let's also add a left arrow icon.

In the main WAD interface, scroll to the top of the Layout tab and find the BUTTON_GROUP_ITEM_1 web item (our main toolbar). Click the Value Help button next to the Back entry in the list of buttons, and click the Value Help button next button to the Icon parameter.

The resulting dialog box (Figure 7.101) will allow you to either enter an image URL or select an image from the MIME Repository on your BW system. In this case, we will use one of the sample images provided by SAP in Business Content, so select MIME REPOSITORY RESOURCE and click the "…" button to the right of the field.

The screen shown in Figure 7.102 will open, displaying the contents of the MIME Repository. The repository can be maintained in Transaction SE80 in your BW system, but you can also click the INSERT button to upload a new image directly from WAD.

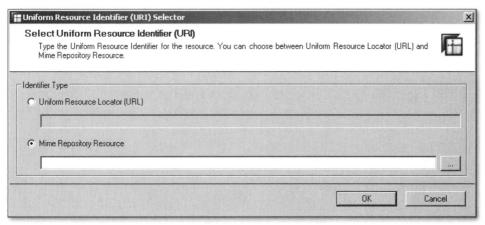

Figure 7.101 Select URL or MIME Repository Resource for Button Icon

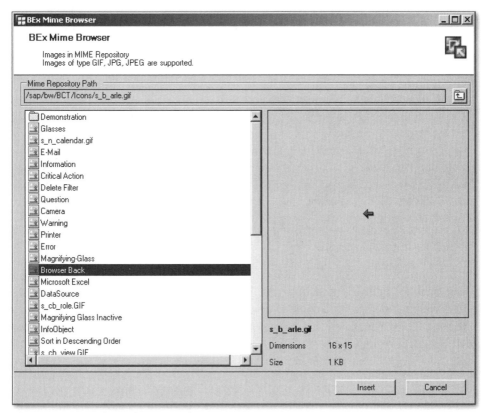

Figure 7.102 List of Sample Icons under Business Content, Icons

To navigate to the sample icons provided by Business Content, double-click the Business Content folder, then double-click Icons. Select BROWSER BACK from the resulting list and click INSERT. (Depending on your system, you may also have several additional icons under the BUSINESS EXPLORER folder.)

A URL beginning with bwmimerep:// will appear in the Mime Repository Resource field. Click OK, and then OK again to return to WAD. Save and execute the web template to see the resulting toolbar, as seen in Figure 7.103.

Figure 7.103 Button Group with Left Arrow Icon on Back Button

Icons can be added to other buttons in the same way. However, don't add icons just for the sake of adding icons — if an icon doesn't clearly associate with the functionality of the button, you are probably better off without it. Alternatively, if the icon is recognizable enough, you can leave off the text description completely.

7.7   A Brief Overview of the Analysis Pattern Template

Earlier in this chapter we saw a screenshot of the standard analysis pattern web template. Now that you have a better understanding of how web templates are put together — especially relating to the nesting of different types of container items — we can take another look at the structure of the template.

Note that this analysis will be done at a high level. For more detailed information about the functionality of web items including lists of properties, see Chapter 8, The Web Application Designer Reference.

You can follow along by opening the 0ANALYSIS_PATTERN web template on your own system, and saving a copy of it so you don't inadvertently change the template. If you cannot open the template, make sure you have been assigned a role with the authorization object S_RS_BTMP configured so you can open templates with technical names starting with 0.

We'll start at the top of the 0ANALYSIS_PATTERN web template layout, seen in Figure 7.104. For a screenshot of the web application, see Figure 7.4 in Section 7.2.1, Types of BI Patterns.

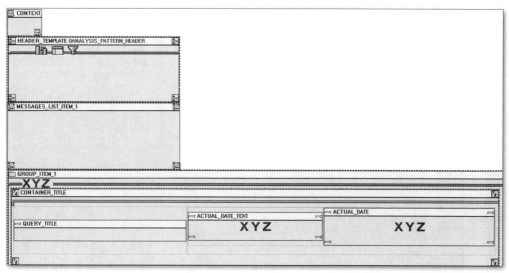

Figure 7.104 Analysis Pattern Web Template, First Screen

The item in the template is a Context Menu web item. This web item can be placed anywhere in the template — it's not actually displayed in the web application, its sole purpose is to configure which items are displayed in the context menu.

Next, we have a web template web item, which loads the contents of the 0ANALYSIS_PATTERN_HEADER. This web item is useful if you have several web templates that share the same header, by including header content in a single web template you can make header changes for multiple web templates at the same time.

A system messages web item is next, so any messages sent by the BW system will be displayed at the top of the web application.

The next web item should be familiar: it's a container item inside a group item, with three text items inside the container. However, instead of a container layout, the designer of this web template opted to use an HTML table (available by selecting Insert Table from the Table menu) to arrange the web items.

This group item (GROUP_ITEM_1) continues just about the entire length of the web template. The group's caption section (the topmost section in the group) displays the CONTAINER_TITLE web item, which includes the query description and the rollup date and time. The group's toolbar section is assigned to the TOOLBAR_ALIGNMENT container item, seen in the next screen of the web template (Figure 7.105).

285

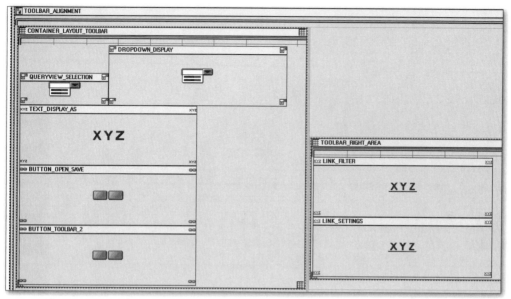

Figure 7.105 Analysis Pattern Web Template, Second Screen

The TOOLBAR_ALIGNMENT container again uses an HTML table to arrange the two container layouts, CONTAINER_LAYOUT_TOOLBAR and TOOLBAR_RIGHT_AREA.

The CONTAINER_LAYOUT_TOOLBAR layout displays the button group BUTTON_OPEN_SAVE first, including the New Analysis, Open, and Save As buttons. Next in the layout is QUERYVIEW_SELECTION, a hidden web item that collects the query views available from the DataProvider.

The next two web items in the layout are TEXT_DISPLAY_AS and DROPDOWN_DISPLAY, which serve as the caption (Display As) and the dropdown menu that allows the user to switch between displaying the table, chart, or both. Finally, BUTTON_TOOLBAR_2 is displayed, including the Information, Send, Print Version, Export to Excel, and Comments buttons.

It is difficult to see in the screenshot, but there is an empty cell in the HTML table between the two container layouts. This empty cell is assigned a width parameter in the XHTML code, resulting in the third cell (containing the TOOLBAR_RIGHT_AREA web item) being pushed to the right side of the header.

The TOOLBAR_RIGHT_AREA container layout item includes two Link items. Link items are very similar to individual buttons within button group items in that they execute commands, but they have the blue underlined appearance of a traditional hyperlink you would see on any web page. The LINK_FILTER item executes a command sequence that shows the FILTER_GROUP_AREA web item and hides the SETTINGS_GROUP_AREA item, while the LINK_SETTINGS item does the opposite.

These two group items are shown in Figure 7.106.

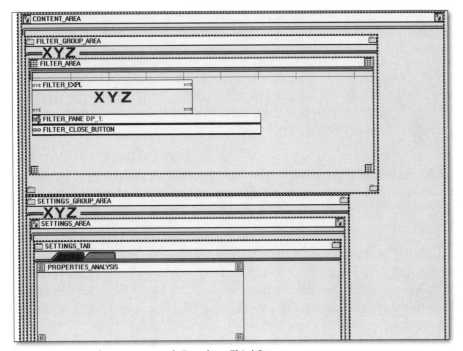

Figure 7.106 Analysis Pattern Web Template, Third Screen

The CONTENT_AREA container you see at the top of this screenshot stretches to the end of GROUP_ITEM_1. This container is the main subordinate web item of the group.

In the first group shown within CONTENT_AREA, you will see a text item, a filter pane item, and a button group, all contained within the FILTER_AREA container layout and the FILTER_GROUP_AREA group. The group in this case is used for cosmetic purposes, as it only includes the FILTER_AREA container layout as the main subordinate web item, with nothing in the toolbar or caption sections.

287

The FILTER_AREA container layout displays its constituent web items in three separate rows: the FILTER_EXPL text item is shown first, then the filter pane itself, followed by the button group. The button group includes a Close button, a Variable Screen button, and a Display All Filters button that opens a new template (0ANALYSIS_PATTERN_FILTER) in a modal dialog, showing the filter selections of the current DataProvider.

Assigning web items to three different rows within a container layout is simply an alternative method for constructing a group of web items with the group item. Using this method changes the look slightly: instead of the web items appearing in slightly separated sections, they all appear within the same blue rectangle.

The Settings section is somewhat more complex. This section has a container (SETTINGS_AREA) included within a group (SETTINGS_GROUP_AREA); the group is again used for cosmetic purposes here, as the only subordinate web item assigned to the group is the SETTINGS_AREA container.

There is only one web item within the SETTINGS_AREA container: the SETTINGS_TAB tab pages item. The tab pages item contains a number of different web items assigned to different tabs — the first one is a Properties Pane item PROPERTIES_ANALYSIS, which shows some of the parameters associated with the ANALYSIS web item (seen later).

The tab pages item continues in the next screenshot, seen in Figure 7.107. PROPERTIES_CHART is another properties pane item; this one displays parameters of the CHART item. Next, are web items that show the Exceptions and Conditions defined in the query, followed by another Properties pane that displays settings associated with the DataProvider instead of an individual web item.

This leads us to the end of the tab pages item. Another button group containing a Close button appears below the tab pages item (but still within the container item). To help visualize which web items are within which containers, WAD uses different colors for different web items. For example, in Figures 7.106 and 7.107, note that the tab pages item is outlined in blue, while the container item is outlined in green, and container layouts are outlined in red. Icons associated with the web item also appear at all four corners of the web item's border.

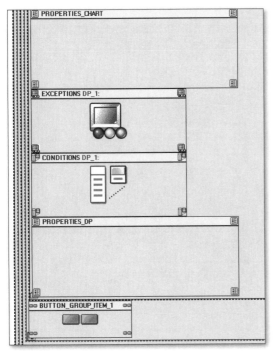

Figure 7.107 Analysis Pattern Web Template, Fourth Screen

The next web item inside the CONTENT_AREA container is the group GROUP_ITEM_2, as seen in Figure 7.108. This group item holds a single container layout item, CONTAINER_LAYOUT_CONTENT. The container layout in turn contains two different web items assigned to two columns: the NAVIGATION_PANE item is displayed in the left column, while the right column is assigned to the DATA_DISPLAY container.

The DATA_DISPLAY container holds just two web items: the ANALYSIS item and the CHART item. The CHART item is hidden by default.

Finally, the last screenshot (Figure 7.109) shows the end of the chart item, the DATA_DISPLAY container, the CONTAINER_LAYOUT_CONTENT layout, GROUP_ITEM_2, the CONTENT_AREA container, and GROUP_ITEM_1. Below this, you can see another web template item connected to the template 0ANALYSIS_PATTERN_FOOTER to allow for common footer content.

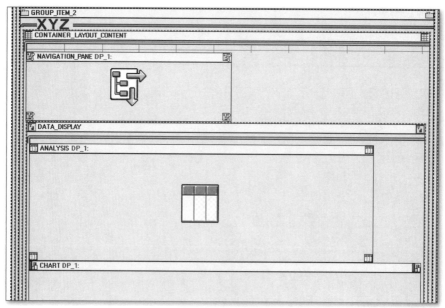

Figure 7.108 Analysis Pattern Web Template, Fifth Screen

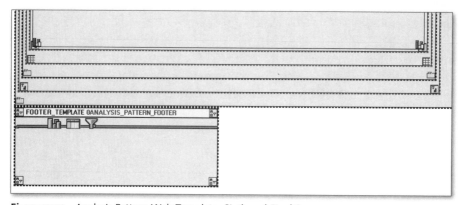

Figure 7.109 Analysis Pattern Web Template, Sixth and Final Screen

7.8 Summary: Web Application Designer

Just as we examined the design side of the BEx analyzer Excel interface in the previous chapter, this chapter focused on designing web applications for execution on the BEx Web engine. Unlike on the Excel side, web applications have their own dedicated design application with a richer feature set.

We started out exploring how to use the pattern wizard to get up and running quickly with relatively basic web applications, then we quickly moved to the most flexible method of web application design: creating a web template from scratch using a series of different web items.

In building our web template, we started with a few basic web items, including the navigation pane and analysis grid. We then arranged those web items using a container layout, and added a toolbar using the button group item. Within the toolbar, we created several new buttons using the command wizard.

Next, we introduced the container and text element web items to add a header to our web application, followed by the consolidation of the header and the toolbar into a single group item.

The next topic outlined different methods for hiding and showing web items, including dropdown boxes, buttons, and tab pages. We also introduced command sequences and looked at why nesting web items is an important concept in web application design. Secondary toolbars with buttons applying to specific web items were also implemented.

We then looked at a few additional techniques for utilizing buttons and commands to improve web applications, including simplifying web item views, disabling interface elements that are not useful, and adding icons to button descriptions.

Finally, armed with the knowledge of how different web items contribute to web application design, we stepped through SAP's standard analysis pattern web template, 0ANALYSIS_PATTERN, taking a brief look at how it is constructed.

In the next chapter, we will take a more detailed look at individual web items and their properties. Unlike this chapter, which was scenario driven, Chapter 8 will function more as a reference.

Web application designer (WAD) includes more functionality than can fit in one chapter, so we will break down components web item by web item in this reference.

8 The Web Application Designer Reference

In the last chapter, we walked through a scenario that involved building your own web template from scratch. While this scenario covered many of the important features needed to build analytical web applications, there is still much of WAD left to explore.

This chapter serves as a reference, looking at each of the web items (including properties), commands from the Business Warehouse (BW) Web Application Programming Interface (API), and a look at the WAD interface in general.

There are four different headings under the Web Items tab in the WAD main window: Standard, Advanced, Miscellaneous, and Data Provider. The first three headings contain different types of web items, while the last heading allows you to set up DataProviders for either query views or filtering purposes.

8.1 Standard Web Items

The web items grouped under the STANDARD heading typically involve communicating with a DataProvider to display data or help navigate a query. A listing of these web items is shown in Figure 8.1.

To access the properties for a web item that has been placed in the Layout tab of the main WAD workspace, click on the web item in the Layout tab and look at the bottom left of the screen in the Properties section. The General tab in the Properties pane handles DataProvider assignments, while the Web Item Parameters tab displays settings specific to the selected web item.

The top of the Properties pane shows the name of the web item, this can be changed by clicking the Rename icon on the right side of the web item name.

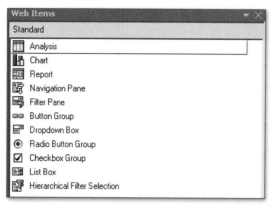

Figure 8.1 Standard Web Items

8.1.1 Common Display Properties

Just about every web item includes a common set of display properties, including the height and width of the web item, checkboxes to set the web item to run the full height or width of the web application, and a parameter that controls the visibility of the web item.

Most web items also have a With Tray option, disabled by default. Enabling this option places the web item within a box that has its own title bar and can be collapsed or expanded. The text displayed in the title is determined by the Caption field as long as the Caption Visible box is checked (otherwise the title of the tray is blank). The style of the tray can be selected (Plain, Transparent, or Filled), and the Expanded parameter determines whether or not the tray containing the web item is expanded or collapsed when the web application is run. The last parameter, Update, controls whether expanding or collapsing the tray triggers an active update on the server (Roundtrip) or happens passively on the client.

8.1.2 Analysis Item

The first web item we will cover is the Analysis item, also known as an analysis grid or table. The DISPLAY, INTERNAL DISPLAY, and BEHAVIOR properties for this web item are shown in Figure 8.2, the internal display parameters are listed in Table 8.1, and the behavior parameters are listed in Table 8.2.

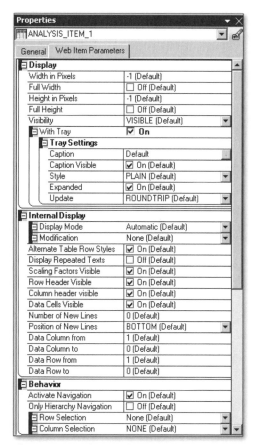

Figure 8.2 Analysis Web Item Properties, Part 1

Display Mode	Choose between displaying the default analysis grid, and displaying data in plain HTML with no formatting (useful when data is being processed by a script). The default setting will automatically select which display mode to use.
Modification	Allows for the specification of modules that can change analysis grid behavior (similar to the Web Design API for Tables in previous BW versions).
Alternate Table Row Styles	Odd and even rows in the analysis grid alternate colors when enabled (enabled by default).
Display Repeated Texts	When disabled (the default setting), contiguous cells that display the same text or key value will be merged.

Table 8.1 Analysis Web Item Internal Display Parameters

Scaling Factors Visible	When checked, this setting displays an additional line in the query output below each column heading indicating the scaling factor for that column.
Row Header Visible **Column Header Visible**	Checked by default, these options display the row header and column header (labels to the left of data and above data, respectively).
Data Cells Visible	This option will hide data cells if unchecked.
Number of New Lines **Position of New Lines**	For input-ready queries, these two settings control the number of new lines added to a table and the position of those new lines.
Data Column From **Data Column To** **Data Row From** **Data Row To**	Limits the number of columns or rows brought in to the web application from the DataProvider. Default settings are From 1, indicating that data will be loaded from the DataProvider starting with the first column or row, and To 0, which means that all columns or rows will be brought in. Columns outside this range are truncated from the analysis grid and are not viewable. To change how many rows and columns are displayed at one time, see the Paging section in Table 8.3.

Table 8.1 Analysis Web Item Internal Display Parameters (Cont.)

Allow Navigation	Allows the user to interact with the analysis grid and change the navigation state. If disabled, the navigation state cannot be changed within the analysis grid.
Only Hierarchy Navigation	If enabled, users will not be able to access the context menu; the only navigation possible will be expanding and collapsing hierarchy nodes.
Row Selection **Column Selection**	Enabling these settings creates an additional row above the first row in the grid (or a new column to the left of the first column) consisting of a series of boxes. When a user clicks on one of these boxes, the entire row or column is highlighted. With the default setting None, this feature is disabled. The Single or Multiple settings allow users to highlight one row/column or multiple rows/columns at a time, respectively. With the Single with Commands option, you can associate commands (via the command wizard) to fire when the user selects and/or deselects a single row or column.

Table 8.2 Analysis Web Item Behavior Parameters

BW users who may be used to working with Excel may miss the ability to highlight specific rows and columns when they switch over to web analytics. The Row Selection and Column Selection properties of the analysis grid duplicate that functionality, and it can be useful to enable it even if you do not associate it with any commands. Because it is a property of the analysis item, you can create a button or other control in your web application to turn it off if it confuses users.

The remaining properties of the analysis item, including DATA BINDING, PAGING, and CELL CONTENT settings, are shown in Figure 8.3 and listed in Table 8.3.

DATA BINDING settings are common among several web items, in the analysis item the only options involve selecting a DataProvider to grab data from and one or more Affected Data Providers to send commands to. You can use the latter option to ensure multiple analysis grids on your web application are kept in sync when the user changes the navigation state.

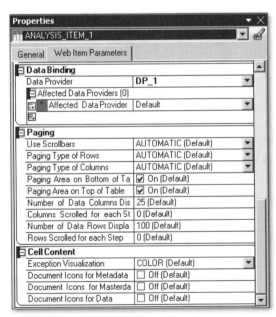

Figure 8.3 Analysis Web Item Properties, Part 2

Use Scrollbars	The default setting, Automatic, will display a traditional scrollbar when data overflows the display area, otherwise the scrollbar is hidden. Note that with typical paging settings the scrollbar will usually be hidden with the Automatic setting; to always show the scrollbar switch this parameter to Enabled.
Paging Type for Rows **Paging Type for Columns**	Choose whether users can scroll through rows page by page, row by row, or let SAP decide with the default setting of Automatic.
Paging Area on Bottom/Top of Table	These two settings control where the paging area appears in the table. You can choose to show the paging area at the top of the table, at the bottom of the table, in both places, or hide it altogether.
Number of Data Columns/Rows Displayed at Once	There are two different settings that control the number of columns and the number of rows displayed per "page." With the default settings of 25 and 100 respectively, the analysis grid will display the first 25 columns and 100 rows of the query. If there are more columns or rows, paging areas will appear to allow the user to step through the data. Use caution when increasing this number, as more data being displayed at one time can cause slow performance.
Columns/Rows Scrolled for each Step	Controls how many columns or rows are scrolled each time the user clicks on a paging button. By default (value of 0), two-thirds of the columns or rows are scrolled. Any other value indicates the actual number of columns/rows to be scrolled. If you change the value of this setting to equal the relevant value in Number of Data Columns/Rows Displayed at Once, data will be scrolled one full page at a time.

Table 8.3 Analysis Web Item Paging Parameters

The final section of the analysis item properties, CELL CONTENT, includes a setting to control exception visualization (whether cell exceptions are displayed with a color, symbol, and/or text) and options to enable the display of document icons for metadata, master data, and InfoProvider data. Business intelligence (BI) documents are discussed in Chapter 4, section 4.7.9, Running Queries on the Web: Business Explorer Analyzer.

8.1.3 Chart Item

Next up is the chart item, which can show a number of different types of charts and graphs. The chart item's properties are shown in Figure 8.4.

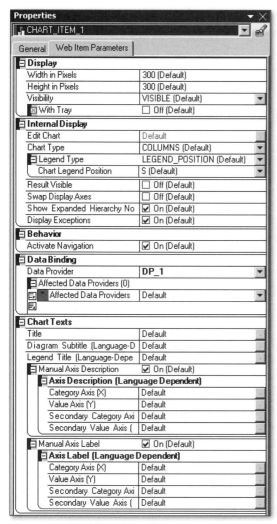

Figure 8.4 Chart Item Properties

The DISPLAY settings are similar to the analysis item, except the Full Height and Full Width options are not available here. The EDIT CHART option under INTERNAL DISPLAY has a number of settings (including a wizard) for configuring the chart, including the chart type, titles, labels, value properties, element properties, and axis settings.

Some of the options from the wizard under EDIT CHART are also available directly on the chart item properties, including the chart type and legend settings. Additional options under the INTERNAL DISPLAY heading allow you to hide or show results in the chart and swap display axes.

When creating a chart from a data set that contains display hierarchies it is important to note the next parameter, SHOW EXPANDED HIERARCHY NODES. By default, lower-level nodes that are displayed in the query are also displayed in the chart, but if you uncheck this setting, the chart will only display the high-level summary nodes of the hierarchy.

The next setting, DISPLAY EXCEPTIONS, is enabled by default, and when checked, any exceptions in the query will be reflected in the chart. The ACTIVATE NAVIGATION setting under the BEHAVIOR heading can enable or disable user interaction with the chart.

After the standard DATA BINDING parameters, the rest of the properties deal with attributes of the chart itself, including chart titles, axis descriptions, and axis labels (such as units or currencies). If you uncheck either MANUAL AXIS DESCRIPTION or MANUAL AXIS LABEL (both checked by default), the system will automatically generate descriptions and labels for each axis, respectively.

8.1.4   Report Item

The Report item allows you to embed formatted reports built with the report designer tool into your web application. This web item is relatively straightforward and offers few options: after the standard DISPLAY parameters, the REPORT DESIGN setting under INTERNAL DISPLAY allows you to select which report to embed in the web template. You can either enter a report name in the REPORT DESIGN field, or click the Value Help button to launch report designer and select a report there.

The other parameters for this web item should be familiar: you can uncheck the ACTIVATE NAVIGATION checkbox to prevent user interaction with the report. The standard Data Binding settings associate a DataProvider with the web item, although the DataProvider will be populated automatically once you select a report.

A screenshot of the report item parameters is shown in Figure 8.5.

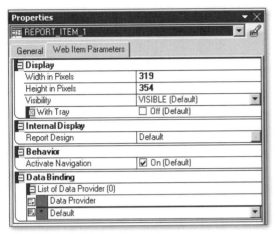

Figure 8.5 Report Item Parameters

8.1.5 Navigation Pane Item

While the navigation pane item provides significant flexibility to users, allowing them to more easily change the navigational state in analysis grids, the web item itself is relatively simple.

Located after the standard Display parameters, the Internal Display section allows you to control which characteristics are displayed in the navigation pane. The Navigation Pane Content setting defaults to All, indicating that the navigation pane will show characteristics drilled down in the rows, drilled down in the columns, and available for drilldown (free characteristics). You can modify this setting to show only one of these three categories instead.

You can also separately specify which characteristics are shown in the Free Characteristics section using the Characteristic List option. If you change this parameter from the default setting of All to List of Characteristics, you will be able to specify which characteristics will be shown. Note that this setting only affects the Free Characteristics section; as long as the Columns and Rows sections are displayed (based on the previous Navigation Pane Content setting), all characteristics in those two sections will be shown regardless of whether or not they are included here.

However, if you have the List of Characteristics setting enabled and you don't specify a characteristic that's drilled down in the rows or columns, that characteristic will disappear from the navigation pane if you move it to the free characteristics section (by removing it as an active drilldown).

Characteristics are automatically sorted in the rows and columns sections based on the order in which they are drilled down. The free characteristics section is sorted alphabetically by default, but if you disable the ALPHABETIC SORTING OF FREE AXIS checkbox, free characteristics will be sorted based on their order in Query Designer.

As with the other web items, the navigation pane item also allows you to disable user interaction and assign a DataProvider. See Figure 8.6 for a screenshot of the navigation pane item parameters.

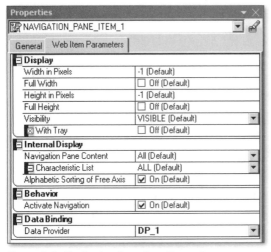

Figure 8.6   Navigation Pane Item Parameters

8.1.6   Filter Pane Item

As we saw in Chapter 7, Section 7.5.5, Placing Items in Tab Pages, the filter pane item allows the user to set up filters on a number of different characteristics. A screenshot of the filter item parameters is shown in Figure 8.7.

The Display parameters are again standard. Under the Internal Display heading, we have an option to change the number of columns characteristics are arranged into within the filter pane. The Max No. of Summary Characters parameter controls the maximum length of the filter summary field (defaults to 20 characters), and the Has Button Row setting determines if the filter pane includes a row of buttons.

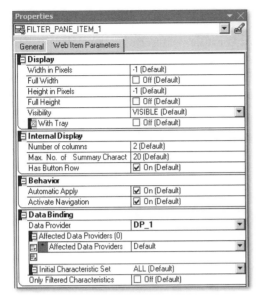

Figure 8.7 Filter Pane Item Parameters

The next setting, AUTOMATIC APPLY, is under the BEHAVIOR heading. By default, the filter pane automatically makes changes when filter values are selected. If unchecked, the filter pane will not make any changes until you click the Apply icon. Note that this setting may not be supported on all versions of BW 7.

The filter pane item is assigned to a DataProvider to load the list of characteristics (based on the first setting under the DATA BINDING header). You can add one or more DataProviders to the AFFECTED DATA PROVIDERS list to make a single filter pane change the navigational state for multiple analysis grids or charts.

The INITIAL CHARACTERISTIC SET parameter controls which characteristics are displayed in the filter pane. The default value shows all characteristics, but you can change the setting to show no characteristics; show only certain specified characteristics (List of Characteristics); or show only rows, columns, or free characteristics (Axes Selections).

Finally, the ONLY FILTERED CHARACTERISTICS option, disabled by default, will display only characteristics that already have a filter value in the filter pane.

8.1.7 Button Group Item

The button group item is one of the most versatile web items, as it can display any number of buttons that can perform a wide variety of commands from the BW Web API. However, other than the assignment of buttons the button group web item itself doesn't have too many parameters.

The only settings specific to this web item are the button width option, which allows you to specify a fixed width for all buttons or leave the default of 0 to automatically determine button width, and the list of buttons. Figure 8.8 shows the button group item parameters.

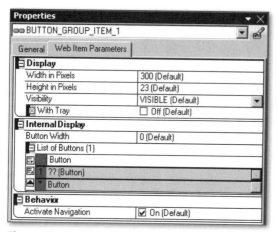

Figure 8.8 Button Group Item Parameters

Once you select a button itself, you can specify the text displayed on the button (the Caption field), a tooltip to be displayed when the mouse is hovering over the button (Quick Info), and an icon. You can also enable or disable the button and modify the button's design.

The Action field is where you enter a command from the command wizard. You can enter another command if you enable the With Release Action setting, which makes the button "stick" in the pressed position when clicked. A second click executes the release action. Finally, you can enable the Execute with Enter setting to fire the button when the user presses Enter .

8.1.8 Dropdown Item

The dropdown item (also known as dropdown box or dropdown menu) is another example of a versatile web item with only a few parameters. The only parameters specific to this web item are MAXIMUM LENGTH OF THE TEXT, which sets a maximum length for each item on the dropdown menu, MAXIMUM NUMBER OF DISPLAYED VALUES (self-explanatory), and DATA BINDING TYPE. The properties screen for this web item is shown in Figure 8.9.

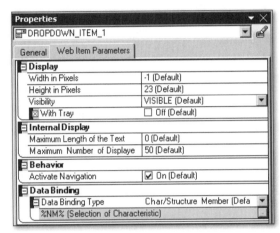

Figure 8.9 Dropdown Item Parameters

The DATA BINDING TYPE parameter has several different settings, explained in Table 8.4.

Char/Structure Member (Default) — see Figure 8.10	Displays the values from a specific characteristic or structure; selecting a value will automatically create a filter for that value. Allows the attachment of an additional action that can be executed before, after, or instead of filtering on the selected value.
Query View Selection	Can display a specific list of query views or show all query views assigned to the query associated with the selected DataProvider. Allows the attachment of an additional action to be executed after the new query view is applied to the web application.
Fixed List of Options	Each item in the dropdown is set up separately to independently execute commands.

Table 8.4 Data Binding Type Parameters

Fixed List of Options: Manual Update	Each item in the dropdown is set up separately to independently execute commands, with the update occurring manually instead of automatically.
Variable Selection	A variable is selected, and the dropdown displays all possible values of that variable.

Table 8.4 Data Binding Type Parameters (Cont.)

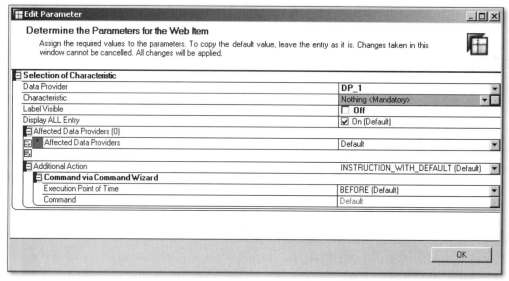

Figure 8.10 Char/Structure Member Parameters

8.1.9   Radio Button and Checkbox Group Items

The next two web items, radio button group and checkbox group, are almost identical except for one major difference: only one value at a time can be selected in a radio button group, while multiple values can be selected in a checkbox group. Both web items are populated by the available values in a specified characteristic or structure. When a user selects one or more of these values and clicks the Apply button, the selected values are created as a filter against the relevant characteristic.

The first INTERNAL DISPLAY parameter for both web items controls whether or not a label is visible at the top of the radio button or checkbox group item. This label corresponds with the description of the characteristic selected. You can also specify a maximum length for each characteristic value and the maximum number of values displayed in the web item.

There is one parameter specific to the radio button group: the DISPLAY ALL ENTRY setting. When checked — the default setting — an ALL item will be displayed along with the characteristic values in the radio button group. Because radio buttons cannot be unselected without choosing another option, the ALL item provides a way for the user to clear their selection. If ALL is selected when the Apply button is clicked, the filter value for the characteristic will be removed.

The next setting controls how many columns the characteristic values in either web item are arranged into. Looking under the DATA BINDING section, we see the familiar DATA PROVIDER and AFFECTED DATA PROVIDERS setting, along with a CHARACTERISTIC drop down that allows us to select which characteristic's values will be displayed in the radio button group or checkbox group.

Screenshots of the properties for these two web items are shown in Figures 8.11 and 8.12.

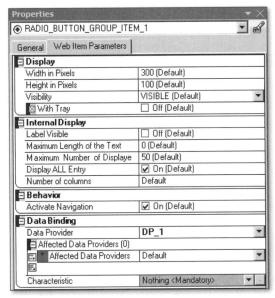

Figure 8.11 Radio Button Group Item Parameters

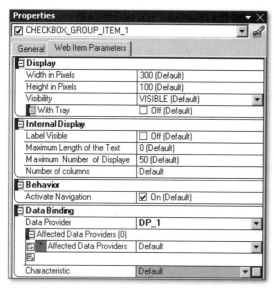

Figure 8.12 Checkbox Group Item Parameters

8.1.10 List Box Item

The list box item is again quite similar to the radio button and checkbox group items discussed in the previous section. As with the radio button and checkbox group items, the list box item displays the available values for a specific characteristic, but it does so in a scrolling list. The height of the scrolling list, and the number of items displayed at one time, is set by the VISIBLE_ITEMS parameter.

The INTERNAL DISPLAY settings are the same as those available in the radio button item, except there is no option to show values in multiple columns.

The parameters for this web item are shown in Figure 8.13.

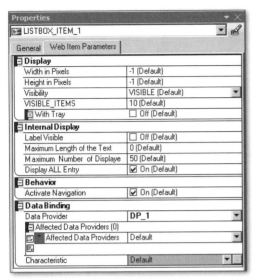

Figure 8.13 List Box Item Parameters

8.1.11 Hierarchical Filter Item

The hierarchical filter item PROPERTIES screen provides an easy way for the user to navigate the display hierarchy for a characteristic and set up filter values for hierarchy nodes or individual values in the hierarchy (see Figure 8.14). The selected characteristic can be displayed at the top of the web item by checking the LABEL VISIBLE setting.

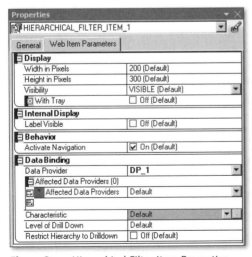

Figure 8.14 Hierarchical Filter Item Properties

As with the previous web items, you must select which characteristic will be shown. The hierarchy shown in the web item will depend on which display hierarchy is assigned to the characteristic in the query definition.

8.2 Advanced Web Items

The next category of web items falls under the ADVANCED heading, as seen in Figure 8.15. Unlike the STANDARD web items, which mostly deal with displaying data and navigating within DataProviders, the ADVANCED web items are primarily used to arrange other web items and provide functionality at the web application level instead of at the DataProvider level.

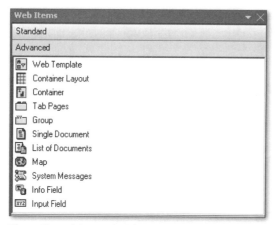

Figure 8.15   Advanced Web Items

8.2.1   Web Template Item

The web template web item is probably the simplest web item to configure, but it also offers quite a bit of flexibility. There is only one parameter for the web template item: you specify another web template to be embedded in the current web template.

When a web application containing a web template item is rendered in the browser, the contents of the specified web template are handled as if they existed in the master template, as opposed to HTML frame tags, which create pages within pages.

Figure 8.16 shows the properties for the web template item. In this example, the contents of the web template 0ANALYSIS_PATTERN_HEADER will be included in the host web application based on the placement of the web template item.

This item is often used to create headers or footers that are shared across several web templates. By allowing multiple templates to use a single header template, maintenance of the header becomes more efficient.

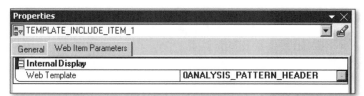

Figure 8.16   Web Template Web Item Properties

8.2.2   Container Layout Item

Next, we have the container layout, a commonly used web item that can arrange web items into a grid of rows and columns. The container layout item was discussed in detail in Chapter 7, Section 7.3.2 Arranging Web Items, but we will go over the available web item properties here, as seen in Figure 8.17.

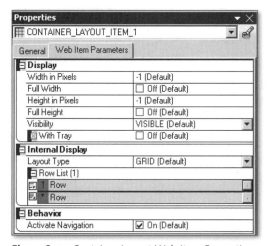

Figure 8.17   Container Layout Web Item Properties

The container layout includes the standard display properties seen in most other web items. The LAYOUT TYPE parameter in the INTERNAL DISPLAY section allows you to change the layout type from GRID, the default setting, to Row Cells Floating or Column Cells Floating. This setting can be useful when web items are assigned to multiple rows — with the default setting, the entire container layout functions as a single HTML table, and all web items are lined up both horizontally and vertically.

If the container layout is changed to Row Cells Floating, each row will be set up as an independent HTML table, so web items within each row are lined up, but web items between rows do not have to be aligned. The Column Cells Floating setting causes each column to be rendered as a separate HTML table with similar results as the previous setting, except within columns instead of within rows. Figure 7.26 further illustrates the differences between these settings.

Clicking on the Value Help button for each Row in the container layout web item properties opens up a new window showing all of the columns in that row. Any number of columns within the row can be assigned to a Subordinate Web Item, meaning the web item specified will be displayed in that column within the selected row. Note that a web item must be dragged within the container layout before it can be selected as a subordinate web item.

For each cell (a column within a row), you can manually specify the width and height, and the rowspan and colspan parameters, which can make the cell span multiple rows or columns within the container layout. You can also indicate where you want the web item to appear vertically or horizontally within the cell: top and left alignment is set by choosing the Beginning setting for Vertical Alignment and Horizontal Alignment, respectively. The Center setting will place the web item in the middle of the cell, and the End setting represents bottom and right alignment.

As with other items, the Allow Navigation checkbox will prevent users from interacting with the container layout item (for example, if the container layout item was set up within a tray).

8.2.3   Container Item

As with the container layout, the container web item can hold other web items, but it does not allow for specifying where each web item appears. A container item is typically used when specifying web item arrangement is not important — each web item inside the container will be displayed sequentially, with line breaks separating each one — or in a situation where only one web item within the container will be displayed at any given time.

The container item can also be used to encapsulate HTML code for inclusion in other web items such as container layouts or tab pages. If you enter the code within the container item, the results of the code will only be visible where the container web item is shown.

There are no special parameters available for container web items other than the standard display parameters and the ACTIVATE NAVIGATION setting (see Figure 8.18).

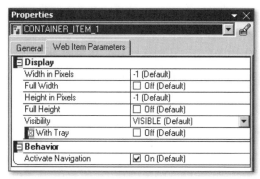

Figure 8.18   Container Web Item Properties

8.2.4   Tab Pages Item

The tab pages item — also known as a tab strip — is essentially a single row version of a container layout item that only displays a single cell at a time. Each cell in the tab pages item is assigned a specific tab, and the user can switch between cells by clicking on the associated tab. See Figure 8.19 for the available properties, and Chapter 7, Section 7.5.5, for a more detailed discussion of this web item.

After the standard display options, the INITIAL TAB INDEX setting under INTERNAL DISPLAY controls which tab is shown initially. The default setting of 1 means that the first tab is visible when the web application is run (assuming the tab pages item itself is visible).

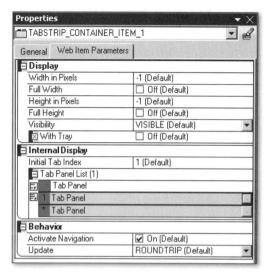

Figure 8.19 Tab Pages Web Item Properties

Each item in the TAB PANEL list represents a single cell assigned to a subordinate web item and a tab associated with that cell. Clicking on the value help button next to any TAB PANEL field will allow the user to change the settings for that cell/tab. The Caption setting changes what is displayed on the tab; an icon can also be added.

You can also set up commands using the command wizard under the Activation Action and Deactivation Action settings. A command set up under the former setting will fire when a user clicks on that tab, and one created under the latter setting will be executed when the user switches from that tab to a different tab. When a user changes tabs, the command in Deactivation Action on the source tab is executed before the Activation Action in the destination tab.

The final setting within the parameters screen for each tab panel field is Subordinate Web Item, where you can assign which web item will be under which tab. As with the container layout, the subordinate web item must be within the tab pages item in the Web application designer Layout tab.

Going back to the main properties pane for the tab pages item, the final setting, Update, controls whether switching tabs triggers an active update on the server (Roundtrip) or happens passively on the client.

8.2.5 Group Item

The group item is a specialized container layout with a predefined visual style that can include a maximum of three subordinate web items on three separate rows. Group items often include a container or container layout (or another group) as the "main" web item on the bottom row, while the top two rows (Caption and Toolbar) contain text descriptions and buttons.

We saw an example in Chapter 7, Sections 7.4.2, Creating and Populating a Header, and 7.4.3, Putting It All Together in a Group, of the group item being used to show a toolbar as the "main" web item and a number of text elements in the "toolbar" item (see Figure 7.40 for an illustration). This example shows that a toolbar does not necessarily have to be assigned to the Toolbar section of the group item.

Looking at the web item properties in Figure 8.20, we again see the standard display settings. One additional parameter is available in the group item, however: CONTENT PADDING. When enabled, this setting will add space around the subordinate web item in each section, allowing more of the visual background applied to each section of the group item to be visible.

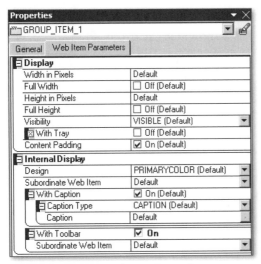

Figure 8.20 Group Web Item Properties

The DESIGN parameter under the INTERNAL DISPLAY section allows you to change the visual style applied to the group item. The first SUBORDINATE WEB ITEM parameter refers to the "main" section of the group item, shown as the last row in the group item if the caption or toolbar are enabled.

315

The next checkbox, WITH CAPTION, controls the visibility of the CAPTION section, the first row in the group item. The caption section can contain plain text (CAPTION TYPE CAPTION, the default setting) or another subordinate web item. The WITH TOOLBAR setting works similarly to WITH CAPTION, except the only option in the toolbar section is to display a subordinate web item.

The WITH CAPTION and WITH TOOLBAR settings are independent, and a group item may only have a main section, a main section with a caption and toolbar, a main section with only a caption, or a main section with only a toolbar. As with other web items discussed previously, a web item must be within the group item on the Layout tab to be assigned as a subordinate web item.

8.2.6 Single Document and List of Documents

The single document and list of documents web items both involve displaying BI documents that have been created and attached to master data, metadata, or Info-Provider data (see Chapter 4, Section 4.7.9, for more information).

Looking at the single document item first (Figure 8.21), after the standard display settings, you can specify the maximum number of lines to be displayed for textual documents, and a default Knowledge Management (KM) document to be displayed if no document is found for the current DataProvider navigational state.

When checked, the DISPLAY WITHIN WEB APPLICATION will show the contents of the document within the web application. If unchecked, a link to the document will be shown instead of the document itself. The next setting, DISPLAY DOCUMENT LIST ITEMS, controls whether or not the list of documents web item is displayed if multiple documents can potentially be displayed. Additional properties for the document, such as who created the document and when it was last modified, can be displayed as well.

The BEHAVIOR parameters control whether the web item can be maintained, whether BI documents can be edited or are displayed read-only, and whether documents from the list of documents web item can be dragged to the single documents web item to be displayed.

As with other web items, a DataProvider must be assigned, as the display of BI documents is dependent on the data being shown in the DataProvider. The DOCUMENT CLASS setting can select between displaying InfoProvider documents (MULTI), master data documents (Reference/CHARACTERISTIC), or metadata

(BW_OBJECT). For the last two options, you need to select a characteristic or meta object to display the relevant BI documents.

If multiple document types are used for a specific InfoProvider, characteristic, or meta object, you can use the DOCUMENT TYPE setting to only show a specific type. For example, if both picture and description documents are available for a certain characteristic, you can create one single document web item to display the picture and another single document web item to show the description by changing the DOCUMENT TYPE setting for each.

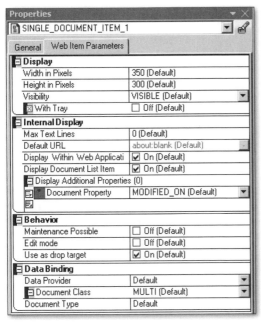

Figure 8.21 Single Document Web Item Parameters

While the single document web item displays actual documents (or a link to a single document), the list of documents web item will display a list of all BI documents that are relevant to the current context of the web application in a tabular format.

The properties of this web item are seen in Figure 8.22. In the INTERNAL DISPLAY section, the format of the table can be specified, including which columns to display (document name, author, etc.), how many documents are shown per page, and whether or not to display a table header.

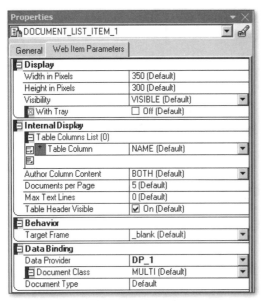

Figure 8.22 List of Documents Web Item Parameters

The TARGET FRAME option under the BEHAVIOR heading will open documents in a new page by default (_blank). Other options include showing the document in the same frame (replacing the web application) or using the whole page (replacing the entire portal environment the web application is running in). The options in the DATA BINDING section are the same as for the single documents web item.

8.2.7 Map Item

The map item utilizes the BEx Map feature to display data in a map-based format. BEx Map functionality is not covered in this book, but the properties screen for the map item is shown in Figure 8.23 for your reference. The properties for this item primarily involve which map layers to display, settings relating to captions, legends, map extents, projections (flat or Mercator), and the visibility of cartography information.

The last setting under the BEHAVIOR section, GEO-FUNCTIONS, controls whether or not to display the geo functions bar (with map-specific features) in the web item.

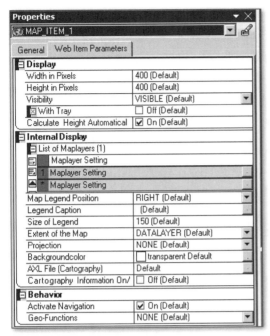

Figure 8.23 Map Item Properties

8.2.8 System Messages Item

The system messages web item is relatively straightforward: it displays any messages (information, warnings, or errors) generated by the BW system. The only options available for this web item are a subset of the standard display properties and the ACTIVATE NAVIGATION option. See Figure 8.24 for a screenshot of the properties for this web item.

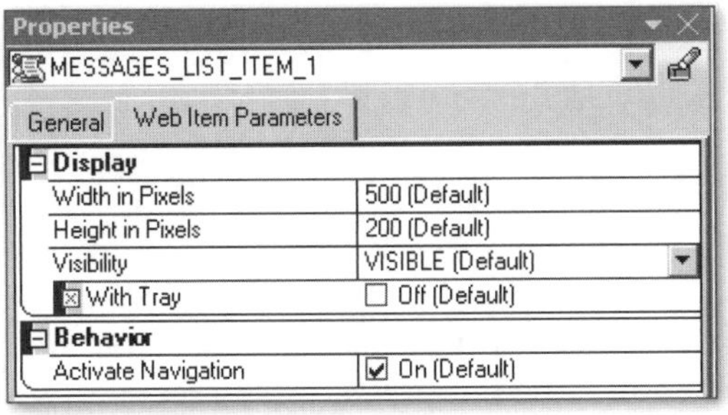

Figure 8.24 System Messages Item Properties

8.2.9 Info Field Item

The info field web item can be used to display a variety of different pieces of information, from text elements associated with the web application to variable and filter values from the DataProvider. The parameters of this web item are shown in Figure 8.25.

Under the INTERNAL DISPLAY heading, the first setting controls whether or not the web item shows headers. The ONLY_VALUES setting will only display the unformatted value of the item shown, without any descriptions.

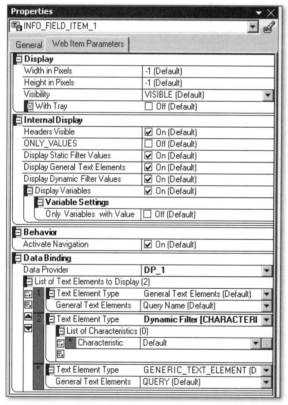

Figure 8.25 Info Field Web Item Parameters

The remaining checkboxes under the INTERNAL DISPLAY heading will determine which information is shown in the web item. You can show static filter values (according to the Filters tab in Query Designer), general text elements (meta information about the web application), dynamic filter values (as specified at query runtime), or variables. If you check the ONLY VARIABLES WITH VALUE checkbox, variables that do not have a default value and have not been populated by the user will not appear in the info field item.

If you only want certain elements to be displayed, you can add them to the list under the DATA BINDING section. If you do not populate this list, all elements of the types checked in the INTERNAL DISPLAY heading will be displayed.

In the screenshot in Figure 8.25, you can see the different options in the LIST OF TEXT ELEMENTS TO DISPLAY for different types of elements. For example, if you select GENERAL TEXT ELEMENTS, you must choose a text element in the next dropdown box. Choosing DYNAMIC FILTER as a text element type requires you to select which characteristic to display dynamic filters for. A list of general text elements can be found in Chapter 6, Section 6.7.2, Constant Text Elements.

8.2.10 Input Field Item

The input field item is often used for BI integrated planning web applications to enter plan values, but it can also be used to allow users to filter by typing in a field directly in the web application. For example, the Set Variable Values command includes a parameter that will read data from an input field item and apply it to a variable.

The input field web item properties are shown in Figure 8.26. The TEXT setting under INTERNAL DISPLAY specifies the default text displayed in the web item, and the TEXT ALIGNMENT setting will show that text aligned to the left (BEGIN), center, or right (END) of the web item.

You can also specify whether a label will be visible next to the input field, and what that label should say. The QUICK INFO setting determines the text of the tooltip for the web item, displayed when the mouse hovers over the input field.

Aside from the standard ACTIVATE NAVIGATION setting that determines whether user interaction is allowed, the input field can be set as inactive by unchecking the ENABLED box. The last two settings can only specify numeric input and determine whether an empty value is allowed.

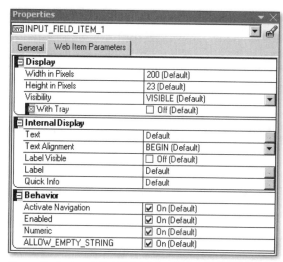

Figure 8.26 Input Field Web Item Parameters

8.3 Miscellaneous Web Items

The next group of web items is clustered under the MISCELLANEOUS heading, as seen in Figure 8.27.

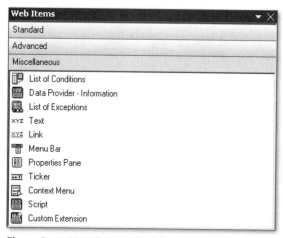

Figure 8.27 Miscellaneous Web Items

8.3.1 List of Conditions Item

The first miscellaneous web item is the list of conditions item, which displays all available conditions associated with the selected DataProvider, along with the status of each condition. Next to each condition, a button is available allowing the user to toggle the condition's state between active and inactive.

Conditions are used to restrict the display of information based on key figures, much like filters are used to set up restrictions on characteristic values. For example, a condition can be set up to hide all rows where a specific key figure value is above or below a certain amount. Conditions are defined in Query Designer.

The parameters for this web item are shown in Figure 8.28. Other than the standard settings available for most other web items, there are no properties specific to this web item's functionality.

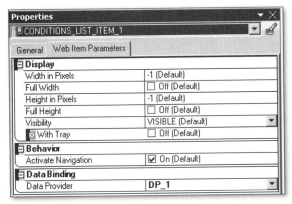

Figure 8.28 List of Conditions Web Item Parameters

8.3.2 List of Exceptions Item

The list of exceptions item, the third web item in the miscellaneous section, displays the exceptions that have been set up for the query in Query Designer. See Figure 8.29 for this web item's parameters.

As with the list of conditions, only generic parameters are available for this web item. The list of exceptions item displays all exceptions defined in the query associated with the selected DataProvider, along with a button next to each exception to toggle the state between active and inactive.

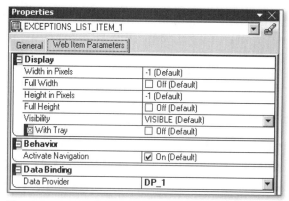

Figure 8.29 List of Exceptions Web Item Parameters

Like conditions, exceptions also are defined based on data in key figures, but exceptions are used to highlight data with different colors instead of hiding the restricted data.

8.3.3 Data Provider — Information Item

The data provider — information web item is different from most other web items in that the results of the web item are not displayed to the user in the web application. This web item generates XML code that is shown in the source text of the web application.

Based on the parameters for this web item (shown in Figure 8.30), you can output the navigational state of the DataProvider and the query results.

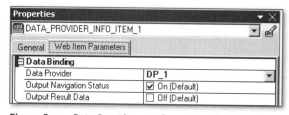

Figure 8.30 Data Provider — Information Web Item Parameters

8.3.4 Text Item

The text web item can be used to display simple text strings, characteristic names, or text elements. Unlike the info field item, the text item can only display one value. You can see the parameters for this web item in Figure 8.31.

The INTERNAL DISPLAY settings determine the text item's tooltip, text color, and design. You can also choose whether or not to enable text wrapping or display the text without formatting.

To select the text this web item should display, you need to choose a category from the TEXT BINDING dropdown. You can choose SIMPLE TEXT, Characteristic (choose a DataProvider and characteristic to display from the new settings that appear), or General Text Elements. Refer to Chapter 6, Section 6.7.2, for a list of text elements.

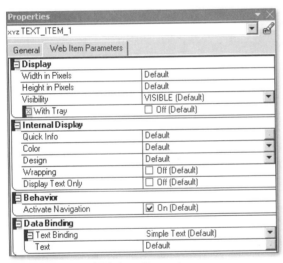

Figure 8.31 Text Web Item Parameters

8.3.5 Link Item

The link web item is very similar to an individual button within the button group item seen in Section 8.1.7, Button Group Item — the main difference is that the command assigned to this web item is executed by clicking on a hyperlink instead of a button.

The parameters for this web item, seen in Figure 8.32, control the appearance of the text link (under the INTERNAL DISPLAY heading) and which command is executed (under the BEHAVIOR setting). You can build a command using the command wizard, or specify a script function to run.

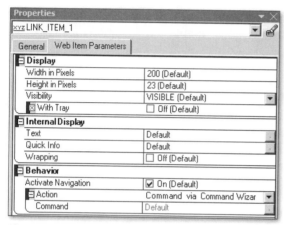

Figure 8.32 Link Web Item Parameters

8.3.6 Menu Bar Item

Another web item that can be used to execute commands is the menu bar item. A menu bar is typically used when it is necessary to allow the user access to a number of related commands in a small amount of space. See the menu bar item parameters in Figure 8.33.

The only parameter directly related to menu bar functionality is the MENU BAR list under the INTERNAL DISPLAY heading. Each item in this list corresponds to a top-level menu, which can be a submenu of other items (GROUPING OF MENU ENTRIES) or act as a button within the menu bar, executing a command when clicked (TRIGGER AN ACTION).

If you click on the Value Help button for a GROUPING OF MENU ENTRIES menu item, you will see the EDIT PARAMETERS screen in Figure 8.34. Much like with a button group, this screen allows you to set up a number of different options, each of which executes its own command. There is one setting here we haven't seen before: if the DISPLAY SEPARATOR ABOVE option is checked, a separator line will appear at the top part of the menu.

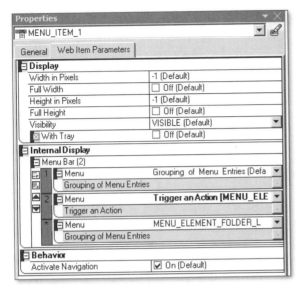

Figure 8.33 Menu Bar Web Item Parameters

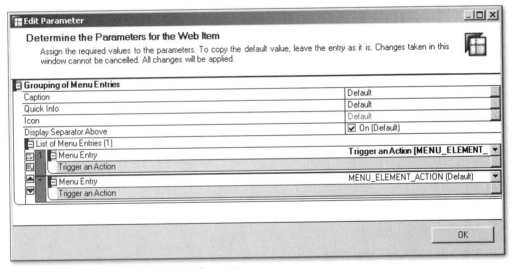

Figure 8.34 Grouping of Menu Entries Parameters

For each entry in the menu, you will need to set the TRIGGER AN ACTION parameters by clicking the value help button on the right side of the field. The resulting screen looks like Figure 8.35.

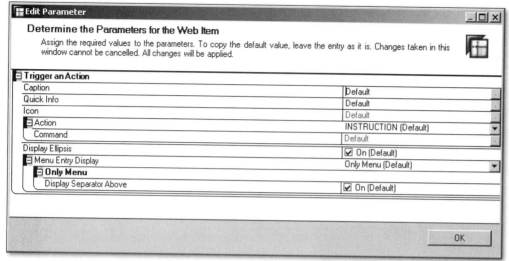

Figure 8.35 Trigger an Action Parameters

Aside from the CAPTION, QUICK INFO (tooltip), and ICON settings we've seen before, you need to specify the type of action: either using the command wizard (INSTRUCTION) or a script function. The command wizard can be launched by clicking the value help button next to the COMMAND field.

Under the COMMAND field, there is a DISPLAY ELLIPSIS option. When checked, this option will display "..." (an ellipsis) after the menu item. An ellipsis is typically used to indicate that a menu option will prompt the user for additional parameters before the command is finally executed.

The final section of this parameters screen controls the display of the menu item itself. You can choose to show the item only within the menu, on the toolbar itself, or both. Selecting any of these options allows you to choose whether or not you want to display a separator bar in the menu, toolbar, or both.

8.3.7 Properties Pane Item

Next up is the properties pane web item. Not to be confused with the Properties screen within the WAD main workspace, this web item will allow the user to change certain properties of specific web items or DataProviders at runtime. The settings for this web item are displayed in Figure 8.36.

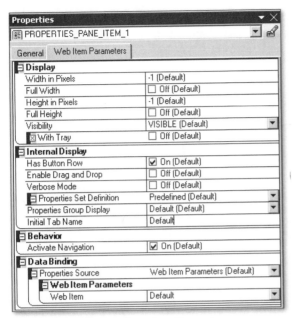

Figure 8.36   Properties Pane Item Parameters

Starting with the INTERNAL DISPLAY settings, the HAS BUTTON ROW setting will display any buttons associated with the selected parameters in the web item. You can also enable or disable drag-and-drop functionality and VERBOSE MODE, which will display the technical name for all parameters.

The PROPERTIES SET DEFINITION setting allows you to choose which specific properties to display. The default value, PREDEFINED, will show the set of properties defined by SAP. You can change this to show all properties, a single group (the technical name of the properties group must be entered along with a description), a single value (again the technical name must be entered with a description), or a matrix layout. The matrix layout option lets you display a number of selected properties in table form.

The PROPERTIES GROUP DISPLAY setting allows you to group properties based on SAP's predefined grouping (the default value), by tab pages, or aligned under the group name (Headline). You can also specify the tab name that is displayed initially.

In the DATA BINDING section, we finally get to choose which type of properties to display. You can choose from the types of parameters in Table 8.5, some of which have additional settings.

Web Item Parameters	Requires selection of a web item, see the relevant section in this chapter, depending on web item chosen.
DataProvider Properties Conditions Exceptions	Requires selection of a DataProvider.
Axis Properties	Requires selection of a DataProvider and an axis (rows, columns, or free characteristics).
Characteristic Properties Characteristic Properties – Input Help Characteristic Properties – Filter Values	Requires selection of a DataProvider and a characteristic.
Properties of Structure Element	Requires selection of a DataProvider and a structure element.
Data Cell Properties	Requires selection of a DataProvider and two structure elements to specify a certain cell.
Properties of All Data Cells	Requires selection of a DataProvider.

Table 8.5 Types of Properties

8.3.8 Ticker Item

The ticker web item allows you to display data from a DataProvider as a moving ticker. Normally, this is not recommended, as most data sets are more easily interpreted by users in tabular or graphical form. The parameter screen for this web item is shown in Figure 8.37.

The options under INTERNAL DISPLAY control the width of characters on the ticker, whether or not the name of the query is shown as a caption, and if a separator is displayed between data records. In the BEHAVIOR section, you can also set a time delay before the ticker starts moving and the speed of the ticker — the number entered in the SPEED IN MILLISECONDS field reflects how many milliseconds the ticket is paused between each character.

Finally, you'll need to select a DataProvider. The query associated with this DataProvider will be broken down, record by record, and displayed in the ticker.

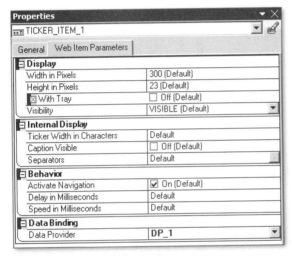

Figure 8.37 Ticker Web Item Parameters

8.3.9 Context Menu Item

Next we have the context menu web item — this web item is not displayed in the web application, it is only used to control which context menu items are displayed in the web application.

The only parameters in this web item (see Figure 8.38) are the context menu items themselves, each can be enabled or disabled independently. For more information on context menu functionality, see Chapter 4, Section 4.7, The Context Menu. Of particular interest is the LOCAL FORMULAS option at the bottom — this web item is the only way to enable this functionality, which is disabled by default. Chapter 4, Section 4.7.8, Calculations and Translations, has more about LOCAL FORMULAS.

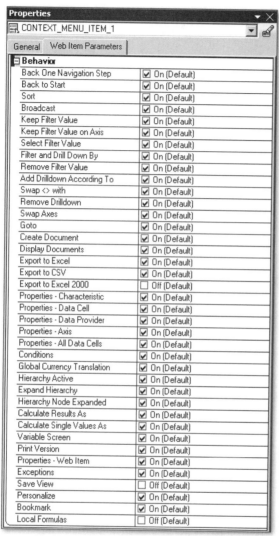

Figure 8.38 Context Menu Item Parameters

8.3.10 Script Item

JavaScript functionality can be embedded in web applications by using an include file uploaded to the MIME repository, or by entering the script directly into a script web item. The options for this web item (seen in Figure 8.39) allow you to select the script language, and enter the script itself by clicking the Value Help button next to the SCRIPT field.

Figure 8.39 Script Item Parameters

After clicking the value help button next to the Script field, a screen similar to Figure 8.40 is shown. The screenshot in Figure 8.40 shows JavaScript code that has already been populated by SAP in the default analysis pattern web template.

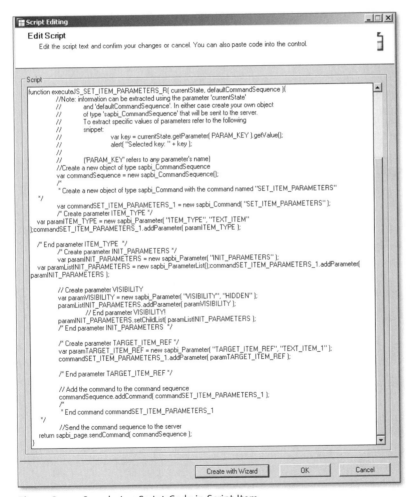

Figure 8.40 Sample JavaScript Code in Script Item

8.3.11 Custom Extension Item

While the script item allows the designer to insert JavaScript code into a web application, the custom extension item does the same with Advanced Business Application Programming (ABAP) code. Once you create an ABAP class, you can include it in this web item (see Figure 8.41 for properties). You can also choose whether or not to pass variable values to the ABAP class, and whether each customer exit can access the navigational state or the result set of the DataProvider.

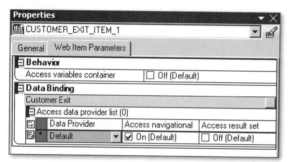

Figure 8.41 Custom Extension Item Parameters

8.4 DataProviders

The final section of the Web Items pane deals with creating DataProviders, which are discussed in greater detail in Chapter 6, Section 6.2.1, DataProviders. There are two types of DataProviders: Query View DataProviders, which return a set of characteristics and key figures based on an existing InfoProvider, query, or view; and Filter DataProviders, which only return characteristics without key figures. The DataProvider section of the Web Items pane allows you to create either type of DataProvider.

When creating a Filter DataProvider, you will see the screen in Figure 8.42. If connecting to an external system using XMLA or OLE DB for OLAP (ODBO), enter the system alias (as defined by the portal landscape) in the System field. You can also specify a "start state" for the DataProvider, based on a query, InfoProvider, predefined filter, or filter view. Another option is a Property List, which can be entered manually.

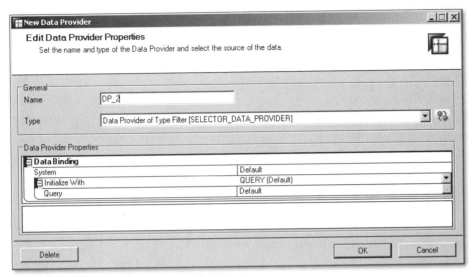

Figure 8.42   Filter DataProvider Parameters

The properties screen for a Query View DataProvider has two views: a simple view (as in Figure 8.43, shown by default) and a detailed view, which is more similar to Figure 8.42. You can switch between these views by clicking the Green and Red icon next to the TYPE dropdown.

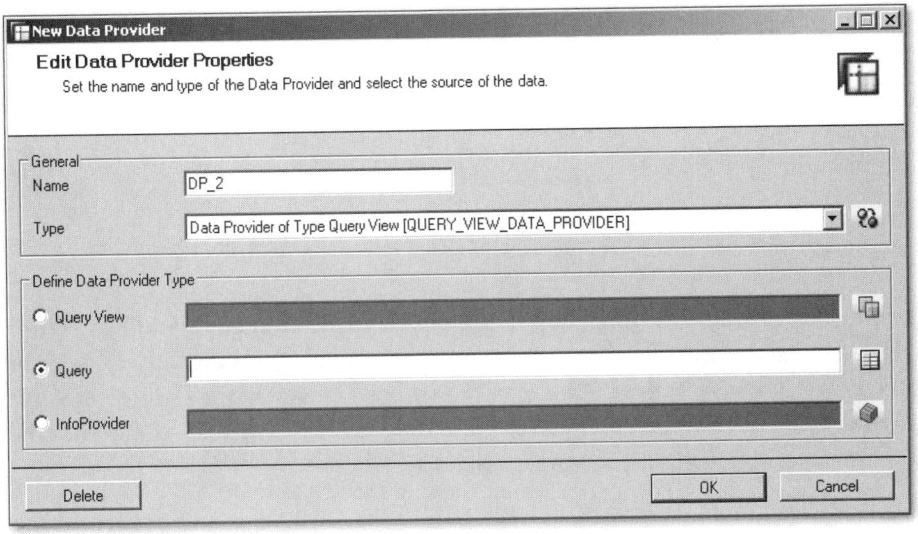

Figure 8.43   Query View DataProvider Parameters

In the simple view, you can choose between a query view, query, or InfoProvider as the starting point of the DataProvider.

8.5 Menu Bar Functionality

The WAD menu bar has some useful functionality available. Most of the menu options are relatively self-explanatory, but there are a few items that bear further discussion.

8.5.1 HTML Tables

We saw in the overview of the SAP-delivered Analysis Pattern template that HTML tables were sometimes used to align web items. To add an HTML table to a web application, you can either select the INSERT TABLE command from the Table menu, or you can utilize the context menu, as seen in Figure 8.44.

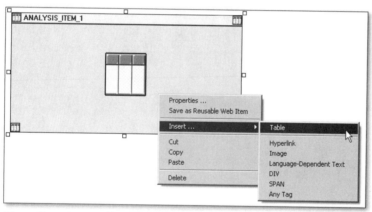

Figure 8.44 Insert Table Command from Context Menu

To the end user, a web application that has web items arranged within an HTML table is indistinguishable from a web application that uses a container layout to specify web item placement. The only difference is maintenance: to move items around within an HTML table, you need to drag them to a specific cell within the Layout tab of the main WAD workspace.

When adding a table, a screen like the one in Figure 8.45 is displayed. You can specify the number of header rows, and the table's width and height, and the number of rows and columns. The table will be displayed directly in the Layout tab in a light gray color.

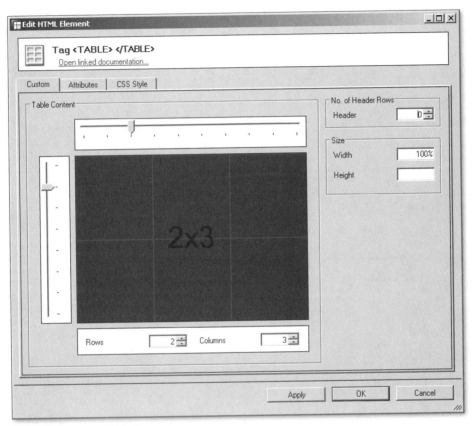

Figure 8.45   Insert Table Parameters

The table menu also allows you to insert and delete rows and columns after the table has been created. You can also merge and split individual cells.

8.5.2   Adding Images

You may have noticed that there are no web items for adding images such as corporate logos or branding elements. To add an image to a web application, click the Insert menu and select the Image option. (You can also add hyperlinks, language-dependent text, and other HTML tags directly to the web application).

The properties box for a new image looks like Figure 8.46. You can specify the image source using a URL, either via HTTP from a web server or from the MIME Repository (as seen in Figure 8.46). Alternate text to be displayed if the image is unavailable can also be set here, and the alignment of the image, border thickness, and spacing.

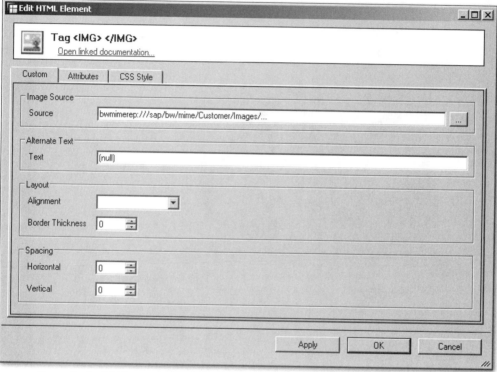

Figure 8.46   Add New Image

8.6   Web Template Properties

Next, we will examine the properties of the web template itself. An easy way to display the web template properties is to click the dropdown box at the top of the Properties pane and scroll up to the very top. The available web template parameters are displayed in Figure 8.47.

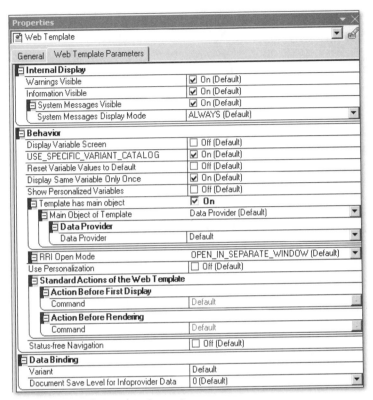

Figure 8.47 Web Template Parameters

Starting with the INTERNAL DISPLAY section, we can choose whether or not to show warnings, informational messages, or system messages in the web application. You can also choose to always display system messages, or only display a particular message once per day.

In the BEHAVIOR section, the DISPLAY VARIABLE SCREEN setting can force the variable screen to be displayed initially when the web application is run (assuming the queries associated with the web application's DataProviders have input-ready variables). Note that the variable screen will still be displayed initially — regardless of this setting — if there are required variables that do not have default values.

The next setting permits the web application to utilize the variant catalog, allowing users to save and load variants within the variable screen for queries. You can also choose to reset the variable values to their default setting as defined in the variable definition.

The DISPLAY SAME VARIABLE ONLY ONCE setting is useful when there are multiple DataProviders associated with different queries, each of which with their own set of variables. If the same variable appears multiple times in the different queries, that variable will only be displayed once in the variable screen of the web application. If you uncheck this setting, the common variable will be displayed once for each query. See Chapter 6, Section 6.2.4, Adding New Analysis Grids, for more information.

When checked, the SHOW PERSONALIZED VARIABLES option will display personalized variables by default in the variable screen. See Chapter 4, Section 4.1, The Variable Screen: Personalization and Variants, for more information about personalization.

You can also choose whether or not the web template has a "main object," which can be a DataProvider or a web item. The main object setting can be used to personalize generic web templates, and the text web item can display properties on the main object of the template.

If the query associated with a DataProvider in the web application utilizes the report-report interface (RRI) feature, the next setting will determine how to launch the jump target. The default option is to open the jump target in a new generic window, but you can also have the jump target replace the current web application, replace the top frame (overwriting the portal framework), open in a window with a specific name, or replace a named frame.

The USE PERSONALIZATION option, when checked, will utilize a personalized web template. The next section, STANDARD ACTIONS OF THE WEB TEMPLATE, allows you to specify a command sequence to be run before the web application is initially run (Before First Display) and before the web application is refreshed (Before Rendering).

The STATUS-FREE NAVIGATION setting is next. When enabled, this option utilizes stateless navigational, which removes the status of the web application from the server after each navigational step. This option frees up more memory on the server and can improve the efficiency of a system with many concurrent users. However, the tradeoff of stateless navigation is that it increases the CPU load, as additional steps must be performed to remove the status after each navigational step.

The last two options, under the DATA BINDING heading, are used to specify a variant for the web application and to change the save level for BI documents. The latter setting has two options: BI documents can be saved at the query level (0) or at the InfoProvider level (1). If users will be saving BI documents in your web applications and you'd like those documents to be available to all queries based on the InfoProvider, you'll want to change this setting to InfoProvider level (1).

8.7 BW Web API Commands

We now move on to the BW Web API, which is implemented in WAD as the command wizard. There are four basic categories of commands in the command wizard: DataProvider commands, planning, web item–specific, and commands that apply to the web template itself. DataProvider commands are in turn divided into several subcategories.

This section will take a look at the commands available in the wizard, category by category. The DataProvider command category will be broken up by subcategory. Each command will be accompanied by a short description of what the command does, including parameters that must be specified.

Call DataProvider Properties Dialog	Opens the properties dialog box for the specified DataProvider.
RRI	Executes an RRI jump from the specified cell in the specified DataProvider to the specified RRI receiver ID (in Transaction RSBBS). The cell can be specified by a data row and data column; or by a row OR column AND a characteristic.
Set DataProvider Parameters	Creates a new DataProvider. For parameters see Section 8.4, DataProviders.
Set Zero Value Display	Change how zeros are displayed in the specified DataProvider. Zeros can be shown with or without currency/unit, as a space, or as custom text.
Set Sign Display	Change how negative values are displayed: with a minus sign before or after the number, or the number in parentheses.
Back to Initial State	Restores one or more specified DataProviders to their initial state.
Back to Previous State	Undoes the last navigation step in one or more specified DataProviders.

Table 8.6 Basic DataProvider Commands

Translate Currency	Specifies a new currency translation type and target currency for one or more specified DataProviders.
Export Data Provider as XML	Exports the specified DataProvider (navigational state or result data) as XML, redirected to a specified URL.

Table 8.6   Basic DataProvider Commands (Cont.)

Set Hierarchical Display of Axis	Changes whether or not the columns or rows of a specified DataProvider are displayed hierarchically.
Set Position of Results Row	Changes the location of results rows for the rows or columns of a specified DataProvider; can be top/left (TOP) or bottom/right (BOTTOM).
Swap Axes	Moves all characteristics and structures drilled down in the rows of one or more specified DataProviders to the columns, and vice versa.
Remove Drilldown	Moves a specified characteristic in one or more specified DataProviders from the rows or columns to free characteristics.
Drill Down a Characteristic	For one or more specified DataProviders, moves a specified characteristic to the rows, columns, or free characteristics. The position on the axis is determined by selecting a parent characteristic or specifying an index number (the first characteristic in the axis is "1").
Exchange Characteristics/ Structures	For one or more specified DataProviders, swaps one specified characteristic or structure with a second specified characteristic or structure.

Table 8.7   DataProvider Commands for Axes

Set Display Attributes	Changes which display attributes are shown for a specified characteristic in one or more specified DataProviders.
Set Presentation	Changes how display attributes are displayed for one or more specified DataProviders; options include short text, long text ,display key, etc.
Display Results Row	Toggles the display of results rows for a specified characteristic in one or more specified DataProviders; results rows can be always visible, always hidden, or displayed with more than one value (Conditional).
Set Sorting	Changes sorting type and direction for specified characteristic in one or more specified DataProviders.

Table 8.8   DataProvider Commands for Characteristics

Set Condition	Creates or changes a condition based on the specified data cell restrictions.
Set Status of a Condition	Changes a specified condition in one or more specified DataProviders to a status of active or inactive. Can also be used to toggle the current status of the condition.
Set Exception	Creates or changes an exception based on the specified data cell restrictions and threshold values.
Set Status of an Exception	Changes a specified exception in one or more specified DataProviders to a status of active or inactive. Can also be used to toggle the current status of the exception.
Call Conditions Dialog	Opens the conditions dialog for a specified DataProvider and condition technical name.
Call Exceptions Dialog	Opens the exceptions dialog for a specified DataProvider and exception technical name.

Table 8.9 DataProvider Commands for Conditions/Exceptions

Set Data Cell Properties	For a specified data cell in one or more specified DataProviders, changes the decimal places, scaling factor, and emphasized status of the cell.
Set Local Calculations	For a specified data cell in one or more specified DataProviders, changes the criteria for calculating the cell's value. See Chapter 3, Section 3.5.5, Selection and Formula Properties, for more information.

Table 8.10 DataProvider Commands for Data Cells

Remove All Filter Values	Removes all filter values for one or more specified DataProviders.
Call Input Help Dialog	Opens the input help (value help) dialog box for the specified characteristic in a specified DataProvider.
Set Filter Values for a Characteristic	Sets a filter for a specified value, operator (equals, greater than, etc.), and sign (including or excluding) for a specified characteristic in one or more specified DataProviders.
Set Filter Values	Sets filters for a specified value, operator (equals, greater than, etc.), and sign (including or excluding) for a list of specified characteristics in one or more specified DataProviders.

Table 8.11 DataProvider Commands for Filter Values

Remove Filter Values for a Characteristic	Removes all filter values for a specified characteristic in one or more specified DataProviders.
Remove Filter Values for a List of Characteristic	Removes all filter values for a list of specified characteristics in one or more specified DataProviders.
Set Filter Values Using Different Sources	Sets filters based on a specified DataProvider selection, variable, or web item for a list of specified characteristics in one or more specified DataProviders.
Set Filter Values Using Filter	Sets filters based on a specified query, precreated filter, or property list, or web item for one or more specified DataProviders.

Table 8.11   DataProvider Commands for Filter Values (Cont.)

Set Hierarchy	Assigns a specified display hierarchy to a specified characteristic in one or more specified DataProviders. Can also change whether or not the display hierarchy is active.
Expand/Collapse Hierarchy Nodes	Changes the expanded/collapsed status of a specified hierarchy node in a specified characteristic in one or more specified DataProviders.
Set Node Alignment	Changes the direction of child nodes in the display hierarchy of a specified characteristic in one or more specified DataProviders (bottom/right or top/left).

Table 8.12   DataProvider Commands for Hierarchies

Call Open Dialog	Replaces the specified DataProvider with an existing query, query view, or InfoProvider as selected by the user in the Open dialog box.
Call Save Dialog	Saves the specified DataProvider as a query view or saves the entire web application as a portal KM document, based on the user's selection in the Save dialog box.
Save Query View	Saves the specified DataProvider as a query view with the specified technical name and description.

Table 8.13   DataProvider Commands for Open/Save Functions

Open Document Browser	Opens a dialog box that displays all BI documents of a specified document type and class for a specified DataProvider.
Open Dialog for New Document	Opens a dialog box for creating a new document based on the specified document type and class for a specified DataProvider.

Table 8.14 DataProviders Commands for Documents

This concludes the DataProvider commands, we will now move on to commands related to planning, web items, and the web template.

Refresh Data	Copies changed data from an input-ready query to the planning buffer.
Save Changed Data	Saves changes made to an input-ready query within a web application; after a successful check, the new data is written to the InfoProvider.
Reset Changed Data	Undoes the data changes made to an input-ready query within a web application. This command cannot undo data saved using the Save Changed Data command.
Set Data Entry Mode	Switches a specified DataProvider with an input-ready query between display mode and change mode.
Execute a Planning Function (Simple)	Triggers the execution of a specified planning function based on a specified Filter DataProvider.
Execute a Planning Function	Triggers the execution of a specified planning function based on specified selections for each characteristic.
Execute a Planning Sequence (Simple)	Triggers the execution of a specified planning sequence.

Table 8.15 Commands for Planning Applications

Call Chart Properties Dialog	Opens the properties dialog for a specified Chart web item.
Call Properties Dialog	Opens the properties dialog for a specified web item, DataProvider, condition, exception, characteristic, axis, data cell, or structure element.

Table 8.16 Commands for Web Items

Set Web Item Parameters	Changes the parameters of the specified web item. Using the Change Object Type checkbox, this command can also be used to change the type of web item.
Back to Initial State	Reverts one or more specified web items back to the initial state they were in when the web application was first run.
Back to Previous State	Undoes the last navigation step for one or more specified web items.
Set Status of Module	Activates or deactivates a specified module (see Modification parameter of Analysis web item) for a specified web item.

Table 8.16   Commands for Web Items (Cont.)

Save Bookmark	Creates a bookmark for the current web application with a specified title.
Load Bookmark	Loads the specified technical name of the bookmark, either overwriting the current web application or opening the bookmark in a new window.
Start Broadcaster	Calls BEx Broadcaster, passing the current navigational state of the web application, a specified DataProvider, or a report web item. Data can be broadcasted via email, to the portal, or to a printer.
Close Browser Window	Closes the current browser window.
Transfer State	Transfers the current navigational state of the web application, one or more specified DataProviders, or one or more specified web items to a new web application.
Set Variable Values	Sets specified variable values for the web application.
Open Variable Dialog	Opens the variable screen for the web application.
Export Web Application	Exports the specified web application (or a list of specified web items) to Excel, PDF, PCL, Postscript, Excel 2000, or CSV format. You can select fit to page options, paper size, orientation, header and footer options, and margins.
Change Web Template	Swaps the current web template with the specified web template, keeping existing DataProviders and web items.
Display Web Template as Modal Dialog	Opens the specified web template in a new window as a dialog box with specified width and height.

Table 8.17   Commands for Web Templates

Close Current Web Template Dialog with Cancel	Used in conjunction with Display Web Template as Modal Dialog: closes the previously opened dialog without applying changes to the original web template.
Close Current Web Template Dialog with OK	Used in conjunction with Display Web Template as Modal Dialog: closes the previously opened dialog, applying any changes made to the original web template.
Set Web Template	Launches the specified web template, either replacing the current web application or opening in a new window.
Back to Initial State	Undoes all changes made to the web application and restores it back to its initial state.
Back to Previous State	Undoes the last change made to the web application.
Delete Personalization	Removes the current personalization status for the web application.
Save Personalization	Personalizes the web application, assuming the Use Personalization parameter on the web template is set. This command essentially creates a bookmark behind the scenes that stores changes made to all aspects of the web application, and this bookmark is automatically loaded with the web application unless it is removed with the Delete Personalization command.

Table 8.17 Commands for Web Templates (Cont.)

8.8 Summary: Web Application Designer Reference

In this chapter, we covered a lot of ground by examining the different features of the WAD toolset. We looked at the different categories of web items, including standard web items that communicate with DataProviders, advanced web items used for arranging other items within the web application, and miscellaneous web items.

We also looked at DataProviders themselves and some of the other functionality available from the WAD menu bar, including organizing with HTML tables and adding images to web applications. The properties of the web template itself were also explored. We closed out the chapter by taking a closer look at the functions of the different commands available with the command wizard.

This concludes our discussion of the reporting and web application functionality available in BW 7, the next chapter will summarize what we have learned on our journey.

From Query Designer to Web application designer (WAD), we have covered the main points necessary to design and build analytical applications delivered on the Web and in Excel.

9 Business Warehouse (BW) 7 Reporting Wrap-Up

By now you should have a good understanding of how to use the various components of SAP's BW 7 toolset to build analytical applications that can be delivered on the Web (with WAD) or embedded in Microsoft Excel (with Business Explorer (BEx) analyzer).

Technology Overview

We began with an overview of the different technologies available in the BW 7 toolset, exploring how they fit together to provide powerful analytics for end users. We discussed the typical progression for building business intelligence (BI) applications based on the needs of different end user populations, including query design, Excel workbook design, formatted reports, creating web applications, and deploying them to the portal. We also talked briefly about Visual Composer (VC), a new development tool that can be used to design business applications by interfacing with different transactional and online analytical processing (OLAP)–based systems.

Designing Queries

A deep dive into the Query Designer toolset was next — we walked through the process for sourcing data from an InfoProvider, setting query-level restrictions, and working with variables and hierarchies. We then built a Key Figure structure to display transaction data and added characteristics to provide drilldown capability to users. The properties of the query and query components were also explored in detail, including the settings relevant to characteristics, axes, structures, selections, and formulas.

Running Queries on the Web

From query design, we moved on to running queries in two separate runtime environments: BEx Web analyzer, and the BEx analyzer Excel-based interface. We started by examining the web-based reporting environment, looking first at the variable screen and personalization options. We then outlined the new drag-and-drop functionality available on the Web with BW 7, the updated interface for setting filter values, and the query properties screen available at runtime. The BEx Web analyzer toolbar was discussed next, including the methods for opening and saving queries and the different export features available: sending queries via email, creating a print version in PDF format, and exporting to Excel.

Running Queries in Excel

Excel-based BW applications were covered next, starting with the different methods for launching the BEx analyzer tool. We then looked at the different features offered by the variable screen in Excel, followed by a discussion of query navigation methods. These methods included drag-and-drop navigation, using the navigation pane, bringing up the navigational state dialog box in the Query Properties, and using context menu commands.

BEx analyzer has its own set of properties — as with its web-based counterpart, we took some time to go over the different settings available in the BW Excel-based runtime environment, along with the Analysis toolbar.

Designing Excel Workbooks

We then moved from BEx analyzer's analysis mode, which is used primarily to run queries, to design mode. In design mode, we explored how to create design items that offer additional analytical functionality to end users. We also looked at the concept of assigning DataProviders to design items to further abstract the query from the runtime environment.

The backbone of an Excel-based BW application is the Analysis Grid and the Navigation Pane, both of which were introduced in this chapter. We then looked at how to add multiple copies of these design items to display multiple queries in a single Excel workbook.

The Button design item was introduced next, along with the Command Wizard, which enables designers to quickly add sequences of commands to buttons within a workbook. Other design items were discussed, including dropdown boxes, checkboxes, radio buttons, and informational displays. We devoted one section to the Workbook Settings box, which contained a number of useful options, including customizing a workbook's interface with themes and integrating Visual Basic for Applications code within BEx analyzer.

Designing Web Applications

In the next chapter, we left Excel behind to focus on WAD, the standalone desktop application that is used to build templates for web applications. We saw the two different paths available for building web applications: the BI Pattern Wizard allows designers to quickly implement simple web applications, while building a web template — either from scratch or based on another template — allows for more flexibility. Most of the chapter was devoted to walking through a scenario involving building a web template from scratch to fulfill various business requirements.

BEx analyzer's design mode has design items that can be incorporated in Excel-based applications. The equivalents on the web side are called web items, and as with BEx analyzer, the core web items of a web application are the Analysis Grid and the Navigation Pane.

A key difference between BEx analyzer's design mode and WAD is the ability to precisely place items at a specific location within the application. On the Excel side, the grid design makes placement relatively simple — but on the Web, arranging web items requires a number of different tools, including the container layout, container, and group web items.

Buttons and the Command Wizard are also available in WAD, and we introduced the button group web item and different examples of commands to provide useful functionality for end users. A number of other web items were introduced as well, including text elements, dropdown boxes, and tab pages.

The last section of the chapter was an overview of the functionality delivered in 0ANALYSIS_PATTERN, one of the standard SAP-delivered web templates. The structure of the web template was covered, along with the reasoning behind each element of the template.

Web Item and Command Reference

The scenario-driven chapter on designing web applications covered most of the basics, but there was still quite a bit of functionality left unexplored. As a result, the next chapter was structured as a more in-depth reference, taking a look at each individual web item available in WAD. All of the BW Web API commands available in the Command Wizard were also covered.

Looking Ahead

This concludes our discussion of BW 7 reporting and web application design. While this book should give you a good start toward building analytical applications for your users, there are additional topics relating to BW 7 that were not covered. Luckily, SAP PRESS publishes books on many of these topics, some of which are mentioned in the following paragraphs.

If you are interested in backend BI development with Advanced Business Application Programming (ABAP), you may want to look at *ABAP Development for SAP NetWeaver BI — User Exits and BAdIs*. For more information on the administration side of BI, check out the book *SAP NetWeaver BW: Administration and Monitoring*. A comprehensive look at BI backend architecture, data modeling, data extraction, and staging can be found in *A Practical Guide to SAP NetWeaver Business Warehouse 7.0*, with more in-depth coverage of data modeling in *Practical Data Modeling with SAP NetWeaver BW*.

For a more in-depth look at information broadcasting, read *Mastering Information Broadcasting with SAP NetWeaver BW 7.0*. The Integrated Planning feature is covered in the book *SAP NetWeaver BI Integrated Planning for Finance*. You may have heard about SAP's BI Accelerator product – get all of the details in the book *SAP NetWeaver BI Accelerator*.

The SAP Portal provides a highly extensible platform for delivering BI applications and offers a number of points of integration with BW 7. You can read more about the portal in *SAP NetWeaver Portal*, and more in-depth looks into integration and portal application development in *Content Integration with SAP NetWeaver Portal* and the *Developer's Guide to SAP NetWeaver Portal Applications*. An in-depth guide to VC applications can be found in the book *SAP NetWeaver Visual Composer*.

Also, keep an eye out for future books covering more advanced topics relating to BW 7 frontend query design, web application design, and BW/portal integration!

For more information and to purchase any of the books mentioned — and others published by SAP PRESS — visit *www.sap-press.com*.

The Author

 **Jason Kraft** has been an avid web developer and graphic designer since the days of NCSA Mosaic in 1993, when he designed the first web site for his high school, the Academy for the Advancement of Science and Technology in Hackensack, New Jersey. Jason received his B.S. in Computer and Information Sciences from the New Jersey Institute of Technology in 2000. After graduating, he joined Johnson & Johnson's IT Leadership Development Program, and was introduced to the world of SAP as a portal developer for the Johnson & Johnson Pharmaceutical R&D SAP implementation in 2002. He transitioned to Business Warehouse development the following year; since then he has continually pushed the boundaries of SAP's BW and portal toolsets by applying his knowledge of web development and usability to design business applications. He currently holds the position of IT Lead in the Business Warehouse team, with primary responsibility for the BW front end, portal integration, and emerging BI technologies. He received his M.B.A. from Santa Clara University in 2010. Jason currently resides in Milpitas, California with his wife Amanda.

Index